Table of Conte

MW00334076

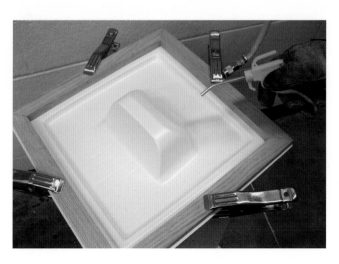

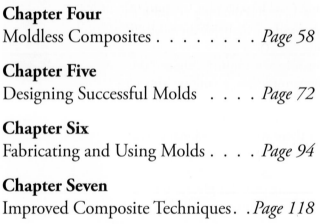

Acknowledgments

My heartfelt thanks goes out to the following individuals for their valuable efforts in assisting with this book on composites:

Charlotte, Eden, Miles and Emmie for all your support, patience, and love…

Professor Ted Shin of Metropolitan State University of Denver for some much needed encouragement...

Terry Dreher and Will Kellog for their shop assistance and occasional photo shooting expertise…

Frank Roundy from Ability Composites for reviewing parts of this book…

All those past student assistants, friends, and acquaintances who have lent their hands and hearts in helping to produce many of the projects and demonstration materials used in this book…

All my previous composites students for their inquiries about how to make "such-and-such" a project using composites, giving me the opportunity to think on my toes while assisting them with just about every possible composites project under the sun…

All those composites enthusiasts out there whose occasional emails and questions keep giving me the opportunity to share my own fabrication experience across the globe...

And to Timothy Remus and the Wolfgang crew for giving me the continued opportunity to share these topics in print.

Preface

In spite of what this book's title might suggest, the information you will get from this book is not the final, authoritative source on composites. Granted, the material presented here is based on over 20 years of my own primary research, real-world experience with composites, and working on and directing countless composite project—so this book is not your typical academic theory-fest of a text. In fact, if you're only looking for composite theory, don't read past Chapter 1 of this book—although the first chapter is still a good bit of background reading for the uninitiated before going hog-wild in the shop. As a life-long learner, I believe in an "open canon" of knowledge, and that no book is the authoritative end to information on a topic. In fact, I feel books are only meant to help springboard us forward into an area of particular interest, and that we *need* to create our own new knowledge beyond that. Consequently, I have edited and updated considerable information from my previous four books on this topic of composites fabrication and geared everything in this book toward some of my favorite people: those who are looking to get their hands dirty in the shop and actually build something cool as they amass their own person knowledge of composites. The information found here is meant to be practiced and refined. It is meant especially for those who want to have something physical to show at the end of the day as a testament to the labor they've expended. It is meant to be *used*.

...But a word or caution: Some readers will find the desire to aim for the highest quality, highest strength (and highest cost) projects first. As a seasoned fabricator, I urge such eager readers to start simple, build up your skills and fabrication complexity over time, and take the act of composites creation one step at a time. It just makes good sense to first learn how to drive with a stick shift using your uncle's old Ford Fiesta before attempting a serious track run in a Ferrari. In short, build your skills in baby steps, even if you have lofty, worthwhile goals in mind...but don't stop aiming for the stars.

John Wanberg
Professor of Industrial Design (and "Mad Scientist")

Chapter One

First, The Basics: What is a "Composite"?

Before jumping headlong into composites fabrication, it is wise to gain a baseline understanding of what basic materials, processes, and properties are involved with composites. This chapter will provide a cursory introduction to some of the fundamental terminology and theory related to composites, and specifically those that can be produced most easily by small shop and garage fabricators.

By its most basic definition, a *composite* is any material made up of two or more dissimilar materials. When used in modern engineering, the term "composite" (typically referred to as an *advanced composite*) generally refers to a class of materials made up of reinforcement fibers embedded in a solidified material whose combined properties exceed those of either of these base materials alone. For the sake of efficiency, this book will only explore the basics of the most easily processed types, or *polymeric composites*— also known as *Fiber Reinforced Polymer (FRP) composites*—although a few other types exist in aerospace and racing.

A wide variety of projects and product possibilities are opened up through the use of composite materials.
Inset: *Advanced polymer-based composites are comprised of a reinforcement and polymer resin joined together.*

Composites are used in many objects that we may see every day—from bicycle frames to storage tanks. Composites offer a high degree of strength for their weight, relatively low-pressure moldability, impact and dent resistance, collision energy absorption, weather and chemical resistance, tunable directional strength, electrical (or dielectric) properties, and even some unique aesthetic qualities. Composites are typically used judiciously when their properties exceed those of other less costly materials and formation methods.

One thing that makes composites especially enticing to do-it-yourselfers is that they can be created using relatively low-tech tools. In fact, a well-outfitted wood shop, with only a modest investment in some other composites-specific tools, will usually suffice for most composite mold-making and part fabrication operations. Even the molds for composites (whether big or small) can be made in a relatively short amount of time, with low labor cost, using inexpensive materials. Once you have created a mold for a composite part, it can be used to make dozens (or even hundreds) of parts if designed and used correctly. In fact, some manufacturers of exotic automobiles have found that composites are more cost-effective than stamped metal body parts in production volumes less than 70,000 units per year.

Polymeric composites do not generally come in readily formable or usable stock shapes in the same way that sheet metals, plastics, or woods typically do—though limited stock shapes do exist for specialty purposes. In fact, the bulk of advanced composites are formed into their final shape based on the following simple composites fabrication recipe:

- Mix together 2 parts *fiber reinforcement* to 1 part *resin matrix*—measured by weight or volume (depending on the specific fiber and resin combination)…
- Add 1 *mold system*—to hold the above reinforcements and matrix in place…
- Provide controlled, sustained *pressure* to the reinforcements and matrix in the mold—to minimize voids…
- Allow the materials in the mold to *cure* or solidify until rigid—to avoid shape deformations…
- Remove these solidified materials from the mold—or *demold* them…
- Finally *trim* the materials to size and *finish* them, as needed—to make them "pretty" and usable.

Using this composites recipe as a guide, let's explore the material components and basic process assumptions behind the creation of a composite part.

Reinforcements

The *reinforcement* in a composite provides *tensile* (pulling) strength and some *shear* (tearing) strength as well—giving them the ability to carry *loads* (or forces acting on them) very effectively in the direction that the fibers are oriented. Raw reinforcements commonly have the appearance of simple fabrics—which they actually are—with

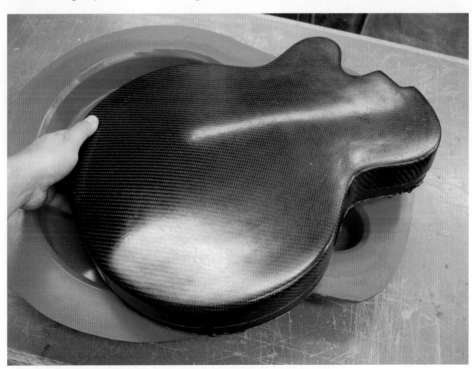

High-quality composites can be built through the use of a mold—shown here with a carbon fiber guitar back over the mold used to make it.

visible threads and a textile-like flexibility that allows them to be draped over a form or mold. They are supplied in rolls of standard widths, similar to average textiles, and can come in several different woven and non-woven styles. A reinforcement's strength is best controlled in tension rather than in *compression* (or pushing)—as compressing the length of these fibers would be akin to ineffectively pushing (rather than pulling) something at the end of a rope.

Matrices

Fiber reinforcements have a great amount of directional strength, but on their own they are about as structurally efficient as a pile of laundry. If these fibers are held together and immobilized in relation to each other, however, they become much more useful. To rigidify these fibers, polymer-based composites employ resins that are either a *thermoplastic* (moldable with heat) or a *thermoset* (solidified by chemical reaction). This resin is forced around the fibers during processing and act as a *matrix* (or a medium that surrounds something else) to lock the reinforcement fibers in place and help distribute loads from one fiber to the next. Composite *matrices* (the plural form of "matrix") provide compressive strength along with additional shear strength to keep fibers from shifting in relation to each other.

Unfortunately, the matrix is the weakest part of the composite, so a composite should have at least enough resin matrix to keep the fibers from moving in relation to each other, but not so much that it will detract from the composite's overall strength. For this reason, an optimally processed composite part should have the proper *fiber-to-resin* ratio. This fiber-to-resin ratio can be measured by either the weight or volume of the two components. Advanced composites contain more than 50% fiber in comparison to 50% resin, with aerospace composites requiring optimized fiber-to-resin ratios roughly between 60/40 to 70/30 percent. Some factors that can compromise the strength of the composite's matrix include impact and overloading, thermal extremes, chemicals, and ultraviolet light.

Layups

To form a composite, the reinforcement and matrix are joined together in multiple layers (called a *lamination* or *laminate*) through a procedure called a *layup*. Layers within a laminate are called *plies* and are built up during molding until they meet the desired thickness for the part requirements.

Either before or during a layup, the reinforcement is infiltrated—or *impregnated*—with liquid resin by rolling, spraying, pressing, squeezing, or injecting the resin into the fibers, or even by applying a vacuum to the reinforcement plies, allowing the pressurized liquid resin to be pulled into and around the fibers.

The methods for creating a composite are grouped into three major layup categories: *wet layup*, *pre-preg layup*, and *dry layup*. At a basic level, wet layup processes include those methods that require the composites fabricator to laminate reinforcement with liquid resin (such as *hand layup* and *spray up* methods)—usually in an *open mold* system (or a mold without a solid top to it). With pre-preg layup, the fabricator laminates plies of reinforcement material that have already been pre-impregnated (hence the name "pre-preg") with resin. Pre-preg material is produced in facilities

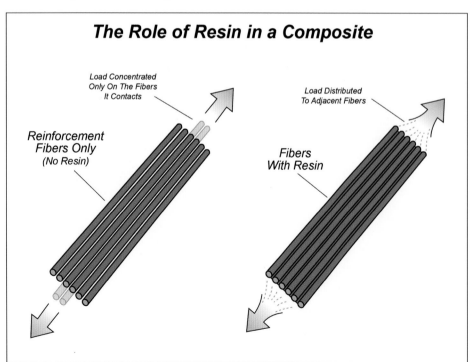

The Role of Resin in a Composite

Load Concentrated Only On The Fibers It Contacts

Reinforcement Fibers Only (No Resin)

Load Distributed To Adjacent Fibers

Fibers With Resin

that tightly control the fiber-to-resin content, and then partially cure the resin to a slightly gelled state (called a *"B-stage"* cure) to produce a composite that just needs a mold, pressure, and heat to cure it. In a dry layup, the fabricator only touches the dry reinforcement during layup, with minimal direct handling of a liquid matrix that is added later. Pre-preg and dry layup procedures generally require more equipment investment and skill to be effective than wet layups, though various "garage" techniques for each of these layup types are illustrated later in this book. (As a side note, 3D printing technologies are currently being developed in the area of 3D printed composites—but size limitations, limited matrix and reinforcement materials, low speed, poor surface quality, and restricted ability to simultaneously control fiber orientation in all axes are some of the formidable obstacles that presently consign these processes to small, prototype parts.)

Laminates

Since a single ply of composite is usually too flexible for most practical applications, multiple plies of resin-impregnated fabric are laminated together to form a unified, multi-layered composite structure. For the purpose of simplified engineering analysis, a composite laminate can be represented as a stack of *planes* (or sheet-like, flat regions) joined together to create the part. Laminate constructions are best at carrying loads that are *in-plane*, or that are in line with (or parallel to) the plane in which the fibers are oriented within the laminate.

One key benefit of laminating composite plies together is that the orientation of the fibers can be arranged to control the directional strength of the composite. When a composite's fibers are oriented in one direction, the composite has significant strength over the fibers' length, yet it will flex and bend (or even fracture) very easily when stressed perpendicular to the fibers. For this reason, it is best to place multiple plies of fibers at different angles in the laminate stack to control the directional strength as needed for the design.

When creating plans to show how a layup should proceed, the composites designer often describes the fiber's directional orientation for each layer in angular degrees as measured from a particular reference direction—which is usually the longest direction found on the composite part. This layup plan is called a *lamination schedule*, and typically includes information about the type of resin and fiber system, along with ply-by-ply illustrations of the ply shapes and fiber orientation for each ply.

Most metals and plastics are generally considered *isotropic* materials, in that their properties are consistent in every direction within the material. Composites, on the other hand, are generally considered *anisotropic* materials, because their material properties are consistent only in the direction of the reinforcement fibers. Laminates that are designed with uniform in-plane properties are called *quasi-isotropic* (meaning "almost-isotropic"), and are made possible by creating equal numbers of plies in certain orientations. Some reinforcement weaves, such as triaxial-woven materials, are specifically made to exhibit quasi-isotropic properties within a laminate.

Pre-preg material is supplied with the proper amount of resin already impregnated into the reinforcement—but it requires special processing techniques to cure it into a usable form.

Along with the conscientious orientation of fibers in a structure, the *symmetry* and *balance* of the laminate plies can be very important in keeping the laminate from naturally twisting, bending or curling. Symmetry refers to the mirrored arrangement of ply fiber orientations in relation to the mid-plane of the laminate. Balanced laminates have a positively angled ply for every negatively angled ply in the laminate and can create a stiffer composite.

Composite Physical Limitations

Composites generally do not have the same *toughness* (or ability to absorb mechanical energy and plastically deform without failing) as many metals do. When metals are loaded and stressed, they pass through a phase of *elasticity* where they will still be able to return to their original shape once unloaded. If further loads are added, metals then become *plastic* and are permanently deformed. Additional loading will eventually cause the metal part to tear or fracture at its final point of structural failure. Composites, on the other hand, are generally considered elastic until they fail—often catastrophically!

If a composite laminate experiences too much physical stress—whether through overload, bending, thermal stress, or impact—the fibers, resin, and laminated plies will fracture or separate, often creating a condition called *delamination* (or "delam", for short). Out-of-plane loads can create *interlaminar stresses* that cause the already-weak resin interface between plies to fail.

Sandwich Composites

One way to add considerable strength and stiffness to a laminate without significantly increasing its weight is through the use of *sandwich core* construction. Sandwich core construction (which differs from a solid, or *monolithic*, laminate) involves creating a laminate that contains a *core material* composed of a lightweight material with high compressive strength (such as foam, wood, or open-celled honeycomb) and adding laminate faces (or *skins*) to either side of the core. When the upper and lower plies of a laminate are separated by a fixed distance, as with the sandwich core, out-of-plane loads are directed through these outer skins and the composite can handle them more effectively.

There is an exponential correlation between the thickness of a cored laminate and the strength and stiffness it exhibits. This is similar in concept to steel I-beams, in that the top and bottom sections bear the majority of the load on the structure, and the middle section of the structure simply holds the top and bottom at a fixed distance from each other so they can work more effectively. The strength of the sandwich construction is then only limited by the compressive strength of the core, the adhesive connection of the core to the laminate plies, and the laminate's own maximum in-plane tensile and compressive strengths. The greater the distance between the top and bottom sections, the stiffer the sandwich laminate. For example, a four ply laminate, if separated by a core to twice its original thickness (with two plies on top and two on the bottom of the core), would be 7 times as stiff and 3.5 times as strong. If that same top and bottom laminate (still at two plies each) employed an even thicker core to take it to 4 times its original thickness, it would have 37 times the stiffness and over 9 times the strength—with very little increase in weight! Needless to say, cores help make good composite structures.

A variety of materials can be used as cores, but the most effective ones are those that are lightweight, have good compressive strength, and are readily bonded with the resin used in the laminate. Some common cores include foam (urethane, PVC,

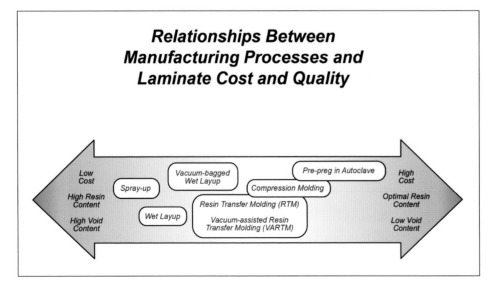

Relationships Between Manufacturing Processes and Laminate Cost and Quality

expanded/extruded styrene), wood (end-grain balsa, plywood), and honeycomb (Nomex, aluminum, and other). For applications requiring low cost and low performance, wood cores work well, while high performance laminates typically use honeycomb cores (but cost more). Moderately price and mid-performance laminates tend to be a good fit for foam cores.

Composite Damage

When composites fracture or delaminate, the results are very similar to broken plywood, where stiff shards or fibers of material are left protruding haphazardly out of the remaining laminate. And when composites are overheated or burned, all that is left is a pile of fibers and charred resin dust. In less destructive scenarios, where the matrix separates but the fibers do not fracture, delamination may appear as a hazy, lightened area in translucent laminates (such as with fiberglass) or as a soft or unusually flexible spot in opaque laminates (such as with aramid or carbon fiber composites). The extent of such damage is often difficult to detect within a composite, and generally requires the use of specialized, *Non-destructive Inspection* (NDI) equipment to assess damage or defects in the composite prior to repair.

Composite Fastening and Joining

Mechanical fasteners will also weaken a composite where load paths formed by fibers of the composite are interrupted to accommodate the fasteners, especially if holes for them are not cleanly and properly drilled. On the flipside of the coin, mechanical joints have the benefit of being disassembled when needed, are less sensitive to environmental conditions, and can be inspected relatively easily.

Adhesive bonding methods can be a good alternative to mechanical fasteners in many situations because they tend to spread loads more evenly at the joint, eliminating

concentrations of stress that are common at the edges of mechanical fasteners. They are also lighter, less expensive, and eliminate delamination issues caused by drilling a hole for a fastener. However, the strength of adhesive joints can be limited by the strength of the adhesive, the curing process used, and the quality of the surface preparation between the mating faces of the joint.

Considerations for Primary and Secondary Structures

In very general terms, composite components— or any engineered components, for that matter— can be sorted into either of the two following types: *primary structures* and *secondary structures*. Primary structures are those that serve very distinct load-bearing, structural requirements, such as a wing spar on an aircraft or frame component on a vehicle. For these structures, the actual manufacturing process can be very critical to the overall component quality.

Secondary structures, on the other hand, are those that typically only need to have enough strength to support their own weight, although they may still have a variety of other important functional requirements. With secondary structures, surface quality may be a high priority for the purpose of aesthetics, marketability, and aerodynamic or hydrodynamic efficiency—so surface filling and coatings may need to be used to cover up imperfections created during fabrication.

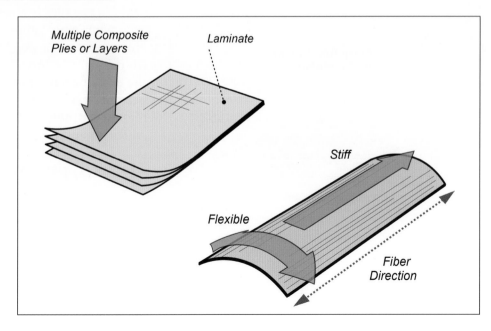

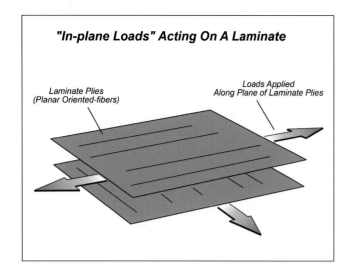

"In-plane Loads" Acting On A Laminate

Laminate Plies
(Planar Oriented-fibers)

Loads Applied
Along Plane of Laminate Plies

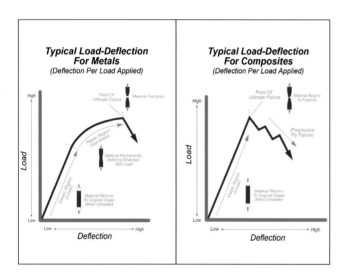

Typical Load-Deflection For Metals
(Deflection Per Load Applied)

Typical Load-Deflection For Composites
(Deflection Per Load Applied)

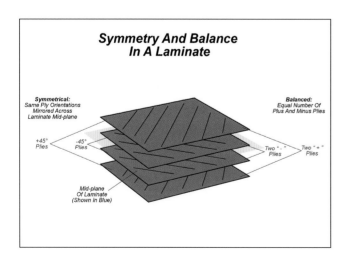

Symmetry And Balance In A Laminate

Symmetrical:
Same Ply Orientations
Mirrored Across
Laminate Mid-plane

Balanced:
Equal Number Of
Plus And Minus Plies

+45°
Plies

-45°
Plies

Two "-"
Plies

Two "+"
Plies

Mid-plane
Of Laminate
(Shown In Blue)

General Composite Types

In industry, several names are given to composites based on their fiber component, and include the following:

- *GFRP* (Glass Fiber Reinforced Polymer) – This is the most common and inexpensive of the reinforced polymer composites and is typically just called "fiberglass".

- *CFRP* (Carbon Fiber Reinforced Polymer) – This composite is widely used in aerospace and racing due to its excellent stiffness and strength.

- *AFRP* (Aramid Fiber Reinforced Polymer) – These composites have some of the highest relative strength due to the fibers' ability to stretch rather than break.

Composites are generally less dense than other traditional materials, meaning that they have greater *specific strength* (or strength-to-weight) than most other materials—which is especially helpful in weight-critical applications.

To observe the relative stiffness of various composites compared to traditional materials, take note of the photo that shows samples of steel, aluminum, balsa wood, GFRP, CFRP, and AFRP. Each of these samples is of the same thickness (.030"), width and length (2" by 11") and clamped to a solid surface. The stiffness of these samples is already somewhat apparent, even when only supporting their own weight. However, once a weight has been applied to each (in this case, a 360g/12.7oz mass clamped onto the end of each sample) the relative stiffness becomes very clear. Steel and CFRP show the highest stiffness, followed by aluminum and AFRP, then GFRP and balsa.

Matrix Types and Properties

In general, the resins that are most easily utilized by home builders fall under the category of *thermoset* polymers. Unlike *thermoplastic* polymers that can be heated and melted many times over (like those found in most recyclable commodity plastics), thermosets generally start off as a liquid and then—through the addition of a catalyst or hardener—solidify in an irreversible chemical process that renders them unable to melt at high temperatures. This chemical reaction, called *cross-linking*, joins the ends of each polymer molecule with others around them to create a single interconnected and very strong macromolecule. Common thermoset polymer matrices used by small shop fabricators include polyester resin, vinyl ester resin, epoxy resin, and urethane resins.

One side-effect of the cross-linking process is the release of heat energy through an *exothermic* chemical reaction. When a thermoset resin is reacting, or *curing*, the amount of heat discharged depends on the rate of cure for the resin system—so fast cure resins tend to generate noticeably higher amounts of heat than do slow cure resins. If a resin is spread into a thin film, the exotherm of the reaction is very minimal and quickly dissipated. However, if that same resin is contained in a cup or bucket, the heat generated by the resin within the concentrated space dramatically increases the speed of the reaction, often resulting in a runaway, premature cure. If left unchecked, this self-feeding reaction can generate enough heat to soften or melt the mixing container, char the resin, and produce noxious smoke or flames. Needless to say, closely monitor the amount of time a mixed resin sits in its container to avoid safety hazards or unnecessarily wasting and pre-hardening of the resin.

Because of the amount of heat generated by mixed resin of different liquid volumes, resin manufacturers list two cure speeds for their products: *pot life* and *working time*. Pot life is the amount of time it takes the curing resin (commonly a 100g sample of material mixed at room temperature) to begin gelling while sitting in a mixing cup. This time can range from a couple minutes to several hours (or even days to weeks), depending on the resin system, the volume of resin mixed, and the resin's temperature.

The working time of a resin refers to the amount of time a curing resin will remain liquid and usable while spread out into fabric reinforcements or in a mold before it begins to gel. A wise fabricator will use a resin system that will provide enough working time to complete the layup before gelling starts, and then will only mix small, manageable amounts of resin at a time to handle the limitations of its pot life. For large wet and dry layups, it is helpful to have an assistant available to mix resin as needed, or to pre-measure several cups of resin with their corresponding cups

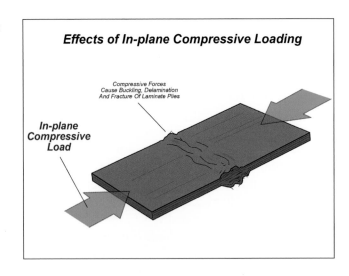

Effects of In-plane Compressive Loading

In-plane Compressive Load

Compressive Forces Cause Buckling, Delamination And Fracture Of Laminate Plies

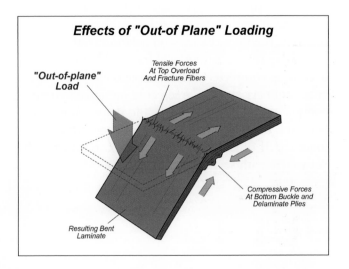

Effects of "Out-of Plane" Loading

"Out-of-plane" Load

Tensile Forces At Top Overload And Fracture Fibers

Compressive Forces At Bottom Buckle and Delaminate Plies

Resulting Bent Laminate

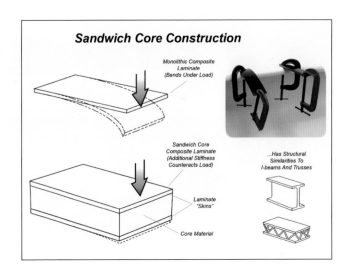

Sandwich Core Construction

Monolithic Composite Laminate (Bends Under Load)

Sandwich Core Composite Laminate (Additional Stiffness Counteracts Load)

Laminate "Skins"

Core Material

...Has Structural Similarities To I-beams And Trusses

of catalyst or hardener for quick mixing and use, as needed in the layup.

Another resin property to consider is *viscosity*, or the resin's resistance to liquid flow. Thinner, or less viscous, resins will *wet-out* (or saturate) a reinforcement very easily. However, thin resin will tend to squeeze out from the laminate when under pressure (such as with vacuum-bagging or compression molding). Thicker, more viscous resins, will tend to help fill in the gaps between woven fiber bundles because they have the ability to bridge small voids more easily. On the other hand, overly thick resin may trap large bubbles and voids in the laminate if not properly *compacted*, *debulked*, or *consolidated* by compressing the laminate against the mold with high pressure.

As a curing resin progresses toward full hardness, it goes through a gel stage that starts as the resin becomes thicker and gelatinous, then hardening to a consistency of hard rubber prior to becoming completely solid. Some builders call this latter, rubbery stage a "green cure". A green-cured composite will still be flexible and deformable (yet delicate), but the laminate plies will be unified together. If timed well, parts can be carefully rough-cut to size with scissors at this stage.

Managing Matrix Weaknesses

During cure, resin adheres most effectively to previously laminated plies in a layup if cross-linked chemical bonds can still be formed with resin that is still wet, or at least tacky to the touch. However, if a resin is allowed to cure completely before the next layer is added, only an inferior *secondary bond* will form with the resin. In secondary bonding, the resin's adhesive strength is limited by how well it can penetrate into the small scratches and surface imperfections of the previously cured layer. Since they are weak and prone to failure, secondary bonds should be minimized as much as possible within structural composites. In some pre-preg manufacturing and repair situations, *co-bonding* joins a previously cured laminate to un-cured pre-preg plies using heat and pressure—producing a bond which is generally superior to that of secondary bonding.

All resins naturally degrade when exposed to ultraviolet (UV) light. Over time, the energy in UV light breaks the chemical bonds in the resin's molecules, destroying its physical strength and ultimately reducing it to a useless powder. To combat this, some resins are enhanced with UV light inhibitors mixed into them by the manufacturer. Composites can also be protected by applying special surface coatings or UV protective paints.

Like adhesives, the resins in composite laminates perform best in shear—or when they are resisting sliding motion between the fibers and layers of the laminate. On the other hand, these resins tend to work least effectively when peeled apart (having poor *peel strength*)—or when the resin-encased fibers or plies in the laminate are being pulled apart from each other. Composites that are subjected to excessive peel-like stresses may eventually succumb to delamination. Consequently, to avoid

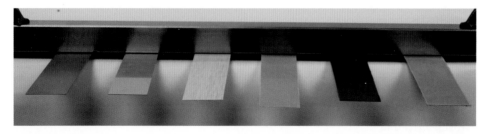
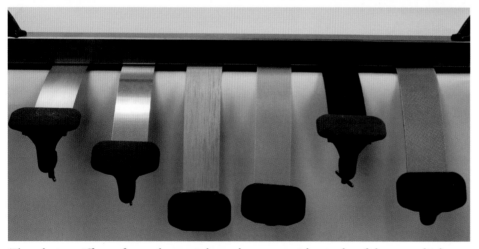

The relative stiffness of several materials can been seen with samples of the same thickness at rest (top), and equally weighted (bottom), including (from the left) steel, aluminum, balsa wood, fiberglass composites, carbon fiber composite, and aramid (Kevlar) composite.

poor management of peel forces, it is generally best to design any composite structure so that forces acting on it are *in-plane* with the laminate and acting in shear (pulling side-by-side) with the resin and fibers, or by creating a sandwich structure to help manage the loads. This same load arrangement also applies to joints, where strap, lap, and scarf joints are preferable to butt joints.

With critical structural composite parts it is important to minimize every possible weakness in the structure, such as *voids*. Voids in the composite—including air bubbles or pockets—cannot carry any load, and will significantly affect the strength of the laminate. If the size and number of voids are reduced through proper resin application and laminate consolidation, the composite will experience a corresponding increase in material strength.

To simplify the resin selection process, this book will mainly focus on some of the most commonly used thermoset resin types, including polyester, vinyl ester, and epoxy resins. These are available at many hardware stores, automotive/body shop supply chains, composites suppliers, or other online sources. They are generally simple enough to use that the average fabricator can competently employ them in most projects with a little practice. In recent years, other specialty resins, such as urethanes, liquid thermoplastic acrylics (polymethyl-methacrylate—or PMMA), and silicones have become more available for use by small shops and fabricators, so this book will briefly illustrate some basic ways to use these materials, as well. When purchasing resins for a composite matrix, keep in mind that you'll typically get the quality you pay for—inexpensive resins tend to give the lowest quality results, and vice versa!

Polyester Resin

Polyester resin (also known as *unsaturated polyester* when in un-cured, liquid form) is the most commonly used resin in mass-production and small composites shops, because of its low cost and adjustable cure time. It is regularly used with a protective coating called a *gel coat*—which is a pigmented or colored polyester resin shell that is sprayed or brushed on.

Polyester resin cures with the addition of a catalyst called *MEKP* (methyl ethyl keytone peroxide)—a chemical which forces the polyester molecules to cross-link. More MEKP will speed up the cross-linking and shorten cure time of the polyester, while less MEKP will lengthen the cure time. MEKP is usually measured in drops of catalyst per ounce of resin, or by a percentage of relative liquid volumes as measured with a MEKP dispenser or with a precision scale (for larger resin batches).

Compared to other resins, polyester is relatively inexpensive. As of the printing of this book, retail prices for polyester resin range anywhere between $25 and $70 a gallon (and even less, when purchased in large quantities or wholesale) depending on the resin's properties and additives. Polyester laminating resins—used to build up multiple laminate plies—tend to be less expensive, but will leave a tacky surface on the cured resin for the bonding of subsequent layers. *Surfacing, finishing, top coat,* or *"waxed" polyester resins* tend to be slightly more expensive but will produce a tack-free surface on the resin once cured because they will seal off oxygen from the resin's surface, allowing it to cure completely. Oxygen can also be closed off from the surface of laminating resin by spraying

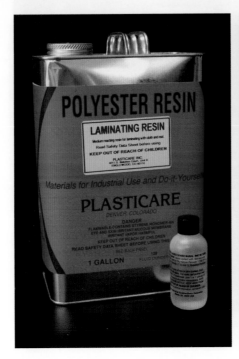
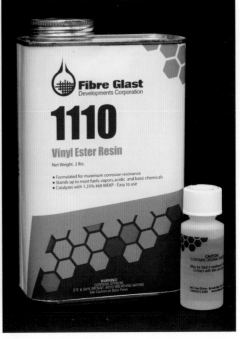

Polyester and vinyl ester resins.

polyvinyl alcohol (PVA) on top of the laminate, and then later washing the PVA off with water once the laminate has cured.

Polyester resins are available in two basic chemical types: *orthophthalic* and *isophthalic*. These names refer to the actual orientation of the molecules in the polyester resin and have a large impact on the final cured resin's properties. For simplicity sake, orthophthalic resins tend to be a little less expensive and common in general-use layups. Isophthalic polyester resins tend to have less shrinkage, higher strength and durability, and higher heat tolerance, so they are widely used in applications that require better performance.

One very helpful property of polyester resin (and vinyl ester resins, too) is that they are *thixotropic* (or become less viscous when agitated), making them easier to work into fabrics—after which they will thicken up and then nicely adhere to the vertical surfaces of a mold until cured. Polyester resin can also be thinned by simply mixing in additional liquid *styrene monomer* (the chemical component that keeps the polyester resin liquid), even to the point of allowing it to be easily sprayed for certain types of layups (or *spray ups*). Styrene monomer liquid will also help in thinning out an otherwise old can of polyester resin that has begun to gel while in storage. Also, because of its styrene monomer content, polyester should not be used directly in contact with Styrofoam (including both expanded and extruded styrene-based foams) or polystyrene plastics, as it will attack these plastics and quickly dissolve them.

Polyester tends to have some of the lowest strength among the common composite resins due, in part, to the high rate of shrinkage it experiences during cure—which amounts to about a 7% volume reduction from its liquid form. When shrinking, stress is built up within the cured resin, taking away some of its overall useful strength. Fiber reinforcements within the resin can help minimize this shrinkage, but it is not usually sensible to employ polyester resin with high performance fabrics.

Another drawback of polyester resin is its dangerous *volatile organic compound (VOC) vapor*. Polyester resin has a very strong, penetrating odor that is produced by the styrene monomer in the resin, but this can be mitigated with proper ventilation and wearable breathing protection.

Vinyl Ester Resin

Vinyl ester resin is used by some builders as an "upgrade" in place of polyester resins. It offers slightly higher performance (in some cases, approaching that of epoxy), excellent chemical resistance, ease of use, less water absorption than polyester, processing similarities to polyester, and excellent compatibility with polyester resins. Vinyl ester costs between $45 and $90 per gallon and has an MEKP controllable cure speed, but will see its maximum performance after *post-cure* heating—as further described below. As with polyester, vinyl ester also shrinks considerably during cure, and also emits an unpleasant styrene monomer odor. Although vinyl ester shares the same reinforcement compatibility limitations that polyester resin does, it is more compatible with epoxy matrices than polyester. When polyester is used over a cured epoxy composite, it may not fully cure because of chemical

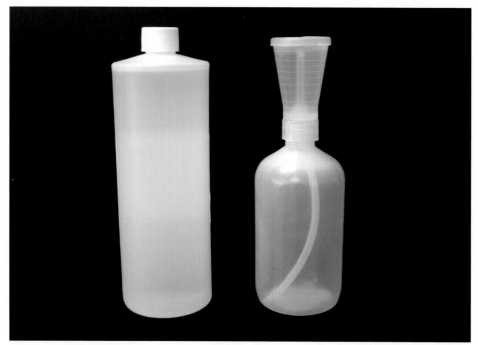

MEKP catalyst for polyester and vinyl ester resins can be easily stored, and can be dispensed with special measuring dispensers (right).

interactions between the two resins—but vinyl ester will generally cure well to either polyester or epoxy. Therefore, when making repairs or bonding composites, vinyl ester resin can work well as a bonding interface between disparate matrices.

Epoxy Resin

Epoxy resins are used in applications where superior strength, durability, and heat and chemical resistance are needed. Epoxies tend to have even higher retail cost than either polyester or vinyl ester resins—ranging from $70 to over $330 a gallon—so cost should be considered in relation to the physical and chemical benefits epoxy can offer. Although epoxies can be used effectively with all fabric reinforcement types, they are especially well-suited for higher performance fabrics where their properties are most beneficial to the overall resulting composite.

Unlike the catalyzed reaction found in polyester and vinyl ester resins, epoxy resin cures through the addition of a hardener in a chemical reaction that actually cross-links the resin and hardener together. Precise measurement of the resin and hardener components is needed to ensure that no excess liquid from either part is left over after the chemical reaction is complete—as this can cause softening or weakening of the final resin matrix.

Epoxies are not typically thixotropic (although thixotropic additives are available for them) but are available in varying viscosities to match the type of layup they are to be used in: low viscosity for resin infusion or transfer molding (dry layup methods), medium viscosities for hand layup (including vacuum-bagging procedures), and high viscosity for compression molding and secondary bonding. While it is possible to apply chemicals to an epoxy to thin it out a bit (including isopropyl alcohol and other commercially available thinners), the mechanical properties of the epoxy are generally weakened by these thinners. Furthermore, it is not advisable to thin epoxies with acetone or lacquer thinner because they will attack the chemical mechanisms that harden the epoxy, making it difficult or impossible for the epoxy to completely cure. Warming epoxy a bit with a heat gun or incandescent light bulb can lower its viscosity, but care should be taken when applying heat to the epoxy as it can speed up the cure time significantly.

Epoxies from different manufacturers will still commonly adhere to each other very effectively. This allows the fabricator to use a *surfacing epoxy* (for

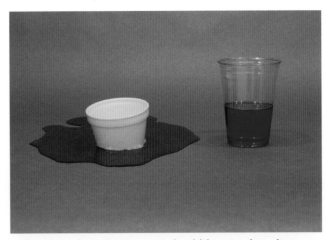

Polyester and vinyl ester resins should be mixed in clean polypropylene (PP), polyethylene (LDPE or HDPE), or PETE containers to avoid chemical incompatibility issues with the container (as shown at left dissolving through a Styrofoam cup).

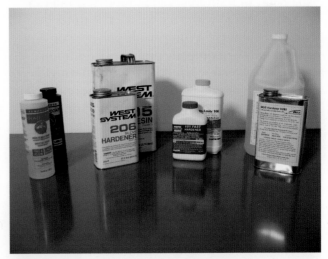

Epoxy resins and hardeners of various types, all with different chemical and mechanical characteristics.

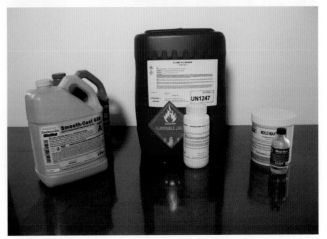

Examples of urethane (left), liquid acrylic (center), and silicone (right) resins.

creating a gel coat-like shell on a mold or part) from one manufacturer with the laminating epoxy from another once the surfacing epoxy has become tacky.

Epoxy resins generally have very low VOC vapors, usually alleviating the need for special respirators. However, they can produce allergic reactions in some people, especially if the epoxy resin or hardener comes in contact with the skin. Even individuals who show no initial signs of an allergic reaction to these liquids can actually become more sensitive to them over time.

Urethane Resin

Polyurethane (or *urethane,* for short) resins have become more popular in recent years for use in composites where flexible or toughened laminates are required. Polyurethane composites (also referred to as *PUR composites*) offer the benefit of a very wide range of resin mixes and properties, and can be manufactured with very quick cycle times (less than ¼ the time of a comparable polyester or vinyl ester parts) when properly processed. Additionally, there is considerably less odor associated with them, although some blends of urethanes still require special ventilation or breathing protection. Urethane resins range from around $50 to over $100 per gallon, and come in a wide range of *durometers* (or flexibilities) and cure times.

Acrylic Resin

Liquid acrylic resin has been used for casting purposes for years (not to be confused with polyester-based casting resins), and has become a welcomed addition to composites. It has a very low viscosity, fast cure time, and relatively good strength properties, making it a good replacement for epoxy, polyester, and vinyl ester in some finely-tuned resin infusion applications. Once cured, acrylic resin becomes a thermoplastic (one of the few resin types that acts as such) meaning it can be later heated and reformed as needed, and even "welded" using heat or solvent-based adhesives. This makes it useful in fabricating pre-formed or stock shape composites for further processing—and it is also a recyclable material. When used in a composite, some formulations of acrylic resin tend to bond best with reinforcement fabrics that are prepared for use with vinyl ester resin (through the specific "sizing" or "finish" applied to them—as described below). Liquid acrylic manufacturers are less common than those for other resins, but a handful of online sources and retailers exist.

Silicone Resin

Silicone resin is rarely used with reinforcement fibers, especially for structural purposes. However, for some applications within soft goods, upholstery, and composites manufacturing, reinforced silicone can be very useful. Silicone tends to have excellent flexibility, and chemical and heat resistance. As such, when paired with a reinforcement fabric, silicone is especially well-suited for some harsh environments that require these resin properties, but with the additional tear strength provided by the fabric.

Post-curing Resin Matrices

The physical properties of many thermoset resins can be enhanced by heating the resin using special post-cure procedures designated by the manufacturer. Most room-temperature cure

Examples of reinforcement fabrics (clockwise from top left): fiberglass, carbon fiber, hybrid weave of fiberglass and carbon fiber, and aramid (Kevlar).

resins do not fully crosslink all of their molecules within the prescribed "full-cure" time designated by the resin manufacturer—even if they may appear to be fully cured. In fact, only about 80-90% of the resin molecules may be cross-linked at the point that the resin feels rigid. To fully realize the strength potential of structural resins—and especially for epoxies used in structural applications—post curing is advisable to expedite complete cross-linking of the resin.

Post curing a resin matrix is performed by adding controlled heating to the composite over a designated period of time (typically just a few degrees per minute), and then slowly ramping down the temperature once sustained post-curing temperatures and time duration have been completed. In most cases, post-curing sequences are best performed while the composite part is still in the mold, as heating of the part will raise the resin's *glass transition* (*Tg*) temperature—or the temperature at which the resin will transition from a glassy (rigid) state to a rubbery state—and may cause warping of an unsupported composite laminate. Without getting too in-depth with the chemical factors that influence these changes, suffice it to say that post-curing drives the Tg several degrees higher than the post-curing temperatures themselves. This can aid in strengthening the composite part and making it more resilient to heat. Post-curing can also help ensure superior surface quality in a part with critical aesthetics by minimizing the amount of *print through*—or the visibility of a reinforcement fabric's weave at the surface of a part, which is commonly caused by shrinkage of the resin during cure.

Reinforcement Types, Properties, and Weaves

Fiber reinforcements are composed of individual filaments that can range in thicknesses from about the coarseness of horsehair to microscopically-finer than a baby's hair. A coating of *sizing* (or *size*) is added to the fibers during processing to allow them to be handled by weaving machinery with minimal fraying. This sizing is then typically removed after weaving and the fibers are coated with a *finish* (or a *coupling agent*) that aids in adhesion of the matrix to the fibers during later resin impregnation processes. It should be noted that within the field of composites, the term "sizing" is widely used to describe *both* sizing and finish coatings used on reinforcement fibers. Some vendors have the ability to add chemical tinting to the sizing or finish of fiberglass reinforcements (rather than as color additives within the glass itself) to produce unique color qualities for a fiberglass composite.

Just as there are several resin types available for use in composites, a variety of different reinforcement fibers are also available for the fabrication of composites, based on the fabricator's needs for the final part. The most common reinforcement fibers are described below.

> Fiberglass is the most common reinforcement used in composites, largely due to its good strength, chemical and heat resistance, low cost and availability.

Fiberglass

Fiberglass is the most common reinforcement used in composites, largely due to its good strength, chemical and heat resistance, low cost and availability. Its two most common grades are *E-glass* and *S-glass*. E-glass is an economical, electrical-grade, general-use fiberglass common in marine, architecture, and automotive applications. S-glass is a high performance fiberglass that has over 25% more strength than E-glass and is used in aerospace, engineering, and racing. When impregnated with resin, fiberglass tends to become translucent and take on the color of the resin surrounding it.

Carbon fiber

Carbon fiber is more expensive than other reinforcement fibers, but is an especially sought-after reinforcement because of its low weight, high tensile strength, and stiffness characteristics. Carbon fiber also has workability and aesthetic qualities that set it apart from other composites. It will generally lay into a mold with less effort than fiberglass of the same weight and can be cut and sanded more cleanly and easily using common tools than either fiberglass or aramid fibers.

Pure carbon fiber comes only in black—although some vendors erroneously sell dyed aramid fibers as "colored carbon"—but it has a unique aesthetic that makes it an attractive choice for unpainted and visible composites. When impregnated with resin, carbon fiber produces a look of woven black silk, producing light reflections that seem to trick the eye. Aesthetics-conscious fabricators find that the most interesting light patterns tend to come with twill weave and spread-tow weaves.

Both *commercial* and *aerospace* grades of carbon fiber are available with varying ranges of strength associated to them. For most small shop applications, though, commercial grades prove to be more cost effective and easier to obtain than aerospace grades—while still fulfilling their project's strength and weight requirements. However, while some fabricators may use the terms "carbon" and "graphite" interchangeably, true graphite fibers have higher strength characteristics (and higher cost) than do typical carbon fibers.

Carbon fiber's fabric weight is often measured in terms of a how many 1000's of filaments are found in a fiber bundle—expressed in *"K"*. For example, 1K fabric has 1000 filaments per fiber bundle whereas 3K has 3000 filaments, 6K has 6000 filaments, and so on. 3K, 6K, 12K, and 24K are common filament counts. 3K fabrics are used for typical layups, 6K fabrics for quick buildup of a laminate, and 12K and 24K are commonly employed as *tooling fabrics* or those that are used to create molds that are made of composites themselves.

Aramid Fiber

Named from a shortened version of its chemical name ("aromatic polyamide"), *aramid* fiber is very lightweight, strong, abrasion resistant, heat resistant, and non-conductive—making it especially useful in tough environments or where safety is crucial. Aramid fiber is naturally yellow in color and is commonly available under the DuPont brand name *"Kevlar"*. It is available in three grades: Kevlar (as a reinforcement in rubber goods such as tires), *Kevlar-29* (for general industrial and armor use), and *Kevlar-49* (for high-performance and transportation applications).

Aramid fibers are notoriously difficult to cut and will tend to become stringy and fray instead of simply shearing if even slightly dulled scissors are used. In a cured aramid composite, some manufacturers employ high-pressure, abrasive water-jet cutting equipment or specialty cutting bits to cleanly carve through their aramid parts.

It is best to use UV protective resins, coatings, or surface treatments in applications where aramid fiber will be subjected to ultraviolet light. Dyed aramid fibers return to their natural yellow color after prolonged UV exposure, and will begin to turn brown and lose their strength.

Hybrid Fiber Weaves

Hybrid weaves are created by interweaving two different reinforcement types together. These weaves create a unique aesthetic—especially when dyed aramid or fiberglass fiber is used in the weave—but can also be used to

Specialty reinforcement fabrics are available in several styles (clockwise from top left): twill-woven carbon fiber with red reflective strands, "honeycomb"-pattern woven fibers, different weave styles of jute natural fiber, spread-tow carbon fiber.

provide different strength characteristics in multiple directions. For instance, prosthetics often use hybrid weaves where good stiffness is needed in one direction, but flexibility is desired in another.

Other Reinforcement Fiber Types

Other specialty fiber types worth exploring as you build with composites include (but are not limited to) the following:

- *Dyneema* – This is a form of ultra-high molecular weight (UHMW) polyethylene that has been drawn out into fiber form. It has excellent resistance to moisture, chemicals, and impact, along with good electrical and antiballistic properties.

- *Zylon* – This is a synthetic fiber with properties similar to Kevlar. It has excellent strength and thermal stability.

- *Aluminized Fiberglass* – This is a type of fiberglass with a shiny, vapor-deposited coating of aluminum on it with a unique "woven metal" aesthetic that produces interesting visual effects.

- *Colored and Black Fiberglass* – Fiberglass is available in a variety of colors for special aesthetic applications. Black fiberglass is sometimes used as a low-cost alternative to a composite that mimics carbon fiber's aesthetic, with the added benefit of improved impact resilience.

- *Quartz* – This is an alternative to fiberglass with higher strength and stiffness, lower density, and nearly zero expansion or contraction over a wide range of temperatures.

- *Basalt* – This is an inexpensive

alternative to fiberglass with even better chemical resistance than glass.

- *Boron* – These are very light fibers with excellent stiffness and strength, and are created by vapor-depositing boron onto carbon or tungsten filaments. Though it is often used in aerospace for applications that require extreme performance, some high-end consumer goods utilize it as well.

- *Natural Fibers* – Several natural reinforcement fibers (derived from natural resources rather than through synthetic formulation in a factory) are now available to fabricators. Natural fiber reinforcements include bamboo, flax, hemp, jute, kenaf, and others. These fibers do not have many of the same high strength characteristics possessed by synthetic fibers, but they are lower in cost, more environmentally sustainable, and still exhibit good resistance to fatigue.

Fiber "Crimp"

The actual straightness of the reinforcement fibers within the composite has an appreciable influence on its strength. When pulled along its length, a kinked or bent fiber will increase in length as it straightens out, detracting from the stiffness exhibited by the fiber. Fibers that are woven into cloth follow a crooked path as they

Different weave styles of carbon fiber (from the left): unidirectional, stitched double bias (+/- 45°), 2x2 twill weave, and triaxial.

21

travel over and under other fiber bundles. However, if a fiber is already straight, it will stretch less than one that has waves or "kinks" in it, giving it more overall stiffness. The degree to which the fibers are wrinkled due to a particular fabric's weave is referred to as the *crimp* in the fabric. Consequently, composites containing reinforcements with low crimp (such as unidirectional fabrics) have higher overall strength and stiffness than those with high crimp (such as woven fabrics).

Woven reinforcements are made from filaments that are bundled into yarns and woven into fabric. In order to be easily woven, fiber filaments are gathered into bundles called *tow* or *roving*, or into twisted bundles called *yarns*. These bundles are then woven together using industrial textile equipment to create either of two types of fabric: woven roving, or cloth (made from woven yarn). Woven roving reinforcements are made of thick filament bundles and tend to come in heavier weights that have wide spacing between strands and accept more resin during layup. Conversely, the tightly bundled filaments in cloth fabrics tend to fray less and create slightly thinner fabrics that use less resin. Reinforcement fabrics that are produced to be flat in their form (rather than tubular or any other cross section) are called *broad goods*—which make up a very large portion of the composite reinforcements industry.

Woven reinforcements are designated and sold in terms of the fabric's thickness (in inches or millimeters), *weight*—frequently measured in ounces per square yard (oz/yd^2), or grams per square meter (or *GSM*), and by the number of yarns found in the weave. These include the *warp* yarns (those that travel the length of the cloth roll) and *weft*, *fill*, or *woof* yarns (those that travel the width of the cloth) per inch of fabric. For example, a particular fiberglass cloth may be measured as .0093" thick, weighing 8.8 oz/yd^2, with a warp count of 54 yarns per inch, and a fill count of 18 yarns per inch.

A reinforcement's weave will affect its directional strength, ability to be wetted with resin, how much resin it can hold, the final surface quality of the composite, and its *drapeability*—or how well it will conform to complex mold shapes. Some common weave types include plain, twill, satin, and basket. Additional specialty weaves such as sock/sleeve/tubing and tapes are also available.

> Woven reinforcements are made from filaments that are bundled into yarns and woven into fabric. In order to be easily woven, fiber filaments are gathered into bundles called tow or roving, or into twisted bundles called yarns.

Plain Weave

This weave style is the most widely available among the common fabric reinforcement types. It is produced by weaving each warp and fill fiber in a simple over-one and under-one pattern which creates a very stable (and symmetrical), easily wetted, but high-crimp fabric. Because of its high crimp, plain weave fabrics can produce small, regularly patterned voids in the surface of a cured laminate where the fibers are unable to lay flat against the mold's face. This is especially common in situations where high pressure has not been applied to the laminate during cure or where heavier fabrics are used. Plain weaves also have difficulty conforming to complex curves and tight radius corners when molded, so they are most commonly used in flat or low-curvature composite parts.

Twill Weave

Twill woven fabrics generally offer the best combination of both drapeability and strength, so they are widely used in applications that require good formability along with high performance. Twill also tends to produce a very desirable aesthetic, especially with carbon fabrics. A very common configuration of this weave is a 2/2 twill in which each warp fiber goes over and under two fill fibers.

Satin Weave

Satin weaves offer exceptional drape to conform with very complexly curved molds, but at the expense of having some of the lowest weave stability. Due to its loose weave pattern, it tends to fray very easily at cut edges when applied in a wet layup, so use care when moving or positioning the fabric after cutting it. *5-harness* (where the fibers go over-one and under-five) and *crowfoot* are common styles for this type of weave.

Basket Weave, Mock Leno, and Other Weaves

Basket weaves are very similar to plain weaves except two or more fiber bundles to go over and under two or more other fiber bundles at a time. They tend to lay flatter than other weaves but are prone to fraying more than a typical plain weave.

Mock leno weaves are thick, flexible fabrics that are often used in the production of *composite tooling* (which are molds made of composites themselves) to bulk up or thicken the composite as quickly as possible. They are typically used behind a lighter, smoother fabric to avoid print-through on the mold surface.

Many other specialty fabrics exist, including those that have their fibers woven into patterns, contain other colored or reflective fibers in the weave, or that are comprised of tow yarns that have been spread out flat (called *"spread-tow"*). Some of these fabrics are produced only for their aesthetic properties, while others (such as spread-tow) offer certain strength benefits.

Stabilized weaves are those that have been specially processed to keep the fabric from spreading or fraying when handled. These types of fabric are used most commonly on the aesthetic surfaces of visible composites where perfect weave alignment is critical. Depending on the type of stabilization processing used, these fabrics may either be unusually stiff, or very flexible.

Stitched Fabrics

Some fabrics are created by laying reinforcements in multiple directions atop each other, after which they are stitched together to form a crimp-free fabric. Double bias weaves are created in this way wherein fibers are placed in +45/-45 orientations and then stitched to hold them together. Biaxial (two opposing directions—along the 0 and 90 degree directions), triaxial (three layers of fibers in the 0, +45, -45, or even 0, +60,

-60 degree directions), and quadraxial (four layers of fibers in the 0, +45, 90, -45 degree directions) fabrics are all common types of stitched fabrics as well. Some heavy-duty *unidirectional* fabrics (further explained below) are also created in this way where the load carrying fibers are all oriented in the same direction, but are stitched together to keep them from splitting apart from each other. None of these types of fabrics are capable of conforming to highly compound-curved surfaces, but are excellent in producing flat or single-degree curved structural composites.

Braided Fabrics: Sock/Sleeve/Tubing/Braided Broad Goods

The terms *sock*, *sleeve*, and *tubing* are all synonymous with a specialty form of fabric weave that comes in a continuous, flexible tube of woven material, resembling a seamless tube sock. This tubular fabric is created by helically braiding a plain weave of yarns fed from spools of reinforcement fibers. When compressed in length, the diameter of the sock increases and, when stretched, the sock's diameter decreases—similar to a novelty finger-cuff. This flexibility in diameter and length is helpful in fabricating hollow, tubular structures, including those that change in diameter along their

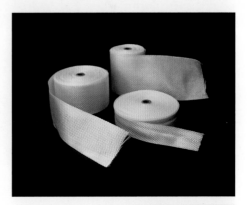

Fiber Direction

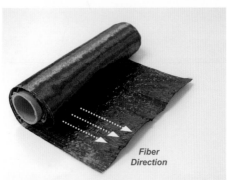

Other fiber forms include (clockwise from top left) sleeve/tube-woven, bi-directional tape, tow, and unidirectional.

length. This form of reinforcement is also available in unidirectional, bi-directional, triaxial, and other specialty braided forms—depending on the needs of the application. It is usually supplied by flattening the sock weave against itself, and then rolling it up for shipping or storage. Additionally, these braided reinforcements can be converted to broad good form by cutting them down one side to produce woven biaxial (+45/-45 degree) and triaxial (0, +45/-45, or 0, +60/-60 degree) fabrics that have excellent drapeability when compared with stitched fabrics of the same fiber orientations—making them especially useful for compound curved shapes.

Tapes

Some specialty reinforcements come woven into narrow *tapes* that resemble their wider fabric counterparts, and include a *selvaged edge*—with fibers woven at the edge of the fabric to keep the rest of the weave from fraying. They come in different widths commonly ranging from 1 to 10 inches and are available in a wide range of reinforcement fiber types. These tapes are especially useful for localized or directional reinforcement of a laminate and for small projects.

Non-woven Reinforcements are available for composite laminates that require special properties uncommon in woven reinforcements. Some of these properties include added strength through very controlled, directional fiber alignment or added bulk with multidirectional fiber placement. To achieve these ends, unidirectional fiber, mat, veil, tow, strand, or roving fiber forms are available.

Unidirectional Fiber

For applications that require maximum directional strength per volume, *unidirectional fiber*, or "uni", is an excellent option. Unidirectional fiber is composed of fibers all oriented in one direction with a light binder or periodic woven fill fibers to loosely hold the reinforcements together. In spite of their excellent strength and fiber consolidation, unidirectional composites tend to delaminate in a composite more easily than those created with woven fabrics because there are no significant fill yarns tying the warp fibers in place. Additionally, they can be very difficult to laminate onto compound curved surfaces, especially if laid onto the mold faces in wide strips.

Mat

Supplied in rolls and used for multi-directional strength and quick build-up of a laminate, *mat* is composed of randomly arranged short fibers held together by a special binder. Mat is used extensively for marine and automotive body repair and for building up FRP molds. Though it has good multi-directional strength, mat has large gaps between the fibers that tend to harbor excess resin, creating a comparatively heavy and more brittle composite.

Veil

Veil is a very thin fabric with a cobweb-like appearance that is very similar to mat, yet is composed of much

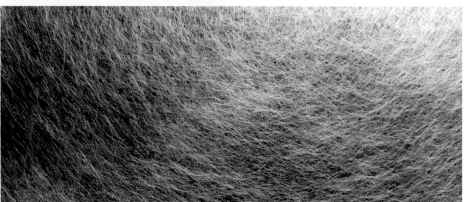

Fiberglass mat (top) is non-woven, as is its more finely-stranded cousin, fiberglass veil (bottom).

finer fibers. Veil is especially helpful in reducing print through that develops when a laminate is heated or exposed to wet environments that would expand and contract the resin and fiber in the composite. Veil can even be adhered to the back of looser fabrics to help keep them from fraying during layup.

Tow/Strand/Roving

Bundled reinforcement fibers that are supplied on reels are referred to as *tow*, *strand*, or *roving*. High-performance fibers, such as carbon and aramid, are typically supplied as tow or strand and are commonly used in filament winding processes. *Filament winding* produces pressure vessels and specialty structures that have incredible strength through specific, directed—and usually automated—fiber alignment.

Fiberglass filaments, gathered together as roving, are also used in filament winding, but are more commonly utilized in spray-ups with a chopper gun. This form of fiberglass is available in large bulk spools that feed the roving out from the center of the spool into the chopper gun.

Conclusion

In conclusion, there are several fiber forms and resins available for a given composites application. Ultimately, the strength of a composite laminate and structure is dependent on the fiber and resin used, the orientation of the reinforcement fibers, the completeness of resin curing, the shaping of the laminate, and the effective use of sandwich core construction.

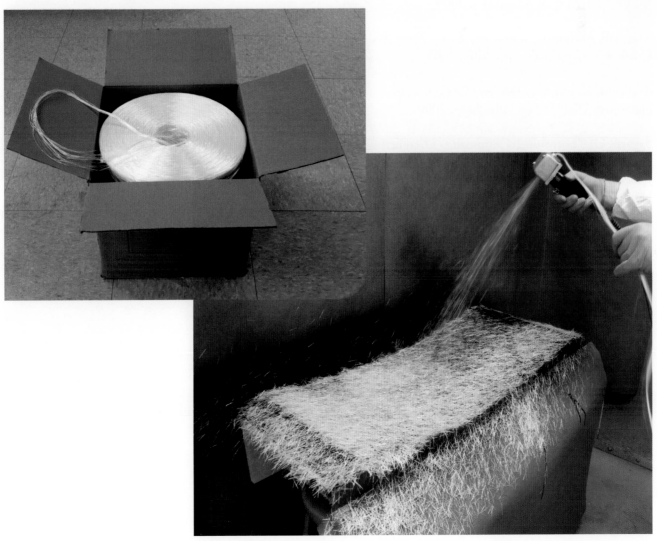

Fiberglass is available in bulk rolls as a yarn-like "roving" material, which is commonly used for spray up processes (shown at right).

References and Resources

Aird, Forbes. *Fiberglass & Other Composite Materials*. New York, NY: HP Books, 2006

Barbero, Ever J. *Introduction to Composite Materials Design*. Boca Raton: CRC Press, 2011

Birch, Stuart "Lotus Small and Maneuverable." *Automotive Engineering International*, 116, no. 6 (May 2008).

Dorworth, Louis, et.al, *Essentials of Advanced Composite Fabrication & Repair*. Newcastle, WA: Aviation Supplies & Academics, 2009

Marshall, Andrew C., *Composite Basics, 7th ed.* Walnut Creek, CA : Marshall Consulting, 2005

McBeath, Simon. *Competition Car Composites*. Sparkford, UK: Haynes Publishing, 2000

Savage, G., "Formula 1 Composites Engineering," *Engineering Failure Analysis* 17 (2010): 92-115.

Sherman, Lilli M. "Polyurethane Composites: New Alternative to Polyester and Vinyl Ester." *Plastics Technology*, Article Post 3/1/2006. www.ptonline.com

Smith, Zeke, *Advanced Composite Techniques*. Napa: Aeronaut Press, 2005.

Stewart, Eric "Epoxy and Fuel Resistance Tests, Part 1: Epoxy Basics." *Kitplanes*, Belvoir Publications (May 2018)

Strong, Brent. *Fundamentals of Composites Manufacturing: Materials, Methods, and Applications, 2nd ed.* Dearborn, MI: Society of Manufacturing Engineers, 2008.

Wanberg, John. *Composite Materials Handbook #1*, Stillwater, MN: Wolfgang Publications Inc., 2009.

Wanberg, John. *Composite Materials Handbook #2*, Stillwater, MN: Wolfgang Publications Inc., 2010.

Wiley, Jack. *The Fiberglass Repair and Construction Handbook, 2nd ed.* Summit, PA: Tab Books, 1988.

Composites World Sourcebook 2017 – www.compositesworld.com/suppliers

High Performance Composites magazine

Composites Technology magazine

Composites World magazine

Composites Manufacturing magazine

www.acma.net

www.arkema.com/en/products/product-finder/range-viewer/Elium-resins-for-composites/

www.azom.com

www.compositesone.com

www.compositeenvisions.com

www2.dupont.com

www.hexcel.com

www.luciteinternational.com
www.matweb.com

www.NEiSoftware.com, *Composite Analysis Compendium*, 2010.

www.sollercomposites.com

www.westsystem.com

Chapter Two

Health, Safety, and Shop Setup

General Health Concerns with Composites

Several guidelines should be followed to ensure safer fabrication when using composites. This chapter provides some basic insights about specific health and safety concerns associated with composites to help fabricators avoid uncomfortable, unhealthy, or life-threatening problems related to vision, hearing, breathing, or skin contact.

First, before using ***any*** of the chemicals associated with composites, be sure to thoroughly familiarize yourself with their related *Safety Data Sheet* (SDS). In most developed countries, an SDS is required information from chemical manufacturers and retailers to explain how their chemicals may affect a person's health, and how to use the chemical safely. SDS are often available through the manufacturers' or retailers' own websites for review prior to purchasing the materials. *Be sure to review this information before using any of the chemicals present in a composite layup or fabrication project!*

Proper facilities and safety gear are imperative when working with composite materials (photo courtesy of Josh McGuckin, www.cameracourage.com)

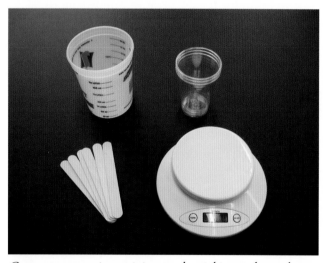

Protective eyewear (top left), hearing protection (top right), breathing protection (bottom left), and hand protection (bottom right) are all required items in a composites shop.

Common measuring, mixing, and weighing tools are shown here.

Examples of air spraying equipment and necessary cutting tools.

Vision Hazards

Eye protection should be worn anytime power tools are being used, open containers of liquid chemicals are present, or dust is airborne in the composites work environment. Goggles made specifically for use with chemicals will provide the most protection from chemical splashes as they cover the face and eyes from all sides. If chemicals do come in contact with the eyes, flush them immediately with generous amounts of water for at least 15 minutes, holding the eyelids open to ensure best washout, and then consult a physician.

Hearing Hazards

Power tools used with composites tend to create noise levels that can damage hearing sensitivity through repeated or prolonged exposure. To avoid hearing loss, use adequate ear protection, such as in-ear plugs or sound-deadening earmuffs anytime loud equipment is in use.

Breathing Hazards

Wood and metal dust from mold making activities can produce generous amounts of nuisance particles that can make breathing uncomfortable. Even worse, airborne dust created by trimming a composite can have especially dangerous long-term effects to your lungs. This is true of the larger particles created when cutting reinforcement fabrics, but also of the fine dust generated when sanding composites. Whenever possible, use a fine particle mask made specifically for working with fiberglass to minimize dust inhalation. Keep a shop vacuum, downdraft table, or centralized dust collection system running closely enough to the cutting area to collect the majority of dust discharged during composite cutting or sanding operations. Airborne dust can also be significantly reduced by employing wet-sanding techniques.

Polyester and vinyl ester resins, liquid acrylic resin, styrene monomer, and the myriad of solvents common to composites fabrication all produce hazardous fumes. To minimize exposure to these, use a snugly fitting NIOSH (National Institute for Occupational Safety and Health) respirator with fresh organic vapor filters. This basic respiratory protection *must* be supplemented with a fresh air ventilation in the composites work area to minimize skin exposure and subsequent absorption of chemical vapors. Use an electric fan, such as a large box fan, as needed to bring fresh air into your work area. Without ensuring such helpful breathing aids, light-headedness, nausea, and neurological impairment may quickly occur. If such exposure occurs, get fresh air immediately and seek medical attention.

Skin Contact Hazards

Fully cured composites are generally chemically inert and present no significant chemical danger to a person's skin, but uncured resins may have serious effects on a person's health, especially as they may cause allergic reactions. This is particularly true of epoxies and the allergic sensitization they can cause. To ensure the safe handling of these liquids, use latex, nitrile, or vinyl gloves on your hands whenever touching liquid or partially cured resins. Special barrier creams made specifically for use with resins can provide added protection and will also help in clean-up after a layup is complete. If you do experience an allergic reaction in spite of adhering to these precautions, immediately discontinue use of the chemicals and contact a physician.

Take special care when handling MEKP catalysts as they can cause chemical burns to the skin. If a spill does occur, completely wash the skin with water as soon as possible, and for a duration of at least 15 minutes. If MEKP gets spilled on clothing, remove the clothing immediately and wash any areas of skin that may have come in contact with the liquid. Contact a physician if any adverse effects occur after water rinsing is complete.

Avoid getting resin on any areas of your body. Protect arms from resin contact to avoid redness and itching from developing on the sensitive skin found at the soft under-part of your forearms. If you do get resin on your skin, do not use solvent to remove it; doing so will simply thin out the resin and allow it to penetrate your skin. Instead, wipe off as much resin as possible with an absorbent paper towel or rag, then use strong soap (such as any citrus-based cleaner commonly found in automotive stores) and warm water to remove the remaining resin residue.

When trimming or cutting a cured composite, protect your skin from the resulting rough or sharp laminate edges which may cause scratches, abrasions, and heinous slivers. Leather gloves, like those common to sheet metal working, can be a very welcome aid when handling such hazardous

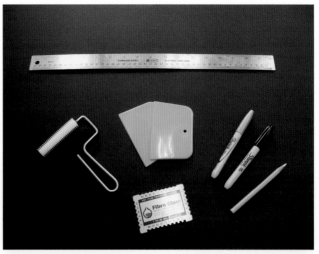

Additional tools for measuring (including gel coat gauge, at bottom), marking, and also applying resin.

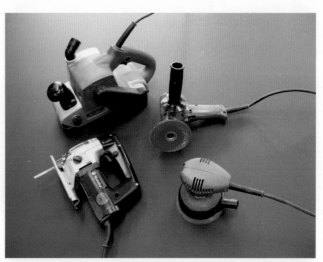

Power tools for sanding and cutting include belt and rotary (and orbital) sanders, and a jigsaw.

Hacksaws (for cutting composites and metals) and handsaws (for cutting soft mold-making materials) are good items to keep around.

29

composite edges. Fiberglass and carbon fiber pieces can be extremely stiff, so use caution whenever near exposed strands or fibers. Clear fiberglass slivers can be particularly difficult to locate, but due diligence in tracking these down can significantly decrease the discomfort they can cause. If stray composite slivers lodge in your skin, simply extract them with tweezers and apply a common antiseptic, such as rubbing alcohol or hydrogen peroxide, to the sliver site and use a bandage to prevent infection.

The fine particles produced during trimming and sanding can also cause considerable irritation when their stiff microscopic fibers lodge in the skin. Some individuals successfully avoid such itchy scenarios by either wearing long sleeved clothing, closing their pores with a gratuitous application of baby powder or corn starch prior to working, or by rinsing their skin with very hot water to sweat the fibers out from their pores after exposure.

Biomechanical Hazards

Working with composites, as with other materials, can entail the use of varying repetitive biomechanical motions of the arms and hands—such as when sanding, waxing, polishing, dabbing with a brush, and using various hand tools and power tools. In the short term, these motions may seem harmless enough, but when compounded over time (especially without physical rest), they can cause repetitive

motion or repetitive stress injuries. Additionally, constant vibration from power tools can cause nerves to inflame in the carpal tunnel of the wrist creating numbness in the fingertips and hand. These injuries can be of serious concern as they may cause long term or permanent damage to muscles, nerves, ligaments, and tendons in the body. When experiencing the physically taxing motions associated with composite fabrication, be sure to take frequent breaks and allow your body time to repair itself.

To avoid accelerated fatigue, wear comfortable, good fitting clothes and shoes. These will make a noticeable difference when engaging in a long layup or extended work day with composites.

Other Concerns

Never ingest the resins, catalysts, hardeners, or solvents used with composites. If such a mishap occurs, follow the chemical manufacturer's recommendations for handling ingestion incidents and seek immediate medical assistance.

Uncured resins and solvents present flammability hazards so store them away from any sources of heat or sparks, including space heaters, open flame shop heaters, pilot lights, water heaters, furnaces, and lit cigarettes. Always ensure that all liquid chemicals used with composites are properly contained, stored, and then used in a well-ventilated, ignition-source free environment.

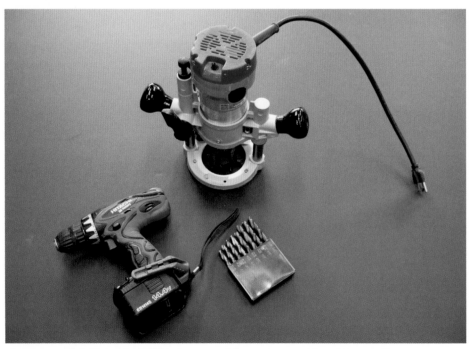

Dispose of resin and solvent-soaked rags in a fire-safe waste receptacle.

On a smooth concrete or tile floor, spilled liquid resins can be as slick as the notorious banana peel. They can also create a difficult clean-up problem if tracked all over a work space. To avoid any potential problems, wipe up spilled chemicals as quickly as possible with absorbent paper or cloth rags, or with absorbent sand, sawdust, or vermiculite. Absorbed chemicals should then be disposed of as local laws require, especially in large quantities.

A router and drill (with drill bits) are good for various mold-making needs.

In addition to these general health and safety concerns, beware of resin contact with clothing or tools. Inadvertently smearing or dripping resin on expensive or important objects can quickly cause costly damage. Wear appropriate work clothing when fabricating composites, such as an old t-shirt, thick but comfortable jeans, and close-toed shoes. Even though shorts may be tempting to wear while working with composites in warm weather, it would be wise to put on pants instead. If resin drips into one's leg hair, or if jagged-edged parts rub against your legs it can cause some very unpleasant or painful problems.

Shop Setup and Layout

Whether starting a composites shop from scratch or upgrading an existing shop to accommodate composites projects, the following guidelines will help in creating an optimal workspace for composites fabrication.

Composites should be created in a room that has a controlled, stable temperature for the duration of the mold preparation, layup, and resin cure cycle. Most resin systems work best at room-temperature, around 75 degrees Fahrenheit (24 degrees Celsius). However if there is any variation in your work area's temperature, it is best if it errs to the side of warmth rather than cold. Cold resin will cure painfully slow, or may simply not cure at all. Warm resin, though, will cure faster than normal, and will at least likely cure completely. Fabricators in warm climates routinely operate with their doors open to the outside air without problems. However, in cold climates, a shop with environmental controls is imperative. Keep in mind that composites should never be laid up in direct sunlight; the UV light and heat created by the sun will quickly cure the resin in a composite—and usually much faster than anticipated!

As mentioned earlier, polyester, vinyl ester, and liquid acrylic resins can be hazardous to breathe for prolonged periods of time, and solvent fumes are generally dangerous in their own right. Even epoxy resins can cause fume hazards if they are allowed to overheat—as with an unattended mixed pot of resin gone awry. Whenever possible, use open windows, dedicated fume hoods, or open-air workspaces to promote positive fresh airflow.

Dust, debris, foreign chemicals, water, and other matter can compromise the resin's adhesion within the composite or cause surface blistering and delamination in the final laminate. Consequently, to guarantee a clean composites environment, it is best to dedicate at least two distinctly separate work spaces in your shop: one space clean enough for quality layups, and one for various messy mold-making, trimming, and sanding tasks. These spaces should be adequately isolated from each other with walls or hanging drop cloths.

Provide generous amounts of easily accessible shelf space to organize tools and materials. Likewise, arrange your workspace so it is free of cumbersome obstacles, unnecessary items, and tight spaces. A complicated layup is far less frustrating when you are not stumbling over car parts, pets, or garage-sale fodder.

Securely store liquid chemicals in flame resistant cabinets and away from access by children or pets.

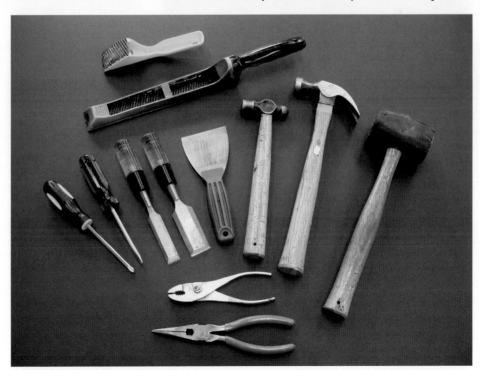

Necessary hand tools include shaper rasps (top), screwdrivers and chisels (left), a putty knife (center), hammers and mallets (right), and pliers (bottom).

31

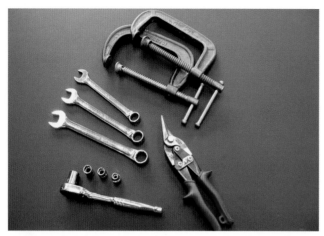

Other needed tools include clamps (top), wrenches (left), and metal snips (bottom right).

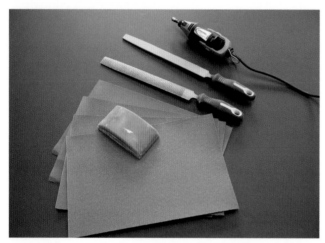

For shaping and finishing purposes, have sandpaper and a sanding block (bottom), along with files (center), and a rotary tool (top).

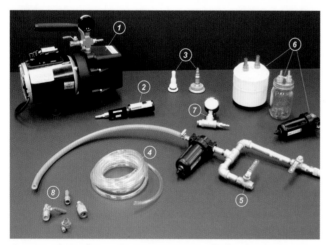

Some tools used in vacuum processes include: 1) vacuum pump, 2) vacuum generator (in place of a vacuum pump), 3) vacuum ports, 4) vinyl tubing, 5) valves for vacuum control, 6) resin traps (a few different styles shown here), 7) vacuum gauge, 8) various hose fittings for the vacuum system.

Store rolls of fabric on shelves (or, if possible, on a roll-stand) rather than propping them up on end—as this will help keep the fabric from slumping and distorting the fabric's weave. Tools and consumables should be stored on shelving or in cabinets so they can be easily accessed but secure from accidentally falling onto your projects.

Make sure to provide space for storing completed, in-use, or archived molds. Molds typically embody considerable investment, so they should be stored in an environment free of excessive moisture, temperature extremes, or physical hazards that may damage them.

One mistake many fabricators make is to underestimate the amount of space needed for composites work. This is especially true of horizontal work spaces, such as a table or workbench space needed for mold prep, cutting, resin mixing, layup, de-molding, and other tasks. As a general rule of thumb, the tabletop area required to perform a layup alone should be at least three to five times the size of the parts or molds you are planning to fabricate. In addition to space for layups, provide room for measuring and cutting reinforcement fabrics. Typically, the area of a 5' x 10' table surface will suffice for this unless you are embarking on a project outside the scope of a reasonably-sized, one-person wet layup. It is also advisable to have separate tables for cutting and layup activities to keep unwanted resin spills from soaking into clean reinforcement fabrics.

Place all necessary resins and solvents within reach so they are readily available during mold making and layup procedures. This includes positioning them in such a way that you will not have to precariously reach over an open mold or layup to access them. Temporarily placing them under the work table or on a shelf near the work space can be helpful in this regard.

If possible, set your work surfaces high enough (preferably at waist height) to be comfortable for leaning or standing over for extended periods of time. Squatting too low or lifting your arms too high for an hour or two at a time can cause considerable fatigue or back pain. In the case of performing layups in large or awkwardly shaped molds, it may help to place the mold on the ground or otherwise alter the height of the workspace for more comfortable access into the mold.

Even if the only space you have available for composites fabrication is in the tool shed behind the hydrangea bush, make sure to sufficiently illuminate your work area. Ample light will help you avoid dangerous obstacles, misplaced items, inadvertent chemical spills, or poorly applied laminate plies.

Lastly, when designating a location for your workspace, try to avoid the "ship-in-a-bottle" mistake—wherein a piece-by-piece fabrication project quickly outgrows its ability to fit through the shop doorway. Use some pragmatic foresight and plan ahead for a way to move your final composite project out of the shop once it is completed—even if it means re-designing the project so it can be broken down into smaller pieces to get it through the door!

Basic Composites Layup Tools

The following is a list of the various tools and materials used in fabricating composites, the majority of which are readily available at most hardware stores—or may already be in your shop.

Measuring and Mixing Containers

General use measuring and mixing containers are available at most paint and hardware stores. For most mixing needs, re-used and well-cleaned plastic tubs (from butter or other grocery items) can be equally effective—and less expensive.

Mixing Sticks

To mix resins thoroughly (and cleanly), clean popsicle sticks, tongue suppressors, or paint mixing sticks all work very well.

Electrical Extension Cord

A heavy-duty electrical extension cord and reliable electrical source is especially helpful when using corded power tools.

Compressed Air Supply, Hoses, and Tools

Several mold making, trimming, and spraying operations are significantly enhanced with access to compressed air-operated tools. Rotary cut-off tools, dual-action sanders, an HVLP sprayer, and an

air blow-gun are not necessarily required for small projects, but can be very helpful in many larger composite fabrication situations. Air tools can also have longer tool life in a composites shop since the air that powers them also blows away abrasive particles, minimizing premature bearing wear.

Digital Scale

For small resin batches, invest in a digital scale that can precisely measure small quantities, such as one that is accurate to 1/10th of a gram. For large batches, a larger scale can be helpful.

Scissors

All-metal scissors (available at upholstery supply shops) will provide the best service life and can be re-sharpened once dull—if re-sharpening services are locally available. If your shop budget is tight, at least get scissors that have all-metal blades (rather than plastic-reinforced blades). Such scissors are typically viewed as a consumable, since they tend to dull quickly. For cutting aramid fabrics, use scissors with serrated blades made of high carbon steel or another very hard material.

Airbrush or Refillable Aerosol Spray Kit

A small hobby airbrush is helpful for applying liquid mold-release evenly to mold surfaces. Some

A pressure vessel (left) is great for producing high-pressure laminates, while a large resin trap (right) is important for big resin infusion jobs.

33

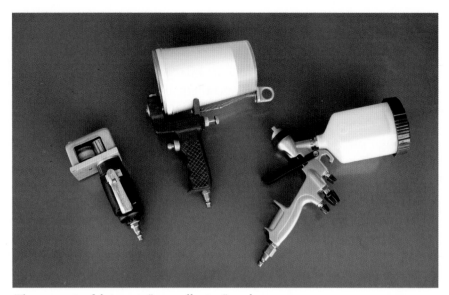

The composite fabricators "gun collection": a chopper gun (left), gel coat cup gun (center), and HVLP spray gun.

manufacturers also make small aerosol spray paint kits that contain a pressurize air can with a detachable and refillable bottle.

Utility Knife

A simple utility knife can be used for cutting tapes, films, and other items. It is also helpful in cutting thick, heavy reinforcements when guided with a metal-edged ruler.

Rotary Fabric Cutter

Rotary fabric cutters are available at fabric stores and are good for cutting thin fiberglass and carbon fiber reinforcements, as well as pre-pregs. The blades are replaceable, and circle-cutting attachments are available for them as well.

Plastic Spreaders

Commonly used in automotive bodywork, simple plastic spreaders are great for spreading resin into flat reinforcements. Once the resin has cured on them it can be easily removed with a quick flex of the spreader.

Resin Rollers

To help consolidate composites and work extra-tacky resins into reinforcements—such as polyester resin with fiberglass mat—these ringed rollers work very well. Disposable and replaceable roller-head types are available at many composite supply stores. Small diameter rollers are best for tight corners and small projects. Large rollers are best for applying heavy pressure to squeeze air out of a thick laminate. "Barrel" rollers have a slight convex shape to them and are good for laminating fibers onto curved surfaces.

Brushes

Bristled brushes have longer usefulness than foam brushes overall when used with

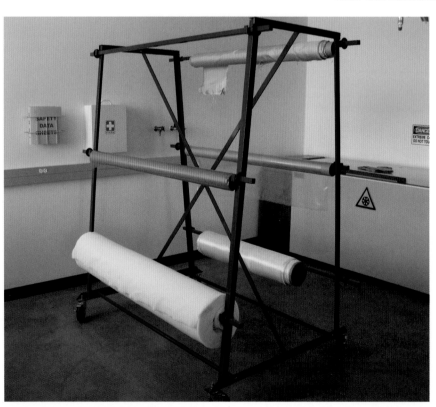

A roll-stand is excellent for keeping fabric and bagging materials organized and clean. Roll-stands like this are also equipped with wheels to easily move the whole rack to the work space.

resins. They are helpful for dabbing resin into reinforcements, especially with large and curved-surface projects. Inexpensive brushes work well for most projects, but remove any loose bristles from them before layup.

Marker and White Colored Pencil

Black, silver, or white permanent markers are indispensable for marking patterns or cut-lines on reinforcement fabrics and cured composite parts. White colored pencil works very well to mark cut lines on dark, coarse, peel-ply treated carbon fiber composites.

Gel Coat Gauge

A gel coat gauge is useful in determining the thickness of a wet gel coat. The gauge has several fingers on it which, when pressed against the gel coat, show how deep the gel coat is.

Fire-resistant Trash Receptacle

Solvent and chemical-soaked rags can pose a fire risk if they react or combust, so place them in a fire-resistant trash container. If such a trash receptacle is not available, at the very least place rags in a metal trash can with a tight-fitting lid. Dispose of used rags daily, as required by local law, to avoid a dangerous build-up of chemically reactive waste.

Mold-making Tools

Foam-shaping Rasp (or Drywall Rasp)

These inexpensive rasps can quickly remove material from urethane or styrene-based foams to rough out a desired form. The cutting screen on most rasps can be replaced once dull.

Electric Buffer

A skillfully used electric buffer is indispensable for quickly polishing large mold surfaces.

Hand Saw or Carpenter's Saw

Simple "old-school" hand-powered saws can quickly shape large, soft materials, such as foam or wood used in mold-making.

Electric Jigsaw

For cutting curved shapes in flat material, an electric jigsaw works well. Use a blade that has teeth to match the thickness of the material to cut: fine-toothed blade for thin and hard materials, coarse-toothed blade for thick and soft materials.

Bandsaw

A bandsaw is especially helpful for cutting various thickness materials with better precision than a jigsaw. This is also good for cutting styrene-based foams in place of a hot-wire cutter.

Drill Bits and Drill(s)

High-speed steel bits work well for drilling in sheet metal and wood, but for drilling into composites, carbide, titanium-nitride coated, or cobalt bits will provide a much longer service life. A drill, whether corded, cordless, or on a drill press, is especially helpful for various mold-making and part finishing tasks.

Router

For making mold roundovers, trimming rough part edges, and making multiple copies of a part using a pattern, a router with carbide bits is helpful.

Sheet Metal Snips

These are good for occasional sheet metal cuts for patterns or molds, and for rough-trimming composite laminates.

General Mechanic's Tools

For various fabrication tasks, procure a set of Phillips and standard screwdrivers, socket wrench and sockets, adjustable wrenches, and pliers.

Various body fillers and filler materials are used with composites.

Hammers and Rubber Mallets

For applying some nicely directed brute force, a ball-peen hammer, claw hammer, and a good rubber mallet are helpful.

Chisels

Chisels come in handy for shaping and refining mold shapes in wood, plaster, and foam, and for certain mold cleanup situations.

Stainless Steel Ruler, Flexible Drafting Tool, and Shape Gauge

Flexible metal rulers, like common stainless steel ones, are excellent for creating smooth curved guidelines for trimming or making patterns. Flexible drafting tools are good for verifying and transferring curves. Where a shape or contour needs to be copied from one area to another, a shape gauge can be additionally helpful.

Vise and Clamps

A simple bench vise is great for securing your work, as are c-clamps and wooden handscrew clamps. Quick-clamps (whether trigger activated or spring-based) can be especially helpful for holding items together.

Tablesaw

For straight cutting large stock and ripping wood to size for plug and mold-making tasks, a tablesaw can be indispensable.

Demolding Tools

Putty Knives

A plastic putty knife can be useful for prying up the edges of a part in a mold to create spaces for wedges to be inserted. Metal putty knives can also help in mixing and spreading fillers.

Plastic or Wooden Wedges

Plastic or wooden wedges (never metal ones) are pushed into thin spaces between the mold and part to help extract it from a mold. These can be made by simply cutting plastic or wood stock on a bandsaw, though commercial types are also available.

Air Compressor and Air Wedge

For some stubborn parts, air injected into gaps between the mold and part can loosen the part and help push it out of the mold. Typical shop air compressor pressure (between 50 and 90 psi) is usually adequate and relatively safe.

Trimming and Finishing Tools

Plastic Tub or Bin

A polypropylene of polyethylene plastic bin helps with wet-sanding or solvent cleaning of parts. Such large, shallow tubs can be purchased at most housewares or home improvement stores.

Rotary Cutting Tools

A rotary tool (either electric or air powered) with cut-off wheel or rotary file attachments can make quick work of trimming a composite part. The use of a flexible "gooseneck" type extension cable can help keep abrasive dust away from the motor and bearings of an electric rotary tool.

A few common consumable items are shown here: mold releases and brushes (top left), various tapes (top right), solvents (bottom left), and towels (bottom right).

Angle Grinder

For thick, jagged-edged composites, a grinder with a thin metal-cutting abrasive wheel can speedily cut through laminate materials.

Sanding Blocks and Files

Sanding blocks and files, are indispensable for creating true surfaces on molds and parts. Likewise, a file can knock down rough, abrasive edges very quickly.

Electric Palm Sander and Belt Sander

Electric palm sanding, belt sanding, or air-powered dual-action sanding can significantly minimize the time and fatigue common with hand sanding.

Hacksaw and Jigsaw

Manual hacksaws and jigsaws are great for cutting small or thin laminates.

Additional Tools

For most common home-built composites work, the above tools should suffice. However, several additional tools can be very helpful in a wet-layup composites shop. These tools include some of the following specialty items, all of which may be purchased from composites suppliers or other online or industrial sources.

Vacuum Pump or Vacuum Generator, Vacuum Gauge, Hose, and Fittings

Many advanced composite processes require a dedicated vacuum pump or vacuum generator. Vacuum pumps are available from many composites and industrial tool suppliers, and can be purchased in sizes that will meet the needs of practically any sized project. A vacuum gauge placed in line with the vacuum can help give a good reading about the level of vacuum, or otherwise show if there are any leaks in the vacuum system.

Resin Trap

When performing vacuum bagging and infusion processes, a resin trap is placed in line with the vacuum to keep stray resin from being drawn into the vacuum pump. These are commercially available, but can also be fabricated using inexpensive materials and air fittings.

Hot Wire Cutter

A hot wire cutter is a high tension, electrically-heated wire that melts through foam with ease. It is commercially available in several sizes or can be built using simple online plans.

Gel Coat Gun

To apply smooth polyester gel coats, especially over large areas, a gel coat gun works wonders. Gel coat guns are powered by compressed air that has around 6 CFM of air flow.

Chopper Gun

This specialized device showers pieces of chopped fiberglass roving into large molds during spray-up processes. Professional versions of these also spray catalyzed polyester or vinyl ester resin along with the fiberglass onto the mold.

HVLP Spray Gun

An inexpensive high-volume, low-pressure (HVLP) spray gun is useful for spraying sealing primer and mold release. A separate spray gun is advisable for applying finishes over a cured composite for best results.

Vacuum Thermoformer

This machine creates open shapes from sheet plastic by heating it and using a vacuum to pull it against a form—and can quickly make disposable

 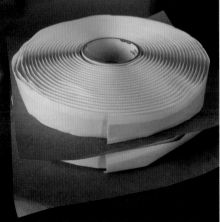

Make sure to never place sealant tape edge-down (the results of which are shown on the left)! Always store it on its side with protective cardboard or rigid plastic between rolls (as shown to the right).

molds for composites. Industrial versions are available, but online plans for smaller versions can be fabricated at low cost.

Pressure Vessel

A pressure vessel (such as a purpose-built type, or a modified paint pressure tank) can produce high-pressure laminates with wet layup composites—and is much cheaper than an autoclave.

Sewing Machine

For some specialized uses, it is helpful to sew reinforcement fabrics prior to layup. Depending on the thickness or coarseness of the fabric used, it may be helpful to use an industrial-grade sewing machine.

Roll-stand (with a Dust Cover) for Rolls of Reinforcements

When using multiple rolls of reinforcement fabrics, a roll stand can provide immense help in organizing and moving large, cumbersome rolls of material.

Fire-proof Cabinets

Though these are listed as "non-essential", some local regulations (especially for businesses) require fire-proof cabinets for storing reactive chemicals.

Wheeled Tables, Shelves, and Dollies

Moveable tables and shelves can be very helpful to reconfigure small shop spaces. For moving large molds and projects, wooden dollies or hand trucks help avoid a sprained back or broken foot.

Down-draft Sanding Tables

A down-draft sanding table can help pull hazardous airborne dust away from a workpiece. Commercial units are available, but online plans can help you build your own.

Water-jet Cutter

Though they can be expensive, abrasive water-jet cutting equipment or services can quickly, accurately, and cleanly cut all types of composites.

Large Oven or Heating Box (for Curing and Post-curing)

A common, surplus kitchen oven can work well to accelerate or post-cure a composite—but use a dedicated oven for post-curing purposes to avoid potential health risks with food preparation in the same oven. An aluminum foil lined wooden box with heat lamps can also provide good results, as long as air is circulated within the box and heating output can be controlled.

Heat Blankets

As with an oven or heated box, common heat blankets—like those used in cold climates or for therapeutic purposes—can be placed in contact with a curing composite (separated by a thin polyethylene or nylon film) to speed its cure or provide low-grade post-curing.

Materials and Consumables

Solvents

Acetone and lacquer thinner are best for cleaning up resin spills and sticky tools. Naphtha and mineral spirits are useful in cleaning up modeling clay, sealant tape, and oil residues. For removing cured epoxy, paint stripper (with methylene chloride) works well.

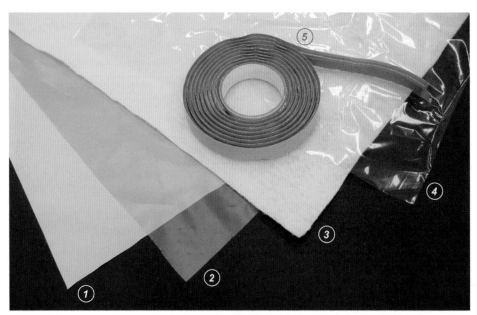

Common vacuum bagging materials include the following: 1) peel ply, 2) perforated release ply, 3) breather/bleeder cloth, 4) vacuum-bagging film, and 5) sealant tape.

Screws, Bolts, and Nuts

A supply of common fasteners in several sizes is beneficial for various mold-making procedures.

Body Filler

Body filler (also referred to as *fairing compound*) is used for filling imperfections and small gaps in mold patterns and parts. General automotive body fillers are adequate for most mold-making uses, while specialty fillers are available for perfecting final part surfaces.

Drywall Compound

Drywall compound is more cost effective than body filler for large mold or mold pattern shaping. It can be sanded very quickly and can be purchased in large buckets, but it is much softer than body filler and can take considerably longer to dry.

Dry Sandpaper

For shaping and smoothing the materials used in composites fabrication, keep some basic sandpaper available in grits ranging from 80 to 220.

Wet-sandpaper (Fine Grits)

A variety of wet-sandpapers from 220 to 2000 grits are used for achieving a high-quality surface finish on parts and molds. For fast material removal, some wet-sandpapers are available as course as 80 grit—a very useful alternative to the dust produced by dry, heavy grit dry sandpapers.

Rubbing Compounds

Rubbing compound is used for polishing out the scratches left in a mold patter or mold surface after sanding. Different abrasive grits are available, depending on the final surface shine you desire for your mold. It is generally advisable to keep multiple rubbing compounds on hand, ranging from course, to medium, to fine.

Cloths

Terry cloths are helpful in wiping up general chemical spills or for buffing wax mold-release. Soft cotton cloths are good for applying mold-release paste wax and PVA. General soft-paper cleanup rags are an inexpensive aid for keeping hands and tools clean during layups.

Mold-release/Parting Wax (Paste Wax)

High-quality mold-release wax (also known as "*parting wax*"), is imperative for quick, effective release of wet layup composite parts. *Don't take a chance with a low-cost substitute (such as car wax)!*

High-temp Liquid Release

Certain liquid releases tend to work better for elevated-temperature cured laminates than paste waxes—and often require less work to apply!

PVA Liquid

Polyvinyl-alcohol (PVA) is a liquid mold-release that is applied and then dried over parting wax. It acts as a water-soluble second line of defense against parts sticking to a mold—at least when used with resins that don't produce water as a by-product of the curing process (as phenolics will do). PVA can be brushed or wiped onto a waxed mold, but is best applied with a small hobby airbrush or refillable aerosol spray can.

Heat Shrink Tape or Tubing

Specialty non-adhesive clear heat shrink tape contracts in length when heated and is used around a mandrel-formed composites to provide fiber-consolidating pressure. Heat shrink tubing can be used for mandrel-formed layups, but is available in limited diameter sizes and must have a special release on it for use with composites. These items are available through some limited composites materials suppliers.

Masking Tape

Common painter's masking tape is great for keeping resin off certain areas of a mold or workspace and for otherwise protecting surfaces from scratches.

Polyethylene Flash Tape

Polyethylene flash tape provides a stretchy, removable mold-release and holds materials in place during vacuum-bagged procedures.

> Specialty non-adhesive clear heat shrink tape contracts in length when heated and is used around a mandrel-formed composites to provide fiber-consolidating pressure.

39

Packing Tape

It has natural release properties and many resins will not adhere to it once cured, so it is useful for various mold-making tasks.

Sealant Tape

Sealant tape is a gummy, sticky, silicone-based material that comes on rolls with removable backing. It is used extensively for vacuum-bagging and dry layup processes but can be very handy for otherwise holding materials in place.

Mastic Tape

An inexpensive replacement for sealant tape, this common construction tape is not as stretchy as dedicated sealant tape, but can still be effective for many fabrication uses, such as temporarily adhering mold-making materials together.

Spray Adhesive

This aerosol-based adhesive is used to tack materials together in a mold during dry layup processes. Special epoxy-friendly versions of spray adhesive are available from some composites suppliers to enhance interlaminar strength of resin infused parts.

Extruded or Expanded Styrene Foam

These foams are used for insulating homes and are readily available at most home improvement stores in large sheets. Because of their relatively low cost and ease of use, they are great for making large, bulky forms, but can be dissolved by polyester, vinyl ester, and acrylic resins—but they can be used in direct contact with epoxy resins without any problem.

Urethane Foam or Vinyl Foam

Urethane and vinyl foams are very stable with all resin systems. They come in a variety of densities, measured in terms of their weight per cubic foot. For example, "10lb foam" is a medium-density foam that weighs about ten pounds per cubic foot. These foams are excellent for building large mold patterns and molds—though they can be a bit expensive—and are easily cut with a handsaw and formed with a rasp.

Two-part Urethane or Epoxy Foam

For filling odd shapes and large gaps, two-part urethane or epoxy foams are available from several sources. They come in various densities and are formed by simply mixing measured volumes of each part together, after which the two chemical components react and foam up to fill whatever volume they are poured into. Take note that some inexpensive, sprayable foams available in cans from hardware stores can become soft again when coated or otherwise removed from contact with air.

Flat or Formable Sheet Materials

Acrylic, styrene, and polypropylene plastic sheets ranging from 1/16" to 1/4" thick are excellent for various mold-making tasks.

Melamine-faced particle board, Masonite, and medium-density fiberboard (MDF), plywood, and oriented strand board (OSB) can make good jigs,

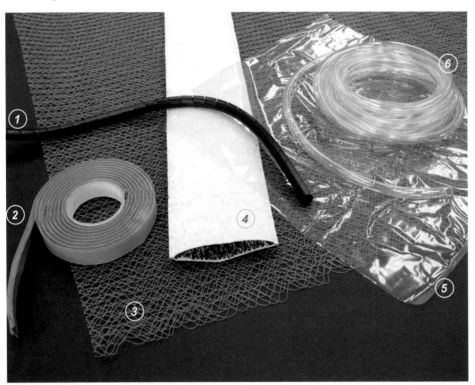

Resin infusion processes require additional materials, such as: 1) spiral-cut tubing, 2) sealant tape, 3) flow media, 4) infusion jacket material (optional), 5) vacuum-bagging film, and 6) vinyl tubing.

mold supports, mold templates and sections, and rib reinforcements—but should be completely sealed prior to using them as a mold surface.

Sheet metal can be formed into durable molds with complex shapes using typical metalworking tools. It can also be polished to a high-quality mirror finish and is great for high-volume production composite parts.

Plastic Film (1mil to 5mil Thick)

Polyethylene plastic film—commonly sold as a painter's drop cloth—can be an excellent, inexpensive option for protecting tabletops and other surfaces from resin spills. These films also work well for separating workspaces or for covering an uncured layup to protect it from shop dust and debris.

Absorbent Sand, Sawdust, or Vermiculite

These materials can be spread over large liquid messes, allowed to absorb for a while, and then scooped up with a shop broom or shovel. Remember to dispose of spilled materials as local safety regulations require.

Gloves (Latex or Nitrile Rubber, or Vinyl, and Leather)

Several pairs of reliable good-fitting, disposable gloves are necessary for general layup and cleanup tasks. Leather gloves are imperative for keeping hands safe around abrasive-edged composites.

Modeling Clay

Non-hardening, sulfur-free, oil-based modeling clay is available from art stores and some composites distributors, and is useful for creating mold patterns, and in various mold-making efforts.

Vacuum-bagging and Infusion Consumables

These are described in more detail in the chapter on *Improved Composite Techniques*, but include the following: release ply film, peel ply fabric, breather/bleeder cloth, bagging film, flow media

Conclusion

Most tools and materials used in composites fabrication are available through common hardware suppliers, although some specialty items can be procured through online composite-specific sources. Always understand the risks inherent with using any of the chemicals, materials, and tools associated with composites, and protect yourself appropriately. Adequately preparing yourself with these items and precautions will set you on your way to successfully fabricating composites—as we'll explore in the next chapter.

References and Resources

Gougeon Brothers, Inc. *West System User Manual & Product Guide*. 2008.

Richardson, T., Lokensgard, E., *Industrial Plastics: Theory and Application, 3rd Ed*. Albany, NY: Delmar Publishers. 1997.

System Three Resins, Inc. *The Epoxy Book*. 2004.

www.avma.org/PracticeManagement/Administration/Pages/MSDS101.aspx

www.compositesworld.com/articles/mold-release-update

www.fibreglast.com

www.grainger.com

www.healthandsafety.curtin.edu.au/Read_SDS_2011.pdf

www.hopkinsmedicine.org

www.msc.com

www.msdsauthoring.com/msds-safety-data-sheet-chemicals-osha-msds-rules

www.osha.gov

www.shopscissors.com

www.sollercomposites.com

Chapter Three

Getting Started with Composites

Having discussed some of the basics tools and space needed to work with composites, this chapter will cover some of the very basic hands-on techniques that form the basis of the many techniques discussed in this book. These techniques include methods for preparing mold surfaces, handling and cutting fabrics, using surface coats and gel coats, and measuring and applying resins to reinforcements.

Working with Molds

Proper preparation and use of a mold is *essential* to the quality of any composite part that comes out

Whether a beginner with composites, or a seasoned pro, the principles for wet layups are all the same—as explained in this chapter.

of it. If the mold surface is not sufficiently smooth, cleaned and waxed, parts will seize to the mold, rendering the part *and* mold unusable—wasting the time and materials invested in the part and mold's creation. To minimize problems, follow these following simple steps when preparing a mold for use with composites.

First, **completely clean the mold surface** with a cloth and warm water, and then wipe it dry with another clean cloth. If cleaning of any stubborn material is needed, carefully scrape it from the surface with a piece of hard wood or hard plastic—always opting to only scrape the mold surface with material that is at least a bit softer than the mold itself, whenever possible. If necessary, apply appropriate solvents, such as lacquer thinner and acetone (for uncured resin), or naphtha (for oil or clay) in sparing amounts to completely clean the surface.

Next, **ensure that all surface imperfections and features are smooth** on the mold prior to actual molding. A mold should be non-porous and have a mirror-like finish to it that is at least capable of showing the reflection of overhead lights in it. A high-quality finish can be created by using wet sandpaper to flatten, smooth, and then refine a surface with progressively finer grits. For flat or low-curvature surfaces, it is best to use sandpaper backed up by a sanding block to help evenly knockdown surface imperfections. These sanding steps can be followed with progressively finer grits of rubbing compound applied to the mold surface with a soft rag to bring the surface sheen up to a high luster.

In the case of molds that have porous or lightly damaged areas, it is best to fill those imperfections in a way that will allow them to release from the cured resin. Naturally releasing flash tape or clear packing tape work well in this regard. For porous areas on the mold face itself, very small holes (such as minute bubbles left in the surface of an FRP mold) can often be filled with parting wax after the mold has been cleaned. Slightly larger holes can often be completely filled with sulfur-free clay and smoothed over. Very large holes, cracks, or other damage may require additional repair to the mold surfaces prior to molding composite laminates on them.

If you are working with a mold that has seams or tight corners—as is the case with multi-section molds or molds with sharp inner corners or tight

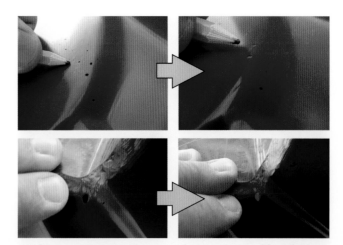

Make sure to start with a smooth, pore-free mold surface. In some cases, small holes can be filled with paste wax (top) or bits of clay (bottom).

Clean the mold surface completely with water or an appropriate solvent, and then apply paste wax (for most room temperature cure resins). Buff this wax film with a clean rag until shiny, and repeat.

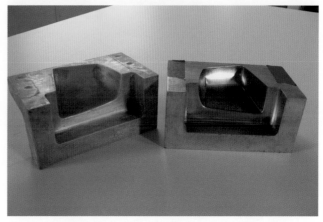

Avoid leaving a thick waxy residue on the surface of the mold (as shown at the left). Instead, buff the mold surface very well after each application of wax to produce a clear, properly waxed surface (as shown at the right).

Sulfur-free modeling clay can be used to fill tight mold corners and seams prior to wet layup.

PVA release is best applied with an airbrush, or a refillable spray tool (shown here).

If wiping PVA onto a mold surface, apply it while still wet on the cloth, and smooth the surface of the PVA as much as possible before it dries.

features—apply sulfur-free modeling clay to fill any gaps with your finger or a rounded stick. Make sure to clean any dust or residue from the mold surfaces prior to adding mold release.

Paste wax will complete the smoothing process by filling in any microscopic scratches to create a highly shined, molding-ready surface. This process of using wet sandpaper, polish, and wax will work well on sealed wood, metal, cast resin, heat-formed plastic, or FRP mold surfaces.

Once the mold surface is smooth and clean, ***apply the appropriate release agents*** for the resin system you'll be using in the composite laminate. *Do not underestimate the importance of properly applied and chemically appropriate release agents when molding composites.* Several release agents are available to match the specific types of resins used to form composites. Paste wax and polyvinyl alcohol (PVA) are most commonly used for low-temperature moldings, and will work well with most resin types used in small shop composites fabrication situations. For higher temperature composites processing, semi-permanent releases are available that chemically bond to the mold surface and produce a heat resistant, long lasting mold release. These tend to be a little more expensive than wax and PVA, but produce very good results.

Always select a wax that has been developed *specifically* for use with your intended resin system and closely follow any special instructions listed on the wax's packaging. With paste wax, this generally entails rubbing the wax on with a cloth, and then allowing the wax to dry away from direct sunlight or heat sources. Avoid applying too much wax; complete coverage with a thin film of wax should suffice for each wax layer. Buff off the wax film with a soft cloth until you can see the shine of the smooth mold surface, and then add repeated wax layers. A new mold will require a minimum of four wax applications. "Seasoned" (or well-used) molds may require two or less wax treatments.

When applying wax to areas with clay on them, be careful to rub the wax very lightly over the clay surface or just use a liquid release over the clay. Avoid picking up any of the clay with the cloth when applying release agents, as it can easily spread onto the rest of the release-coated mold surface.

Apply polyvinyl alcohol (PVA) onto mold surfaces when a full-coverage, water soluble thin film is needed as a backup release agent—as with some large polyester and vinyl ester-based laminates. PVA is best applied with a spray gun in multiple coats, allowing it to dry completely between coats. It will be evident that the PVA has dried completely when it has lost its surface sheen. PVA can also be applied by generously wiping it onto the mold surface with a rag, but will likely produce faint wipe lines in the final laminate's surface due to slightly uneven application. PVA release films can be fragile and will tear easily, so use care and avoid touching the surface after it has dried.

Shield the mold from any dust or foreign matter (including curious fingers) that may otherwise damage the prepared mold surface. Use a painter's drop cloth, such as an inexpensive 1-mil to 5-mil polyethylene drop cloth, to protect the mold until all the materials for layup are ready.

Working with Fabric Reinforcements

Using reinforcement fabrics requires a certain degree of finesse, so **use care when handling reinforcement fabrics** to avoid disrupting the weave, soiling the fabric, or unevenly draping it into a mold. Reinforcement fabrics are best stored when rolled onto a cardboard or plastic tube to avoid creasing the fabric. They should be stored horizontally by placing them onto shelving, or by using a roll-stand (where a rod passes through the inner support tube of the fabric roll) to support the fabric material as cleanly as possible. Shelving for roll storage can be mounted to walls, above work spaces, or even from the ceiling to save space. Never store fabric rolls vertically—the fabric will inevitably slough down the roll over time and disrupt the weave! Fabrics should be protected from dust, debris, and chemicals by wrapping them in craft paper, butcher paper, or plastic film. It is also a good practice to label the fabric roll with a tag at its end to easy identification—especially when it is wrapped in opaque paper. Reinforcement scraps or off-cuts can be stored in a box or bin for later use in bulking up a composite tooling layup for small projects.

A fabric's thickness can be simply measured with calipers. The final laminate thickness will typically be more than just the added thicknesses of the plies, though, as the resin content of the laminate will add more thickness to it. High-pressure laminates (those created under high pressures during processing) tend

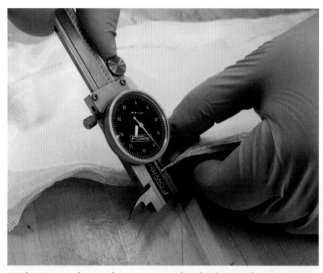

Calipers can be used to measure the thickness of reinforcements.

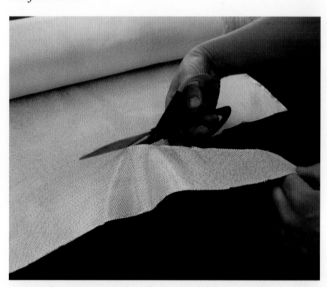

Serrated scissors work best for general fabric cutting.

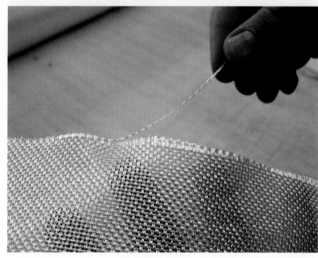

To keep stray fibers from falling into the layup, loose strands can be removed from cut edges.

Patterns can be made by placing fabric (of the same weight and weave of material that you'll be laying up) onto the mold surface, followed by marking the edges of the shape…

…then removing it from the mold and straightening out the weave.

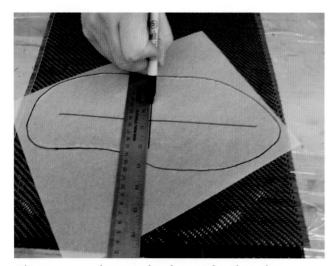

This pattern outline can then be transferred to other materials (along with marks that indicate the weave direction.

to have the tightest material consolidation, and are comparatively closer to the actual added thicknesses of the plies.

Most raw **reinforcements can be easily cut with sharp scissors.** Finely serrated and all-metal scissors tend to work well for most reinforcements, but aramid fabrics cut best with dedicated, serrated scissors. Several composites suppliers sell scissors made specifically for cutting aramid fabrics—which tend to be more expensive than regular scissors, but are well worth the cost difference.

To ensure straight cuts in loose fabrics (such as twill or satin), pull several strands from the fabric near the intended cut location by snipping through the selvaged edge of the fabric, then pull two or three weft/fill/woof threads from the fabric. The remaining gap in the fabric will mark the area to make a straight cut—even if the fabric itself is slightly warped.

When cutting patterned shapes from fabric, first straighten out the fabric by carefully pulling on the far edges of the fabric with your palm holding the weave flat against a table top. Pull the weave along each of the general directions of the yarns contained within the fabric. Once straightened, the pattern can be carefully marked on the fabric and cut with scissors or a rotary cutting blade. To keep loose weave reinforcements from fraying during pattern cutting, thin veil material can be attached to the fabric with spray adhesive, and then cut prior to lamination—and the veil will help hold the loose fibers in place.

For relatively flat composite parts, patterns can be made by laying paper or poster board onto the mold surface, and then trimming them to the size of the ply, as needed. However, this technique of patternmaking works only marginally well on complexly curved surfaces. Patterns for more complicated molds can be made by using a scrap of fabric similar in thread weight and weave to the material that you'll be using. This raw fabric can then be placed in the mold, formed to match the curvature of the mold, marked, removed and flattened, and then traced to create the correct ply shape. Note that some fabric weaves can be opened so much that the part will be weakened. When a part is too curved for practical fabrication from a single continuous piece of material, multiple pieces can be laminated together, as long as the edges of the plies overlap well and are reinforced by successive layers.

Working with Resin Matrices

Because of the liquid nature of resins, the most accurate way to measure them is to use a digital scale with a 1/10th gram increment. Such scales have become much less expensive in recent years and work very well for measuring small batches of resin. Resin can also be measured using a balance scale set to the specific weight ratio for a given resin type, or can be metered out by special hand pumps that measure out the resin in specific volumes with each stroke of the pump—although these can require priming, and they tend to work intermittently if air gets into them, creating uneven resin mix ratios.

When using polyester and vinyl ester resins, volumetric measurements tend to work best—especially for small batches. The liquid resin can be easily measured by volume in ounces, and the MEKP catalyst can be added using the cc/ml measurements on the catalyst container or MEKP dispenser.

Liquid acrylic (PMMA) and its catalyst (a proprietary mix that includes benzoyl peroxide) are typically mixed by weight, with 2% catalyst for thick parts, and 3% catalyst for thin parts.

Gel Coats and Surface Coats—Their "What", "Where", and "How"

Some composites may experience excessive abrasion, encounter high humidity (which causes fabric print-through), or require special coloring or surface effects. For these applications, a coating of resin—called *a "gel coat" or "surface coat"—is generally applied to the mold prior to the composite being laid over it*. The term *gel coat* generally refers to special-purpose, gelled polyester resin coat, whereas a thickened epoxy resin coat is called a *surface coat*. Such surface treatments are common in boats and hot tubs, but are also beneficial anywhere a durable or protective surface is needed at the expense of added weight to the composite.

Whenever using polyester, vinyl ester, or acrylic resins, make sure to mix them in a container made of polyethylene, polypropylene, PETE, or un-waxed paper to avoid resin attack on the mixing container. *Always completely mix the resin and catalyst/hardener* by scraping the bottom and sides of the mixing container to force all available material into the chemical reaction.

More permanent patterns can be made using rigid materials, such as cardboard or thin plastic.

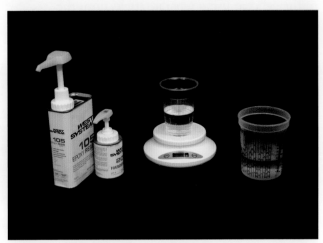

Resins can be measured with dispensing pumps, a digital scale, or a marked cup.

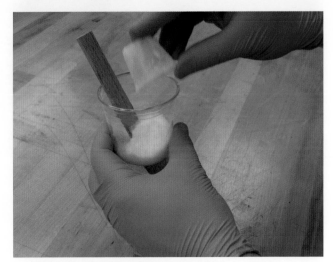

Resin can be thickened by thoroughly mixing in colloidal silica—adding in sufficient material until it reaches the needed viscosity.

Polyester gel coats come clear or in a variety of pigmented colors. They will accept fillers, such as glitter, special effect flakes, or grip enhancing grit, and can be easily color-matched with an existing paint color. Before adding your own pigments to a gel coat, be sure to **thoroughly mix the pigment in its container**. Pigment particles tend to settle to the bottom of the container over time. Use a clean stick to add pigment to the gel coat mixture in amounts recommended by the pigment manufacturer. First dip it into the pigment container, then scrape the pigment from the stick onto the interior rim of the gel coat mixing container so it can be easily stirred in by a separate mixing stick.

If a color *blend* is required (such as when creating a special purple through the mixing of a blue and a red pigment), slowly add the pigments to the gel coat using separate sticks until the desired color is obtained. **Avoid accidentally cross-contaminating pigment color containers** by inadvertently inserting a pigment-coated stick from one color into another. Likewise, avoid getting any gel coat resin in the pigment container. If adding glitter flake (or other additive), again, make sure that it is fully mixed before application.

When using an epoxy lamination resin system in a composite, apply an epoxy surface coat instead of a gel coat. These are available from several manufacturers, but it is not difficult to mix your own surface coat when needed. Thickening additives and pigments are available for this specific purpose, and can be mixed to the proper viscosity prior to actual application of the surface coat into a mold. To create your own thickened epoxy resin for use as a surface coat, first choose a resin with a pot life 30 minutes or more—though a longer pot life is needed to cover large mold surfaces. Next, measure out the correct ratios of hardener and resin in separate containers. Slowly add an appropriate thickening agent (such as colloidal silica) to the measured resin, stirring it as thoroughly as possible to minimize any clumping of the thickener in the resin. Add only enough thickener to bring the epoxy mixture to the viscosity of where it stops dripping from the mixing stick. Add pigment to the thickened resin in the same manner as with polyester resins (discussed above). Mix the resin and hardener as completely as possible to avoid leaving soft spots of poorly cured resin in the surface coat. Finally, add thickening agent to the mixed resin, as needed, to bring it to a creamy peanut butter-like consistency. *Do not apply thickened epoxy with a spray gun—it is not thixotropic, so it will clog the gun!* Instead, **apply epoxy surface coat with a brush**—this will still produce good results, and can be applied up to 1/8" thick.

To create a custom surface coat, pigment can be added to thickened resin.

48

If using a cup gun or spray gun to spray a gel coat, first catalyze the gel coat with MEKP as directed by the manufacturer. Some specialty gel coat guns actually mix the gel coat as it is being sprayed—in which case you should follow the instructions specific to the gun, adjusting for proper catalyst mixture in the spray. *Most professionals prefer to spray gel coats* (rather than brush them on), but when fabricating small molds or parts, a high quality brush and some careful application will still work well and save some spray gun clean-up hassle. *Apply gel/surface* coats in long, continuous strokes rather than in short back-and-forth movements. This will minimize bubbles created in the coating during its application to the molding surface.

If using a brush to apply the gel/surface coat, spread it on in a couple thick layers, rather than in many thin layers, as you would with paint. Thicker layers create less bubbles at the mold surface and are more self-supportive when brushed on—but keep in mind that overly thick coats can develop significant heat during the curing process. Overheated resin can cause discoloration and release problems, especially where clay or wax fillets are present in seams and corners, since they can soften or melt, and mix into the curing resin. When applying multiple gel/surface coats with a brush, allow the first coating layer to cool and cure to a tacky state before applying additional coats.

If spraying on a gel coat, do so in thin layers, opting to use a spray gun made specifically for applying gel coats, such as a cup gun that holds the gel coat in a removable paper cup and has an easily cleaned spraying orifice. A standard HVLP spray gun, though still usable with gel coats, is not recommended because of the extensive, difficult cleaning required immediately after spraying; gel coat guns are significantly easier to clean—and last much longer! If you must use a paint gun with gel coat, however, styrene monomer can thin it a bit so it will flow better through the gun—but be aware that adding more than 20% to 25% styrene (by volume) to the gel coat can make it overly brittle. Also, be sure to use goggles and a respirator when spraying gel coat since the atomized styrene-based resin can cause acute respiratory and eye irritation.

A gel coat thickness gauge (available from resin suppliers) is helpful in monitoring the thickness of your gel/surface coat. A typical gel coat thickness is between 12 and 20 mils (.012" and .020") and can be measured with a gel coat thickness gauge at the time it is applied. To use a gel coat gauge, simply press the edge of the gauge onto the uncured gel/surface coat; the highest gauge finger to have resin on it will indicate the gel/surface coat thickness. Keep in mind that a gel coat will shrink in thickness

Thoroughly mix pigment into thickened resin, adding more thickener as needed to obtain the correct consistency.

49

by about 20% to 30% during cure, so spray it slightly thicker to compensate for this dimensional change if coating thickness is critical. Additionally, with good planning, different colors of gel/surface coat may even be applied in the same layup by masking the mold surfaces in stages to produce an interesting aesthetic/graphic effects.

In order to promote good polymer cross-linking and bonding between the gel/surface coat and the laminate laid up over it, *the laminate should be applied while the gel/surface coat has firmly cured, but is still tacky*. In this way, gel/surface coats differ from *flood coats* (or aesthetic top coatings) that are applied onto an already fully-cured composite. This tacky state of a resin can be readily determined by touching a discrete section of the resin-coated surface with a gloved finger. If resin sticks to your finger, it is not quite ready; but if your finger leaves a sticky impression on the surface without picking up any resin, the coat is ready for layup of the laminate over it.

Using Tooling Gel/Surface Coats

Opaque tooling gel coats or epoxy surface coats produce a more durable surface than typical gel coats and are best used when fabricating composite tooling. Polyester tooling gel coat and epoxy surface coat resin can be a little more expensive than gel coat resins, but their increased toughness is well worth the cost difference. The application of tooling gel/surface coats is exactly the same as for other gel/surface coats.

Approximating Material Quantities Needed for Layups

Make sure to *have enough resin and reinforcement on hand to complete a project before starting the layup* by approximating your material needs beforehand using simple material measurements and weights. First, measure the overall length and width of the mold with a flexible tape measure, rounding up to the next whole number, and then multiply these two measurements to get the overall surface area. Next, multiply the surface area by the number of layers in the laminate to find the total material surface area to be used. Lastly, multiply this by the weight per unit area listed by the material supplier or manufacturer to determine the total reinforcement weight for the project. This final reinforcement weight can then be used to find approximate resin amounts, as described below.

Gel/surface coats should be applied in long, single-directional brush strokes.

For fiberglass laminates, resin quantities can be approximated by matching the same weight of polyester or vinylester resin to reinforcement material weight when using woven fiberglass, or by adding nearly twice the weight resin to reinforcement when using mat fiberglass. Approximate resin weights are as follows:

Vinylester resins = 9lbs/gallon
Polyester resin = 8.8lbs/gallon
Epoxy (with hardener) = 8lbs/gallon
Acrylic resin = 7.9 lbs/gallon

Notice that epoxy and acrylic weigh slightly less than polyester and vinylester resins, and remember that carbon fiber and Kevlar fabrics have less density than fiberglass, so resin weight will take up more of the total weight in the composite (for the same volume fraction). As a result, plan to have at least 1.3 pounds of epoxy resin per pound of carbon fabric, or 1.6 pounds of epoxy resin per pound of Kevlar fabric. For example, to make a six layer laminate that is 2 square yards (or 18 square feet) using 1.5 oz fiberglass mat, the reinforcement materials would weigh a total of 162 ounces (or about 10.1lbs) and therefore require about 20.2lbs (or about two and a third gallons) of polyester resin. Based on their particular layup methods and experience, fabricators may use slightly more or less resin than this, but these calculated amounts are good approximations. Simple material and resin calculators are also available online— with an exceptionally handy one being located on the www.fibreglast.com website.

Plan enough time to do a correct layup, and **employ skilled help when creating large mold layups.** As a rule of thumb, a properly catalyzed gel coat can take about an hour to cure after application before it is to the tacky state, and ready for layup. As far as planning for actual layup time, a single skilled worker can typically hand-laminate six layers of 1.5 oz fiberglass mat to a 10 square foot mold surface in about a six to seven hour period—equal to a moderately sized mold in a full eight-hour work day. Additional skilled workers assisting with a mold layup will typically bring the lamination time down by a couple hours per person—so a layup that requires one person six hours to complete could feasibly be done in only four hours with two people, and in roughly two hours with three people (as long as they don't get in each other's way).

For large jobs, gel coat can also be applied with a gel-coat cup gun (as shown here).

A gel coat thickness gauge indicates how deep the gel coat is on the surface.

A gel/surface coat is not ready for layup if it is still wet (as shown at left). When it is tacky, but doesn't leave a resin residue on a gloved finger (as shown at right), it is ready for laminate layup over it.

Applying Resin into Reinforcements with Basic Wet Layup Techniques

Pour some laminating resin into the mold, and then use a squeegee or brush to level the resin over the tacky gel/surface coated faces. This initial coating of resin will allow better wet-out of the first fabric layer from beneath, allow it to be re-positioned (if needed), and also help hold it in place. Next, carefully place the first layer of reinforcement fabric into the mold, avoiding any tugging of the fabric that may distort the weave. Apply light, sweeping pressure on the fabric with your fingers to temporarily tack the fabric ply in place in the mold. Perform additional resin infiltration and void removal by using a squeegee, spreader, roller, or brush. A squeegee or spreader work best on flat mold faces, but can be used to quickly impregnate fabrics prior to placing them in a mold. Rollers are best used with mat and veil fabrics on large or lightly curved mold faces, especially when wetted with polyester or vinyl ester resins. Brushes generally work well for all types of resins and mold shapes—especially in removing air bubbles and voids—although they wet-out fabrics a bit more slowly than squeegees, spreaders, or rollers.

If resin from below the first layer of fabric

does not fully wet it out during lamination, simply add more resin to the top and spread, roll, or brush it into the fabric until the fibers are fully wetted. When fully impregnated with resin, fiberglass will go from opaque to transparent, whereas aramid fabrics will become deeper in color once saturated. It is difficult to see when carbon fiber is fully wetted out because of its matte black color, but it will begin to show slightly more surface sheen when saturated.

Additional reinforcement plies can be applied one at a time, as designated by the lamination schedule using the same impregnation methods listed above.

Reinforcement fabrics can also be saturated with a more controlled amount of resin prior to placement in a mold using "wet pre-preg" lamination techniques. The simplest method of wet pre-preg lamination includes placing dry reinforcement material onto plastic film sheeting secured to a table top, pouring resin onto the reinforcement ply, spreading the resin evenly throughout the fabric, carefully peeling up the wet pre-preg ply from the table top, positioning it in the mold, and pressing it down onto the mold surfaces with a spreader, roller, or brush to remove any voids.

An even less messy version of this process is performed by placing dry fabric onto a piece of plastic film, pouring a measured portion of resin onto the

Apply laminating resin over the gel/surface coat…

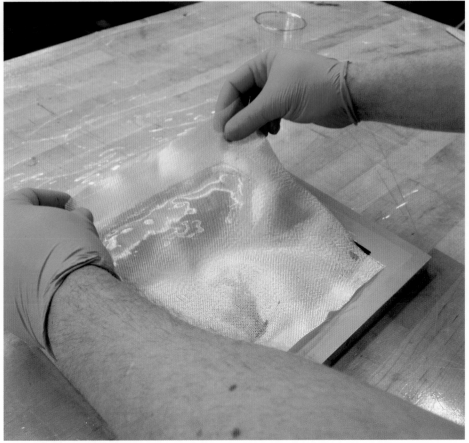

…and then add a layer of reinforcement material.

53

Smooth out the reinforcement, and add just enough resin to saturate any dry spots in the fabric.

Repeat the last two steps (applying a laminate ply, and then adding more resin) until the necessary thickness of material has been built up.

fabric, applying a top sheet of plastic film, and then using a squeegee or spreader to push the resin uniformly throughout the fabric sandwiched between the plastic films. Remove the top plastic film, position the fabric wet-side-down onto the mold surface, remove any large voids, and then peel off the remaining plastic film from the wet pre-preg ply. Remove any small remaining voids with a spreader, roller, or brush.

Once the layup is complete, the laminate can be allowed to cure in the open air, or vacuum bag processing can be performed (as described in the chapter on *Improved Composite Techniques*). The length of time required for full cure of the lamination depends on the particular resin system, the thickness and temperature of the laminate, the presence of UV or infrared light, ambient temperature, and the temperature of the mold. While many common resins will cure to a gel state at room temperature within a couple hours, it is often recommended to leave the laminate in the mold for at least twelve to twenty-four hours (or more) to allow it to fully harden. Some resins may require a post-cure cycle in which additional temperature is applied, so be sure to follow the resin manufacturer's recommended curing instructions for your type of resin.

After demolding a composite, be sure to **check the final surface coating of the laminate** for any pinholes, pores, or soft spots that may have been left in the gel/surface coat due to poor processing. These imperfections may need to be corrected (as described in the Demolding, Trimming, and Finishing chapter) prior to putting the laminate into service.

Spray-up Composite Techniques

Spray-up processes are great for producing large parts that need to be bulked up and fabricated as quickly as possible. Gel coats are typically used in conjunction with spray-up techniques and can be applied with a cup gun. After applying the gel coat to the mold and allowing it to tack up, spray an even coating of catalyzed resin across the mold surfaces using a cup gun. Next, use the chopper gun to completely cover the resin coated mold with fiberglass, loosely guiding the fiberglass roving into the gun with a gloved hand. Use a smooth, side-to-side motion to systematically and evenly cover the mold surface. When the mold is sufficiently coated with fiberglass strands, use the cup gun to apply more resin over the fibers. Spray the resin from high above the fibers at first, coating them with enough resin to immobilize them on the

Fiberglass will become clear when properly impregnated (left), aramid fabrics will become deeper in color (center), and carbon fiber will gain additional sheen (right).

To perform fiberglass spray up, first apply gel coat to a waxed mold surface and allow it to tack up (as previously explained).

55

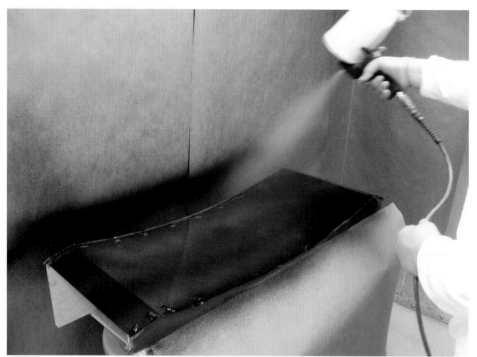

Once tacky, apply laminating resin to the gel coat with a cup gun…

mold surface. If resin is sprayed too closely, these fibers can be blown off the mold surface.

Use a roller or brush to press down on the fibers and better consolidate the composite. After consolidating the fibers, use the cup gun to apply another coating of resin to the part, followed by another pass with the chopper gun and subsequent consolidation with the roller or brush. Continue these steps until the laminate is built up to the desired thickness. Be careful to not build up the laminate too fast as this may cause excessive exotherm in the composite. As a general rule of thumb, allow the laminate to cool and tack up after every .25" of buildup. Lastly, remember to clean up any resin and fibers from the rollers with acetone immediately after lamination is complete.

Conclusion

Very basic wet layup techniques can be mastered through the practice of some simple mold preparation, material planning, gel/surface coat application, and lamination steps. Spray-up processes can also be performed through a slight variation of these steps with the additional use of a cup gun and chopper gun. The next chapter will explore fabricating "moldless" composites—or laminates created without the use of a mold.

…and then spray chopped fiber onto the wet resin with a chopper gun. Guide the roving strand into the back of the gun with one hand, while moving the gun back and forth over the mold with the other hand for even coverage.

Use a back and forth motion with a roller to consolidate the material, and then repeat the last two steps (applying resin with a cup gun, and then adding chopped fiber with the chopper gun), until the proper material thickness is achieved.

References and Resources

Wanberg, John. *Composite Materials Handbook #1*, Stillwater, MN: Wolfgang Publications Inc., 2009.

Wanberg, John. *Composite Materials Handbook #2*, Stillwater, MN: Wolfgang Publications Inc., 2010.

Smith, Zeke, *Advanced Composite Techniques.* Napa: Aeronaut Press, 2005.

Warring, R.H. *The Glassfibre Handbook.* Poole, Dorset: Special Interest Model Books, Ltd., 2003

Wiley, Jack. *The Fiberglass Repair and Construction Handbook, 2nd ed.* Summit, PA: Tab Books, 1988.

www.compositesworld.com/articles/mold-release-update

www.axelplastics.com

Chapter Four

Moldless Composites

One method of composites fabrication that is invaluable for one-of-a-kind prototyping is *"moldless" composite* construction. These types of composites save considerable cost and effort when only one copy of a part is needed. To create moldless composites, the fabricator can either manipulate stock composite pieces, or otherwise layup the composite over a suitable form that holds a laminate in place until it has cured. Solidified moldless composites may then be removed from the temporary form, or the form may remain as part of the composite's final structure. Moldless composites are also especially helpful in developing a form over which a mold can be produced.

Molds are not always needed to fabricate a composite project—as evident in this one-off hood scoop made using some of the "moldless" composite techniques demonstrated in this chapter.

Prototyping with Stock Shapes

One of the easiest means of producing a complete project without the need for a mold is to modify existing stock composite shapes for a particular one-off purpose. At most, such cut pieces may need to be held in place with an ad-hoc jig, clamps, or adhesive while they are bonded and further reinforced—but the considerable time and expense of mold making can be altogether avoided. Stock shapes can be quickly trimmed with a hacksaw or rotary cut-off wheel (as shown in the chapter on *Demolding, Trimming, and Finishing*) and then sanded with 80-grit sandpaper prior to bonding, making sure to create a uniform, rough surface.

To create a coped cut to join round stock pieces, a spindle sander (if available) can quickly create the needed cut shape. When sanding the stock pieces, make sure to sand slowly to avoid creating too much heat—which can damage the matrix. Always use fresh sandpaper and slow to moderate sanding speeds, and then clean the sanded area with acetone.

Do not use polyester resin to bond epoxy-based stock materials since it will not properly join them together. Also, make sure to mask off any areas not included in the bonding process to simplify cleanup of the final piece. If needed, stock pieces can be tacked in place with a spot of superglue gel, and then instantly solidified in place with some superglue accelerant. Well-placed clamps can help in securing pieces together while any adhesive cures. Transition fillets can be made by thickening up mixed resin using equal parts glass microspheres and colloidal silica to a consistency of peanut butter, and then applying it to the joint. Once cured, sand these fillets smooth with 80-grit sandpaper and overlay them with laminate material.

Pre-cured laminates adhere best to each other when pressure is applied to them through the joint material. Right-angled joints can held together with clamps over angle iron or aluminum pieces (with release or packing tape coating on them) to create the needed pressure. For complex, rounded corners, partially cured (to a thick, sticky, and gelled state) resin-impregnated unidirectional reinforcement can be applied in thin strips to wrap the joint for additional strength. These reinforcements can be better consolidated using pressure imparted by vinyl electrical tape (applied adhesive-side-out) that has been stretched and wrapped over the joint.

Stock round tubes can be easily coped to fit and join with other tubes using a spindle sander of their same diameter.

Use 80-grit sandpaper to completely roughen the bond area of a joint, and then clean the bond site with acetone. (Note: masking tape can help keep the roll-wrapped carbon fiber tube clean below the intended bond area.)

Superglue can be used to temporarily tack the joint together, and can then be instantly bonded using a spritz of accelerator.

59

Fillets and transitions for the joint can be created with mixed resin and a 50-50 blend of colloidal silica and glass microspheres.

Smooth out any ridges on the joint with 80-grit sandpaper, and wipe it clean with acetone prior to adding laminate material.

Unidirectional reinforcement works very well for joints like these. Here, resin was applied to unidirectional carbon fiber, allowed to gel, and then it was cut into ½" wide strips.

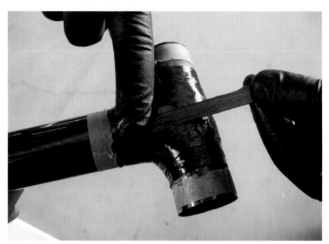

The tacky,-gelled-resin carbon strips can be easily tensioned and lashed around a joint.

Electrical tape can then be stretched sticky-side-out around the laminate strips to provide consolidation pressure to the joint.

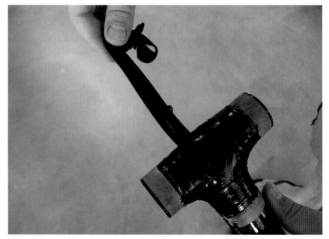

Once the resin in the joint has fully cured, the electrical tape can be removed and the joint can be further cleaned up with some light sanding.

Thin acrylic matrix composites (created by using infusion processes described in the chapter on *Improved Composite Techniques*) can be thermoformed to make bends using a heat gun or strip heater. When heat is applied to the bend, a slight whitening will occur to the resin, but when cooled, it will return to normal. Apply pressure to the bend line during bending to minimize delamination that can occur as the inner corner of the bend encounters high in-plane compressive forces. Hold the bent laminate in place until the acrylic matrix has fully cooled.

To join acrylic matrix parts together, sand the bonding surfaces as detailed above, then apply an appropriate acrylic adhesive to the joint. Clamp the parts together so the adhesive and the acrylic in the laminate can co-mingle, and allow the bonded area to fully dry before removing the clamps.

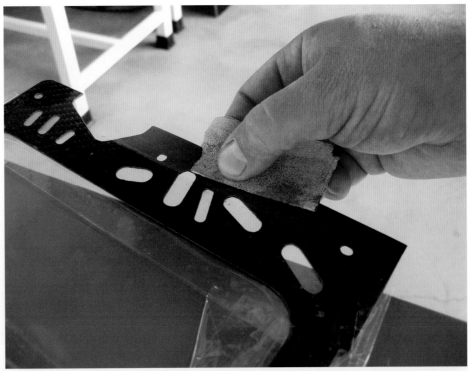

For bonding right-angled joints, prepare the bond site by sanding it with 80-grit sand paper and wiping it with acetone. The assembly of a support bracket for some racecar electronics is shown here using 1/8" thick carbon fiber sheet.

Composite "Origami"—Foldable Moldless Composites

Flat, flexible sheet materials have been used for centuries to form structures that derive their strength from folds made in them. Certain composites fabrication techniques use these principles to produce foldable structures—including making them weather resistant, collapsible, and easily transportable. This can be done by laying out fiberglass fabric over a fold pattern, and then applying masking tape on either side of the fold lines. Low-durometer silicone (such as a flexible

Angle aluminum sections that have been release coated (with wax or packing tape) work well as forms for joints like this. V-cut wood blocks can help support the aluminum.

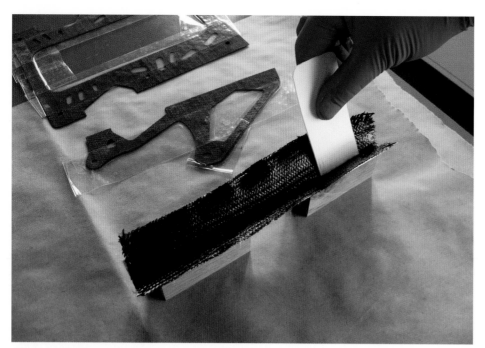

Shore A-10 or Shore 00 material) can then be impregnated into the fabric at the fold line between the masking tape and allowed to cure. Next, remove the masking tape and impregnate the remaining raw fabric material with an appropriate polyester, vinyl ester, epoxy, or acrylic resin. Once this resin has cured, the rigid sheet can be folded along the silicone fold lines into the desired structural part.

Use a spreader to squeeze resin into some reinforcement tape (or strips cut from fabric) and then place the wetted strips into the angle form.

An adaptation to this moldless fabrication method includes masking off the fold lines, instead, and then impregnating the open areas of raw fabric with mixed resin. Once cured, the structure can be folded and additional resin can be added to the raw fabric folds to create a fully rigidified structure.

Skin-over-foam Moldless Composites

"Skin-over-foam" composites are made by laying the composite over a sculpted foam form, often to permanently encase the foam in it—which is especially helpful in quickly creating one-of-a-kind parts, or for developing a mold pattern. These composites also have the added benefit of increased rigidity and impact absorption because they create a sandwich structure using the foam within them as a core. Truly hollow composites may also be created using this method by using styrene foam as a form for an epoxy laminate, and then dissolved out the

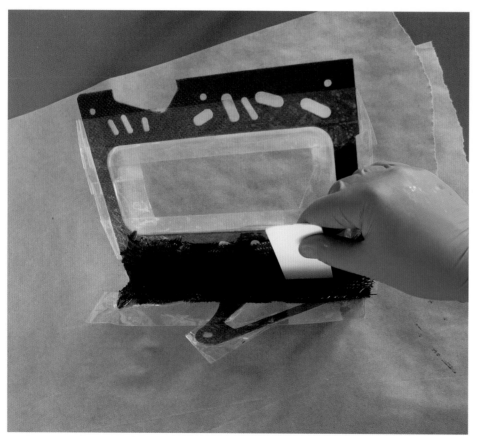

Add the pieces that will be bonded together, and then apply more wetted reinforcement strips over the joint.

foam with solvent once the composite has cured.

Styrene foam can be rough-cut by slicing and breaking it to size with a utility knife (as is done with wallboard) or quickly cutting it with a handsaw. Denser foams can be cut with a bandsaw, tablesaw, or handsaw. When using foam sheet that is too thin for your needs, additional sheets of foam can be laminated together with spray adhesive, thickened epoxy, or urethane-based adhesive (such as Gorilla-brand glue). Dense urethane and epoxy foams can be laminated together using thickened epoxy. Keep in mind that if the adhesive between the foam layers is harder than the foam itself, will remove the foam material faster than the seam adhesive—leaving hard, rib-like ridges in the surface of the shape.

Next, shape the foam as needed, but avoid complex shapes with too much detail; it will be difficult to adhere the laminate to sharp corners, edges, or small details with the composite material. In general, the minimum laminate radius that will effectively adhere to a form is about ½" radius when using up to 10oz woven fiberglass fabrics— and thicker fabrics will require even larger radii.

To use templates as a guide for hot wire or handsaw shaping of large profiles in styrene foam, align the templates on adjacent faces of the foam, and then adhere them to the foam with spray adhesive. For some applications it may be necessary to adhere foam

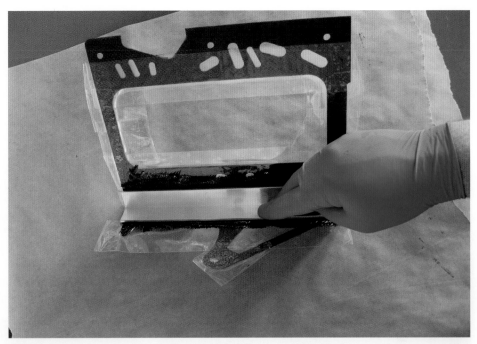

Place another release-coated angle form on the opposite side of the joint…

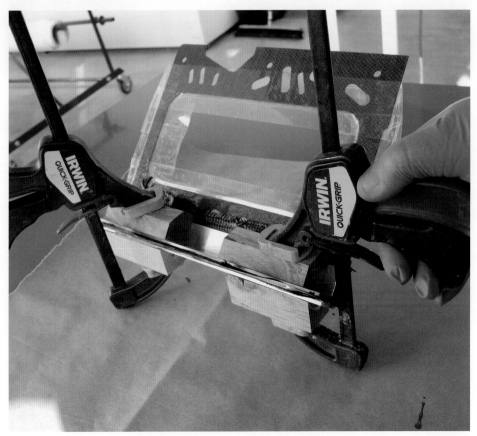

…and then apply clamps to consolidate the joint until the resin cures. Again, v-cut blocks work well here to give the clamps a flat surface to press against.

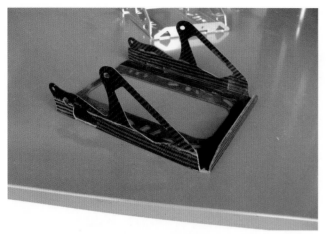

These steps can be repeated for any remaining joints. After trimming, this support bracket is ready—and it weighs significantly less than the aluminum version of the bracket.

To create bends in thermoplastic composite sheets (as with this acrylic matrix panel created using resin infusion), mark the location of the bend, and place it over a strip heater (made for heat-bending plastics).

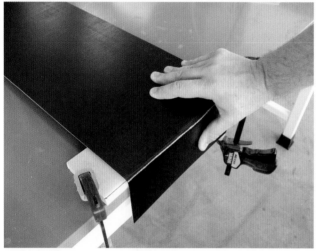

When the joint is hot enough to bend freely, bend the laminate over a generously-curved corner. (MDF with a 3/8" radius edge was used as a form here.)

Tight bends will likely cause delamination of the laminate at the inside of the bend—so large radius bends are best, and apply heavy, radial pressure to the bend while bending.

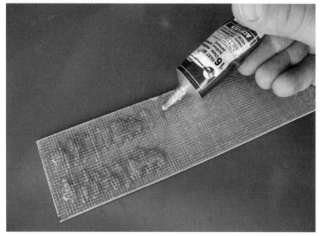

To bond thermoplastic matrix composites, use a solvent-based adhesive that is compatible with the matrix material.

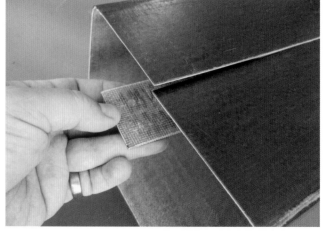

As usual, lap joints work best for bonding composites. A strip of material can be used to lap two butted edges.

to the template sections and then remove the foam until the sections are visible. A reversible form of this method entails pressing external, removable templates into the soft foam, then shaping the foam until the traces of the template have disappeared.

Test fit a ply of reinforcement fabric material over the foam and add relief cuts (or *darts*) anywhere it will not lay down on the surface well enough. Pre-cut and stack up all needed plies prior to layup. Use a brush to completely wet the surface of the foam with mixed epoxy. Carefully place the first layer of reinforcement fabric onto the resin-wetted foam, and avoid tugging or distorting the fabric too much. Apply light pressure on the fabric with the resin-wetted brush or spreader to help work the resin through the fiber. Continue building up the remaining layers and resin to complete the layup, adding relief cuts as needed in the fabric to help it conform to the surface of the foam without creating large ripples and voids. Overlapping the fabric at the relief cuts will cause it to be thicker than necessary, but this can be corrected by sanding the laminate down in these areas after cure. Excessive buildup can also be minimized if these overlapping sections are offset from each other from one ply to the next. To enclose a foam shape on all sides with laminate material, lay up one side first, allow it to cure to a tacky state, and then turn it over and finish with a second layup that overlaps the edges of the first layup.

Once the laminate has fully cured, it can be trimmed and finished using the guidelines in the chapter on *Demolding, Trimming, and Finishing.*

Rigid Sheet-based Moldless Composites

Rigid sheet material can also be used to create a base form that will support a moldless composite laminate, yielding a sturdy final part. Any self-supporting sheet material that is chemically compatible with (and will bond to) the laminate can feasibly work with this fabrication method. This includes plywood, corrugated cardboard, foam sheeting (urethane or styrene-based), and "foamcore" (available at most office supply stores). These materials can be joined together using miter cuts, dados, fasteners, adhesives, slotted fittings, and a variety of other methods. However, these sheet materials are generally limited to planar shapes and single-degree curves—and often only when *kerfed* (or relief-cut partway through the material at regular

Apply clamps to the joint for best bonding results.

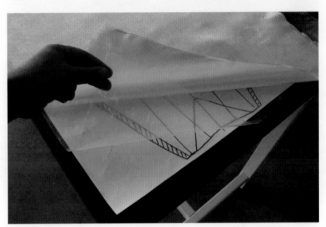

To create foldable, "origami"-style composites, place a drawing of the intended fold lines under clear plastic film, and then place a couple plies of translucent fiberglass material on top.

Apply masking tape to any areas that should not be impregnated with resin. For this foldable kayak demonstration (based on the Oru Kayak), the fold lines were left unmasked so they could be impregnated with silicone resin, first.

65

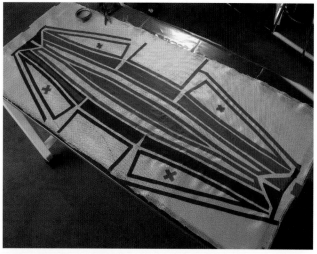

Once completely masked off, the reinforcement material is ready to accept resin.

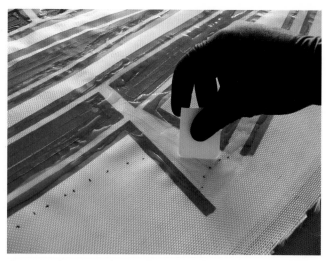

Squeeze resin into the reinforcement fabric with a spreader, but avoid getting resin in unwanted areas during this process.

After the resin has cured, remove the masking tape.

As silicone was used to seal the fold lines with this part, laminating resin was used to wet out the remaining dry cloth without concern about additional masking.

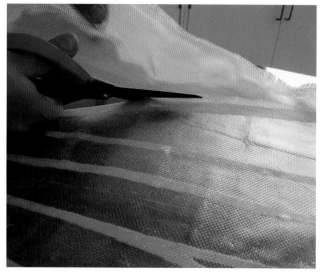

After the laminating resin has cured, use scissors to trim off any excess material.

The composite can then be folded, as intended.

intervals) and carefully bent to create the curve. Thick sheet materials are generally inadequate for creating compound curved faces unless they are heat formable—as is somewhat possible with thin vinyl foams. With a little practice, though, rigid sheets can still be used to create a wide range of usable shapes. For areas of a project that may require compound curved faces, styrene of urethane foam material can be laminated onto the rigid sheet materials with adhesive and then shaped down as needed to create the curved surfaces.

Strong, rigid sandwich structures can be fabricated by laminating composite materials over *both* sides of the base sheet material, as well. To create a skin-over-foam moldless composite sandwich structure, first laminate the composite materials over one side of the sheet material form, and then allow it to cure. Next, trim back and chamfer the edges of the support material to provide a good transition between the two opposing composite faces. Finally, layup additional plies of composite laminate over the other side of the sheet material, ensuring that the laminate comes in contact with the chamfered edges of the core to produce a secure secondary bond to the edges of the original laminate skin. Once the composite has fully cured, the laminate can be trimmed and its surfaces smoothed as needed.

Framework-based Moldless Composites

Another viable moldless composite lamination technique involves using wire, wood, and fabric as a support framework for a composite laminate. This one-off construction method can produce relatively large or flowing shapes and is only limited by the fabricator's own ability to create a suitable frame structure that can adequately support the weight of a taut laminate laid over it.

Wire frameworks can be connected to each other using techniques of bending, lashing, soldering, or tack welding—depending on the type of wire material used and its particular thickness. Copper wire can be soldered with a gas torch while steel wires are much more effectively linked using tacked or spot welded joints. After joining the wire framework together, ensure that these wire-to-wire connections are secure enough to avoid structural failure during composite lamination over them.

With wooden frameworks, boards can be cut and slotted together, or sections can be cut from

The final 1/3 scale-model kayak is now ready for testing in real water.

To build up enough thickness for some projects, styrene foam can be: 1) sliced with a knife and snapped apart, 2) sprayed with spray adhesive, 3) joined to another piece of foam, and then 4) trimmed as needed with a hot wire, bandsaw, or handsaw.

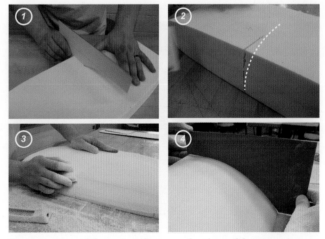

Because styrene foam is soft, it can be shaped by: 1) pressing a template into it, 2) leaving a line from the template, 3) sanding it down to the indented template line, and then 4) checking the shape with the template.

Complete any shaping to the foam, as needed, and then apply mixed epoxy directly to the surface of the foam.

Laminate all the required plies of material to the foam…

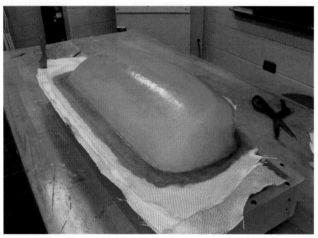

…and then allow it to fully cure prior to final trimming and finishing.

Foamcore board works very well for creating rigid, moldless composites.   Trim and bend patterns can be drawn directly on the surface of the material…

…and then the foamcore can be trimmed with a knife. Fold lines can be made by removing only one side of the material with a knife.

Hot glue can be used to help hold pieces in place.

Epoxy and reinforcement material can be applied directly over the foamcore (but polyester and vinyl ester will attack the foam within).

The laminate can then be green-trimmed or allowed to fully cure before final trimming.

To create a sandwich core laminate, the foamcore can be trimmed back and edge-chamfered on the un-laminated side…

…and additional laminate material can be added to match up with the previously cured edges. This laminate can then be cured and finished, as needed.

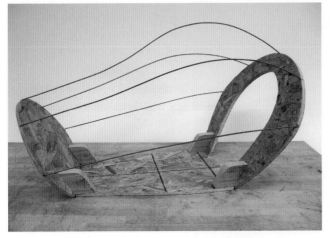

Wire or wood frameworks can also be used to form composites without a mold.

Stretchy material (as with the fleece shown here) can be stapled directly to a wooden frame…

...and then wetted with resin so additional laminate plies will adhere to it.

plywood and mounted at uniform spacing from each other on a support structure (explained in the next chapter). Even woven reed can be used to produce very organic and fluid forms. Wooden frameworks have proven to be especially helpful in classic aircraft and car audio fabrications since they can also be used for mounting additional components.

After creating the framework, stretch flexible fabric over this frame to act as a bridge between the gaps of the frame members. Fleece (like that used in jackets), thin cotton-poly knit fabric (commonly found in T-shirts), Lycra/Spandex blended fabrics, and even some "stabilized" reinforcement fabrics can work well for this task if they stretch well but are not overly elastic and droopy. To simplify the stretching process, fabric can be secured to the framework using strategically applied spots of hot glue, superglue, or even stapled directly to a wood framework. A single layer of fabric is usually sufficient to support the first couple layers of laminate material laid over it.

Next, saturate the support fabric with resin, and then apply the first layer of reinforcement fabric. Build these layers up slowly to avoid over-stretching the support fabric beneath the composite. Once a couple of layers of laminate have been laid over the framework and allowed to cure to a "green", tacky state, the shape will be considerably more supportive for additional bulking layers—which can

Reinforcement material can then be laminated over the form and allowed to cure.

then be added up to the needed thickness for the laminate. After completing all lamination steps, allow the composite to fully cure, and then finish it as described in the chapter on Demolding, Trimming, and Finishing.

Conclusion

One-of-a-kind, secondary structures can be fabricated using a wide variety of low-tech methods. These various methods can be adapted and manipulated to produce a creative range of final solutions, depending on the fabricator's particular needs. When one-off creations will not suffice, however, mold design and mold-making steps may be needed to aid in producing multiple copies of a part—as outlined in the next two chapters.

Surface filling, finishing, or upholstering is then possible over the laminate, as demonstrated in the chapter on Demolding, Trimming, and Finishing.

References and Resources

U.S. Patent # 212016000094U1 - Collapsible Kayak with Large Cockpit

Wanberg, John. *Composite Materials Handbook #1*, Stillwater, MN: Wolfgang Publications Inc., 2009.

Wanberg, John. *Composite Materials Handbook #2*, Stillwater, MN: Wolfgang Publications Inc., 2010.

Wanberg, John. *Composite Materials Handbook #3*, Stillwater, MN: Wolfgang Publications Inc., 2013.

www.compositesworld.com/blog/post/cw-talks-explores-foldable-composites-with-joseph-choma

www.rqriley.com/frp-foam.htm

www.hotwirefoamfactory.com/home.php

www.techlib.com/hobby/hotwire_foam_cutter.htm

Chapter Five

Designing Successful Molds

Actually making a mold for your composites project will provide you with the ability to quickly create replacement parts, copies of a part for testing purposes or to sell your parts to others—along with a myriad of other benefits. Mold-making is a very broad subject, but this chapter will discuss some of the basic principles that can help in designing effective molds for use in a small shop setting.

What Makes a Good Mold?

A well-designed and fabricated mold adheres to a few design principles that will ultimately allow the mold to ensure the following:

- Smooth surfaces on the final composite part
- Clean removal of the cured part from the mold

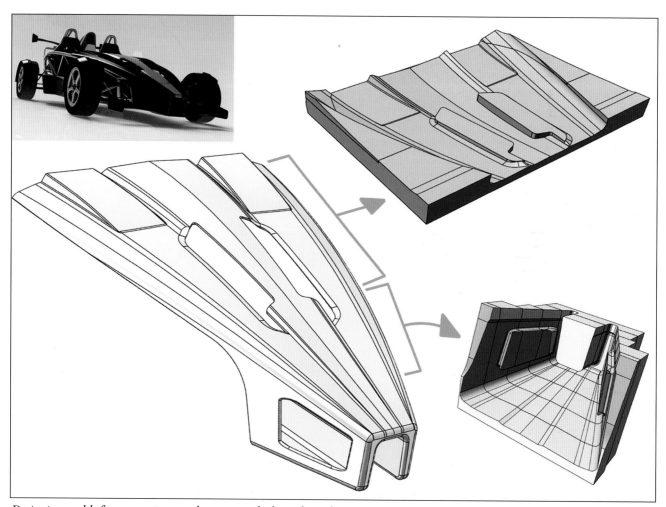

Designing molds for composites can be a particularly tricky task as times (as with the multi-section molds required for this racecar), but this chapter will outline several of the mold design considerations needed to make practically any composite molding job a success.

- Dimensional and geometric accuracy of the part it forms
- The easiest possible use of the mold, including its storage and transportability
- Chemical compatibility between materials used in the molding process
- Proper mold shape while resisting the pressure, forces, and heat that occur during lamination, curing, and demolding
- Very few (if any) physical changes to the mold due to good forethought and mold planning
- A reasonable mold lifespan and minimal mold wear while forming the needed number of parts
- Relative cost-effectiveness in mold and part fabrication

Example of a male mold—used to create a part with a smooth inner surface.

General Molding Terminology

Let's get started in our discussion of mold design by covering some of the terminology common to the art. Laminates are always smoother where they come in direct contact with the mold surface, and a mold that is used to form a part with a smooth inner (or concave) surface is referred to as a *male* mold. Conversely, a mold that is used to form a smooth outer (or convex) surface on a part is called a *female* mold. An *open mold* is one that is rigid on only one side—often for use with hand layup, spray

Example of a female mold—used to create a part with a smooth outer surface.

73

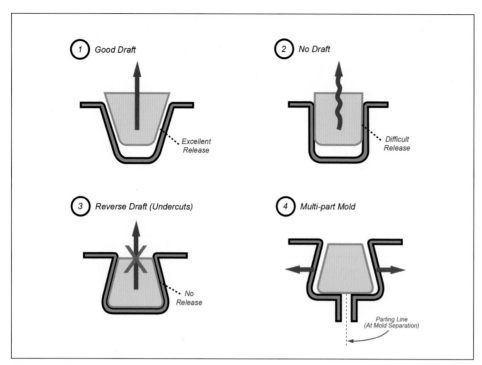

Good draft is required for all molded composite parts, as illustrated with the examples above.

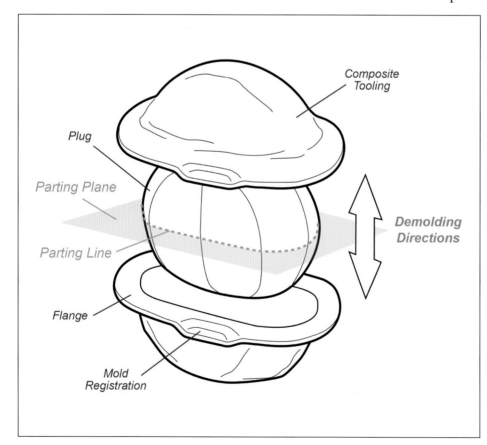

up, and vacuum-bagging processes. Conversely, a *closed mold* has rigid top and bottom sections that are closed together to form an enclosed cavity, as with inflatable bladder, trapped rubber, or transfer molding systems. *Matched molds* are a type of closed mold, but often used with industrial resin transfer molding and compression molding processes that create parts with smooth surfaces on both mold-contacting sides of the laminate.

Draft is the angle of the part's sides in relation to the direction that it will be removed from the mold (or *demolded*). *Positive draft* will allow a part to be easily demolded and will minimize mold wear, while *negative draft* or *reverse draft* will prevent it from being demolded or cause premature wear on the mold. A simple example of draft is found in the standard plastic ice cube tray in your freezer. Without positively angled sides, the brittle ice cubes formed in the tray would be difficult or impossible to remove—leaving us sipping warm drinks. Some part features (such as lips, protrusions, and ledges) may create *undercuts*—or localized areas that counteract the laminate's ability to be easily demolded and must be accounted for in the design of a mold.

Bosses (protruding features used to mount something to the part), *ribs* (thin protrusions used to reinforce a wall on the part), and *gussets* (angled, rib-like features used to support a boss or wall) are commonly found on injection molded and welded parts, but they also appear on some composite parts. For better moldability in composites, these features are often designed slightly differently from their plastic or metal counterparts.

Flanges are extensions to the edge of a mold face that make it easier to handle the mold and apply special processing materials to them. *Trim lines* are marks in a mold that indicate where a finished part is to be trimmed after molding. *Backup structures* are specialized supports added to a mold or mold pattern to help keep it rigid during layup, demolding, and transportation. *Mass-cast* molds are those that are created through the pouring of a liquid material (such as fluid plastic resin or molten metal) into a form, which then solidifies and creates the mold shape.

Various types of hollow, enclosed, and complex shapes can be molded using a *mandrel, mold core*, or *insert*—which are all specialized internal molding components. A mandrel is a long, straight or tapered, rigid mold around which a composite is formed. It is often demolded after cure through the use of a jig or press. A mold core is used to create internal cavities in a composite part. Some mold cores are considered *captive molds* in that they remain in the final molded composite—as with the hollow, thin-walled aluminum tanks around which composite pressure tanks are commonly formed. Other types of mold cores can be removed, destroyed, or dissolved out of the part—as with cores made of plaster, styrene foam, wax, or specialty dissolvable materials (called *soluble cores*). Still other types of internal molding aids are expandable, such as rubber inserts or inflatable bladders, and apply pressure to the curing laminate, after which they are removed. For areas with tight corners or details, an *intensifier* (often made of a flexible material, such as rubber) is used along with pressure to help force the composite tightly into place and to minimize voids.

Multi-sectioned molds break apart into multiple pieces to aid in the demolding of negative draft or undercut features—

with each mold section being well drafted in the direction that it is demolded from the laminate. The edges where mold sections meet are commonly comprised of *matched* flanges—or walls that extend perpendicularly from the mold faces—typically with *registration* features that are shaped to help the mold sections fit together cleanly and securely. The flat flange surfaces where these mold sections meet is referred to as the *parting plane* because this is where the mold *parts*, or separates. The *parting line* is the separation on the mold faces, where this parting plane comes in contact with the actual molded part. The parting plane and corresponding parting line may be angled, jogged, or curved as needed to meet the forming and demolding requirements for the part.

When creating composite tooling, cast molds, or vacuum-thermoformed molds, the original component around which the mold is created is referred to as the *pattern, plug*, or *master*. There are slight nuanced differences in these terms depending on the area of industry using them, but in this particular book the term *mold pattern* is used to describe any form over which a mold is created.

With those terms and definitions out of the way, next we'll cover a few important guidelines that will help guarantee good result with a new mold design, regardless of the size or complexity of the project.

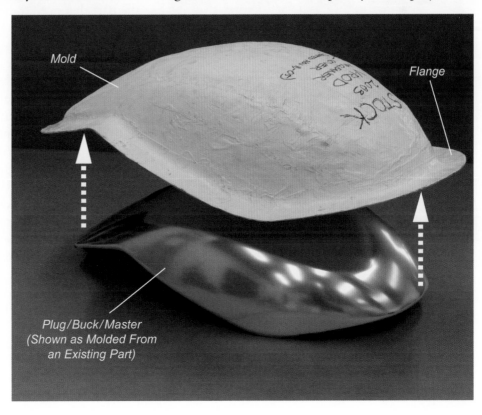

Mold

Flange

Plug/Buck/Master
(Shown as Molded From
an Existing Part)

Using a Caul Plate for Smooth Surfaces on Both Sides of a Vacuum-bagged Part

Bagging Materials

Caul Plate (Sheet Metal)

Composite Laminate

Mold

Analysis of Part Top:

Emblem Mounting Holes (To Be Smoothed Over)

"Class A" Surfaces

Mounting Holes for Rear Wing

Rear Light Mounting Holes (Across Rear)

License Plate Mounting Holes (X4)

"Class A" Surfaces

Rear Light Access Hole

Trunk Lock Mounting Hole

Analysis of Part Bottom:

Sections Removed For Weight Savings And Bonding Access

Trunk Hinge Mounts (Weld Nuts)

Rear Wing Hardware Access Holes

Lock Hardware Access Hole

Trunk Latch Mounting Plate and Hardware

Rear Light Hardware Access Holes

Rear Light Access Hole

Rear Light Mounting Holes

"Weep" Hole (for Water Drainage)

Analysis of Part Release Direction:

Top Side Release Direction

Bottom Side Release Direction

Parting Line (At Edge)

* Top and Bottom Parts Will Need To Be Adhesively Bonded Together After Molding

Practical Molding Considerations

Determining the successful moldability of a composite design requires a practical analysis of its shaping complexity, including its draft and undercuts, surface texture, and functional features—and then simplifying the design (as needed) for better moldability. A mold must be the *identical geometric inverse* of the finished part—or shaped as though the part were simply subtracted out of the mold material, leaving a cavity the shape of the part itself. Visualizing this can be difficult for complex parts, but is easily achieved when a mold is formed *over* a mold pattern—as when fabricating composite tooling—or when using drawings or computer modeling software.

Identify Aesthetic Surfaces

When considering the actual moldability of a composite part design, first find any surfaces on the part that need to have a high quality finish for aesthetic, fitment, ergonomic, structural, coating, aerodynamic/hydrodynamic, or other purposes. These surfaces will likely need to come in contact with a mold face for the best surface quality, so they may dictate the most effective demolding direction and corresponding draft considerations. If only one side of a part must contact the mold, a relatively simple, open-faced mold may suffice, though it will inevitably leave a rough surface on the non-mold-contacting side of the finished part. When a flat panel or slightly curved part has two opposing aesthetic sides, a *caul plate* (a release-coated panel that is rigid or semi-flexible) can be used to produce smooth surfaces on the non-mold-contacting side of the laminate. Other more complex parts may require fabricating a *set* of molds to form features found on both sides of the part (as explained below).

Determining Demolding Direction and Degree of Draft

Every face on a part must have some degree of positive draft in order to be easily released from a

mold-contacting
...ine the shape of
...les to determining
...riving to find the
...umber of surfaces
...om the mold
...of the part are
...ection, reassess the
...ther direction will
...g direction is not
...in, a multi-section
...be necessary (as

...o create the
...mold face can
...nical or aesthetic
...y speaking, deep
and narrow parts demold most easily with at least
5 to 15 degrees of draft, whereas shallow and wide
parts can work well with only 2 to 5 degrees of draft.

Employ a protractor or other angle-measurement tool to assess the draft on a mold pattern in relation to the direction it can best be demolded. Note that certain roll-wrapped or mandrel-formed composites are often created with zero draft—but these are the exception, not the rule—and they require special demolding methods (as explained in the *Demolding, Trimming, and Finishing* chapter).

Identify Important Functional Features and Hard-to-mold Areas

Check for areas of a part design that need to maintain very specific measurements for fitment, performance or other functional purposes. This may include positioning mold faces to accurately control the dimensions of the part, or to manage the placement of important functional features—such as threaded inserts, holes, slots, bosses, pins, ribs, etc.

Mounting flanges, edge lips, or tabs can create undercuts that counteract the demolding direction, so their molding needs to

be carefully considered or their shaping otherwise altered. Also, identify areas on a part that are especially small, detailed, textured, narrow, thin, sharp, or particularly inaccessible. As a rule of thumb, if you cannot get your fingers into a tight mold detail, it will be difficult for composites to conform to it without special accommodations—likely causing large voids or resin pooling in those areas of the finished laminate.

Additionally, sharp corners (whether internal or external) typically require a minimum ½" radius for effective open mold wet layups. For vacuum-bagged and infused laminates, ¼" radius is the recommended minimum corner sizing. If tighter corners are imperative, they will require an intensifier or high pressure processing method (such as an autoclave, pressure vessel, or compression molding) to facilitate good contact with the mold corners.

Simplifying or Smoothing Features and Surfaces for Better Moldability

Flat parts are always the easiest to form—which is why they make great practice pieces for beginners—but curved parts can still be molded with relative ease. The more complex the part, though, the more complex the molding process, so always consider the simplest design to do the same job. For example, some assemblies of parts can be combined into a single part, while some parts may need to be broken down

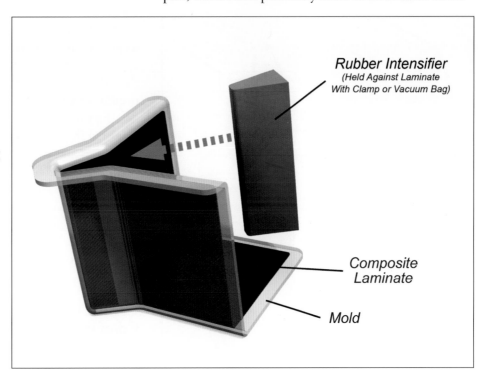

Rubber Intensifier
(Held Against Laminate With Clamp or Vacuum Bag)

Composite Laminate

Mold

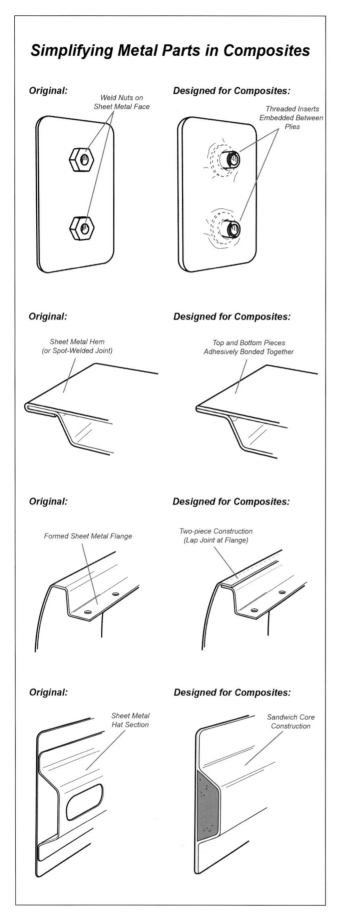

Simplifying Metal Parts in Composites

Original:
Weld Nuts on Sheet Metal Face

Designed for Composites:
Threaded Inserts Embedded Between Plies

Original:
Sheet Metal Hem (or Spot-Welded Joint)

Designed for Composites:
Top and Bottom Pieces Adhesively Bonded Together

Original:
Formed Sheet Metal Flange

Designed for Composites:
Two-piece Construction (Lap Joint at Flange)

Original:
Sheet Metal Hat Section

Designed for Composites:
Sandwich Core Construction

into multiple pieces for molding and then later joined together. In some cases, cut-open sections in a surface may need to be closed off to simplify the mold design, and sandwich core construction may need to take the place of stiffening ribs.

Holes are commonly drilled or cut into a composite part *after molding* rather than being molded into it to simplify the molding process. Slight relief marks or scribed lines in a mold can be used to denote the exact locations for drilled holes or cuts on molded components when computer-controlled trimming methods are not available.

Always remove extraneous "adornment"—such as emblems, trim, hardware, etc.—from a mold pattern so it will be easier to mold. When small details or slight undercuts simply cannot be avoided on a part, flexible silicone molding techniques (such as *mother molds* described in the next chapter on *Fabricating and Using Molds*) can be utilized.

When a mold pattern contains permanently attached hardware (such as weld-nuts, hinges, or brackets), the existing hardware can be used to mold "location hardware" into the composite tooling. This can be done with waxed, removable fasteners that aid in embedding secondary hardware into the mold (as demonstrated in the *Fabricating and Using Molds* chapter).

Remove small dents, surface waves, hail damage, "orange peel" paint texture, rust (including rust-bubbled paint), flaking clear coat, and even scratches from a mold pattern prior to molding over it. Modeling clay or soft wax can smooth out dips, wrinkles, and imperfections on a mold pattern prior to mold-making. Additionally, the mold surface should be wet sanded and polished to a high sheen until it is highly reflective.

If a mold pattern is well-drafted and has only minimal imperfections (i.e., with only minor blemishes and no deformity in the part), light repairs can be made up in the tooling created from the mold pattern—*but only if absolutely necessary* as this can inadvertently alter the shaping of the mold faces. To do this, first form and remove the tooling from the mold pattern, and then carefully wet sand and polish the flaws left in the mold surfaces afterwards.

Considerations for Using Sandwich Cores in a Mold

Composite sandwich cores can be applied over an entire laminate structure, or also used for localized laminate stiffening. Cores are most easily applied over flat mold surfaces, but can also be adapted to single degree-curved molds by scoring or kerfing the core material. For compound curved surfaces, the core may need to be cut into smaller conformal sections—although thin PVC foam can be thermoformed to fit a mold prior to adding it into the laminate. If both of the facing laminate skins of the sandwich construction have different shaping to them, the composite skins may need to be molded separately, secondarily bonded together at their edges, and then filled with expanding foam through access holes created in the laminate.

Flat sandwich cores are easily formed using compression molding, but the compressive force of the molding process must not exceed the compressive limits of the core material's strength. Cores can also be used with vacuum-bagging and resin infusion processes, but ensure close fitment of the core to the laminate materials to avoid excess resin or void formation at the laminate-to-core interface.

Adding or Subtracting Features from Existing Parts or Patterns

When adding material to a mold pattern to create a "positive", convex shape (like an integral scoop on an existing hood) it may be best to add geometry to the mold pattern *prior* to forming tooling over the pattern. However, when subtracting material to make a "negative", concave feature (like a NACA vent recessed into an existing body panel), modify the mold pattern by cutting into it and doing all necessary body work before replicating it. If you need to avoid modifying the actual mold pattern itself, create tooling over the mold pattern as usual and then modify the mold by appropriately adding material to it after demolding the pattern.

Alternative Molding Considerations

To enhance moldability of a complex part, consider alternative molding methods that may obtain the same results. For example, could those one-of-a-kind curved composite handlebars be created using moldless techniques, or could they otherwise be assembled from multiple stock pieces? If your one-piece composite wing would seem to require a large and complex multi-sectioned closed mold system with bladders, could it be made as a moldless part, or possibly re-designed to be molded

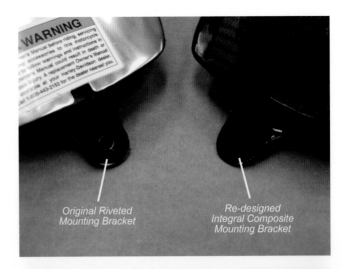

Original Riveted Mounting Bracket

Re-designed Integral Composite Mounting Bracket

Before creating molds for a part like this trunk lid, it must be completely stripped of every additional component on it.

Remove all extraneous parts from a mold pattern that may otherwise complicate the mold-making process.

79

Aluminum tape is useful for covering and smoothing over rough or damaged areas on metal parts.

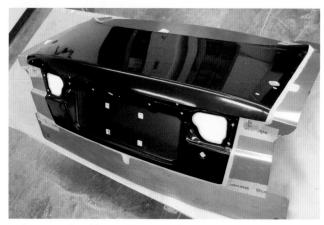

After considerable preparation, this trunk lid is now stripped, smoothed, and ready for composite tooling to be laid up over it.

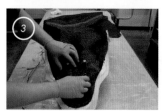

Captive hardware can be created by: 1) placing a waxed fastener into the needed hardware (in this case, an unwaxed T-nut), 2) laminating around the fastener to retain its position, 3) completing any other lamination around it, and then 4) removing the fastener from the hardware after the laminate has fully cured.

in open-faced molds and then later bonded together instead? Does your part really need a mounting tab bolted to it, or could the mounting tab be formed into the part instead? Looking at your design from a different point of view may greatly streamline your mold making endeavors.

Considerations for Hollow, Flexible, or Large Mold Patterns

Hollow parts (such as fluid tanks or tubular frames) can be notoriously tricky to form, often requiring complex, multi-sectioned closed molds. If the hollow part has a smooth outer surface, this will likely require the assistance of internal pressurization methods (such as internal bladders) to hold the laminate against the mold surfaces during cure. In some cases, parts like these may need to be molded in separate pieces and then later bonded together.

To build a mold for a hollow part, first determine a parting line at the transition where draft reverses between the top and bottom halves of the part or pattern. Secure the mold pattern to a flat base, and then place one arm of a framer's square against the base and the other arm of the square against the part. Drag the square around the entire mid-line of the part and mark successive points at the tangency between the square's vertical edge and the part surface. Connect these points with a marker to produce a reference line that can be used for the parting line between the two halves of the mold set. Tooling can be built with matching flanges that meet at this parting line (as described below).

When using flexible mold patterns, strengthen them so they will be strong enough to withstand the weight of composite tooling formed over them. This can be done by securing scrap wooden blocks to the back of the mold pattern to support it over a flat table top, or by using two-part expanding urethane foam to fill the release-coated cavity under the pattern. Simple egg-crate support structures fabricated from cardboard scrap are also effective, but for large or heavy flexible parts, plywood and common home-construction 2x4 boards can make especially cost-effective supports.

Mold Pattern Support Structures

Some large mold patterns may be best supported by placing them directly on a level shop floor, while other mold patterns may need to be accessible from all sides, requiring a center support member through its end or side that will allow the pattern to be rotated. Some patterns may even need a lifting base built into them so they can be easily raised—or they may be so large that they require scaffolding for multi-story access.

Other elaborate constructions (such as vehicle bodies) can be best formed using mold patterns that break up into multiple pieces to ensure proper fitment between molded sections. A variety of assembly features can be molded along with these sections to guarantee that the composite pieces formed in them will fit together solidly once completed.

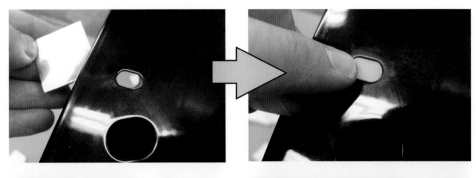

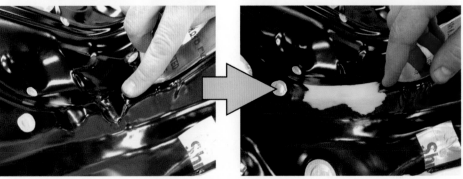

Holes can be smoothed by backing them up with aluminum tape and filling them with clay (top), and complex shapes can be simplified by adding clay over them (bottom).

Considerations for Molding Tow/ Roving-based Composites

When laying up tow or roving in a filament would layup, the reinforcement yarns must be held under tension throughout the entire lamination process. This can be done by either pulling it against a mold wall, or wrapping it around a support framework that holds it securely in place. Due to this tensioning requirement, negative shapes—or those that indent *into* the general shape of the part (rather than out of it)— are generally avoided.

For filament wound structures with thin walls, a mold face (formed by a mandrel, soluble core, or captive mold) is typically used to hold the tow or

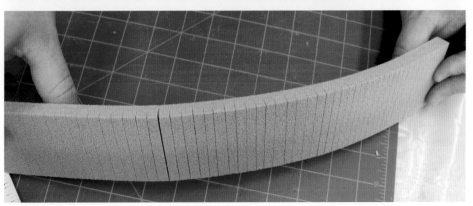

Slight curves can be created in foam by "kerfing" it with slits cut into it at uniform depths and widths.

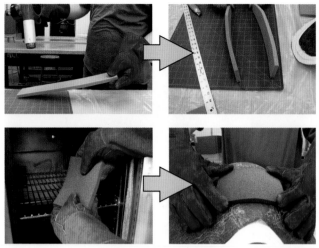

PVC foam can be softened with a heat gun (top), or warmed in an oven (bottom) and then formed and cooled to its final shape.

roving in place. Filament is applied over the mold faces to the right fiber orientation and thickness, cured, and then the mold core or mandrel is removed—so plan ahead for an acceptable way to extract the core.

In certain lattice, skeletal, or grid-type filament constructions, sections of reinforcement act as thin, load-bearing members of the structure. The *nodes* (or connection joints between these load-bearing elements) can be immobilized for better load control on the structure by creating solid adhesive connections, or by wrapping additional yarns of material around the joint (typically with aramid fiber)—similar to lashing with rope.

When devising a support framework for lattice and skeletal filament windings, determine the best way to disassemble, break down, or remove the framework from the part after it has cured. This may involve using supports that are joined together to a central core with fasteners, or by employing a soluble core material.

Planning the Mold or Mold System

A mold can be planned out so that it is directly fabricated, or it can be formed over an existing mold pattern. Direct mold-making can save considerable time and expense, but it requires the fabricator to skillfully visualize and construct the mold based on the part's geometric inverse—which can be complicated for anything other than simple parts without the aid of computer modeling software (as described below).

Mold-making over a mold pattern, on the other hand, requires the fabricator to build the exact form of a part, and then form an

Adding Positive Mold Features

Original Part

Feature Added To Original Part

Mold Formed Over Part and Feature

Final Part With Positive Feature Added

Adding Negative Mold Features

Mold Formed Over Original Part

(Mold Removed From Part)

Feature(s) Added To Mold

Final Part Removed From Mold With Negative Feature(s) Added

Creating a Parting Line Reference on a Mold Pattern

Bad Parting Line Reference:

Angle Too Shallow Here

Good Parting Line Reference:

Good Balanced Spacing Above and Below Parting Line

Bad Parting Line Reference:

Angle Too Shallow Here

actual mold over it—which is usually accomplished using composite tooling, thermoformed molds, or mass-cast resin molds. This method does not require complex computer models, and can be used for practically any level of mold complexity.

Planning the Location and Size of Mold Flanges

Mold flanges for flat parts can be created most simply when extended out tangentially from the surface of the part. If flanges are fabricated on the edges of a deep, vertical-sided part, they will generally be most useful when constructed at an angle or when perpendicular to the side of the part. This helps provide clearance for the fabricator's hands and arms to fit into the mold cavity during layup. Additionally, make sure the mold flanges are wide enough for adhering the sealing tapes used in vacuum-bagging processes, the vacuum or resin supply lines used with infusion, or extra-wide flanges required for double-bagged infusion processes. In general, 2" to 4" wide flanges work well for most small to medium parts, but 4" to 6" of width is recommended for molds used with double-bagged infusion processes.

To build flanges in composite tooling with a mold pattern, *flange forms* (or temporary supports at the edge of a part) are used to prop up the composite tooling during layup. Flange forms can be made from a variety of non-porous sheet materials or resin-compatible

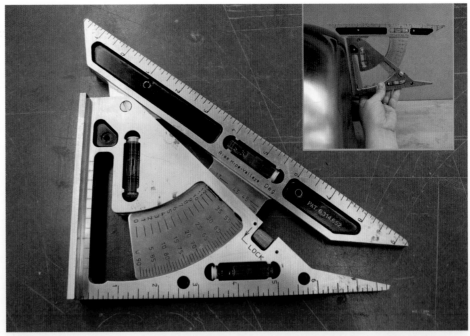

A protractor will work well for measuring draft angles, but a "pivot square" (shown above), available from the C.H. Hanson Company (www.chhanson.com), can be an especially helpful tool.

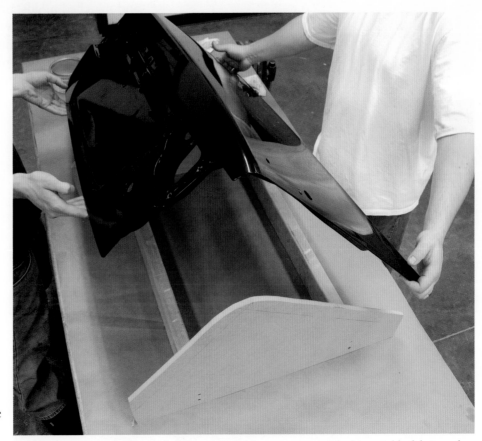

Backup supports may be needed for some mold patterns, as with this quickly fabricated wood structure added beneath this large part.

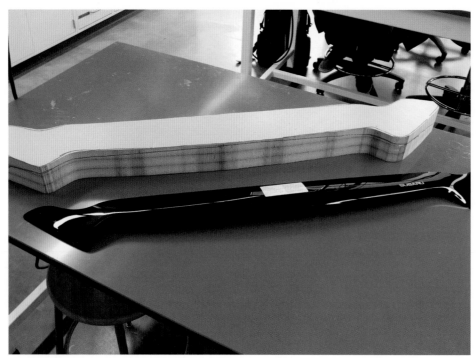

materials and are attached to the mold pattern using methods described in the next chapter.

Flanges for vacuum-bagging molds must be smooth to minimize vacuum leakage issues. However, bear in mind that the flanges used in multi-part molds may require additional width, alignment hardware, or registration marks (as described below) to make sure the mold sections fit correctly with each other—so they are more difficult to fully seal when used with vacuum bagging applications.

Some flexible mold patterns (like this plastic bug shield) may require a more elaborate support structure. Here, a laminated styrene foam support has been cut to match the profile of the part…

Devising Multi-sectioned and Matched Molds

When constructing multi-sectioned, closed, and matched molds, first determine where it would be most effective to locate the parting line and corresponding flanges for the mold sections. Formulate a good means of fabricating the flange forms and their required width, and determine an adequate means of registering the mold sections to each other to ensure proper mold alignment (as discussed in the next chapter).

Matched molds can be used for parts that need to be smooth on both sides—but they are also helpful for parts that require back-to-back bonding of two mating laminates. For example, most vehicle hoods and trunk lids have a smooth-faced top component bonded with another smooth-faced structure beneath them. With these parts, separate top and bottom molds can beF formed of the mold

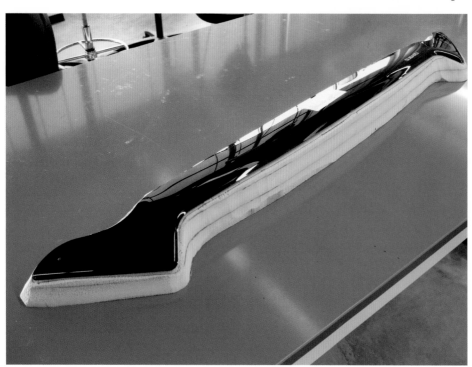

…and then sculpted down with a shaper rasp to adequately support the part.

84

pattern's surfaces, using registry features between the two molds to ensure perfect alignment between the molded and bonded components.

Planning for Appropriate Mold Strength

For a mold to sufficiently support itself throughout the molding and demolding processes, it should be at least 3 to 4 times the strength of the laminate formed in it. This is especially critical for parts with tight tolerances and geometric accuracy requirements. Additionally, when using high pressure forming methods in a mold, machined metals, mass-cast resins, or highly reinforced composite tooling are recommended.

Planning for Various Mold Sizes

Small or deep parts can be difficult to demold without a wide enough mold flange against which to exert sufficient demolding forces on the finished part. Consequently, small parts usually benefit from a larger flange that can be laid over with excess laminate material for the sole purpose of accommodating wedges for easier demolding. Removal hardware can also be laminated into the part itself—such as extraction bolts that can be pulled on during demolding. Other special demolding provisions may include using knockout pins embedded in the mold, incorporating screw-type hardware into the mold to push out the part, or even embedding inflatable sections into the mold to help eject the part.

Examples of Mold Pattern Structures

Internal Wooden Structure

Plywood Templates Mounted to Central Steel Support (Strongback)

Flat Shop Floor or Plywood Base

Wheeled Base

Mold patterns can be supported in several ways, depending on the access needed around it during fabrication.

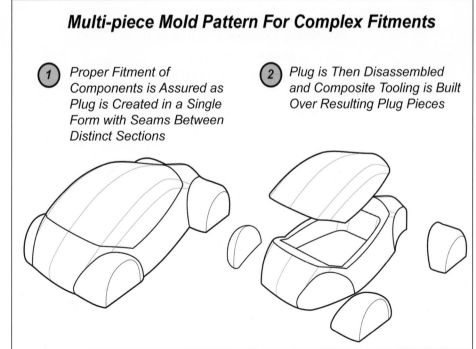

Multi-piece Mold Pattern For Complex Fitments

① Proper Fitment of Components is Assured as Plug is Created in a Single Form with Seams Between Distinct Sections

② Plug is Then Disassembled and Composite Tooling is Built Over Resulting Plug Pieces

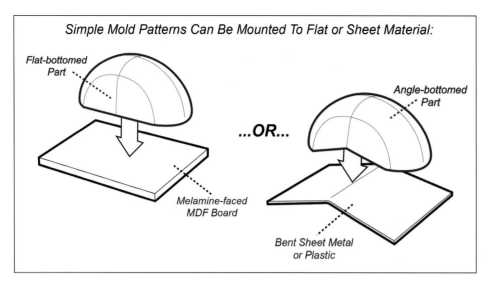

Simple Mold Patterns Can Be Mounted To Flat or Sheet Material:

Flat-bottomed Part

...OR...

Angle-bottomed Part

Melamine-faced MDF Board

Bent Sheet Metal or Plastic

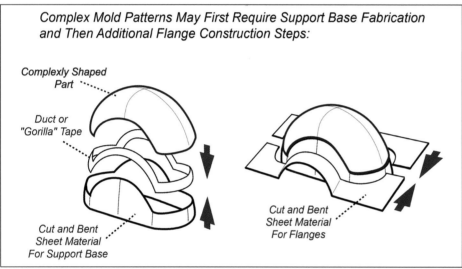

Complex Mold Patterns May First Require Support Base Fabrication and Then Additional Flange Construction Steps:

Complexly Shaped Part

Duct or "Gorilla" Tape

Cut and Bent Sheet Material For Support Base

Cut and Bent Sheet Material For Flanges

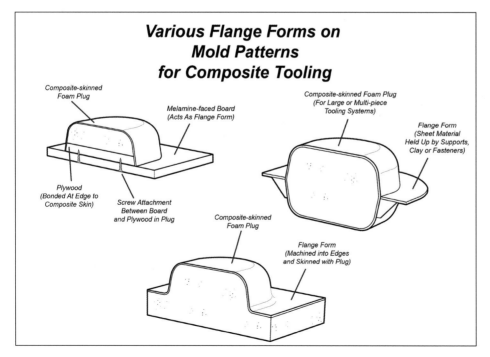

Various Flange Forms on Mold Patterns for Composite Tooling

Composite-skinned Foam Plug

Melamine-faced Board (Acts As Flange Form)

Plywood (Bonded At Edge to Composite Skin)

Screw Attachment Between Board and Plywood in Plug

Composite-skinned Foam Plug (For Large or Multi-piece Tooling Systems)

Flange Form (Sheet Material Held Up by Supports, Clay or Fasteners)

Composite-skinned Foam Plug

Flange Form (Machined into Edges and Skinned with Plug)

Most medium and large-sized molds usually need backup supports to help rigidify them. This may entail laminating plywood or urethane foam ribs (or even egg-crate structures) to the back of the mold, but may include welded-tube frameworks (made of steel or aluminum) bolted to the mold.

For transporting larger molds, casters (whether removable or fixed), runners beneath the mold (for a fork lift or pallet jack access), or rigging (for use with overhead cranes or lifts) can all be welcomed mold additions.

Computer-based Mold Pattern Planning and Digital Output Methods

A variety of computer modeling programs can be used to create a mold design and then assess its draft, interference and fitment with other parts, as well as determine a part's final weight, center of gravity, or how (and where) it may fail when overloaded. With Boolean functions in the software, the part can also be subtracted from a block of virtual material to create the inverse (or mold) of the part for direct mold fabrication, or the mold surfaces can otherwise be copied from the designed part and thickened to create a mold shell.

Post-processing software creates CNC control codes from the three-dimensional computer model data in order to move the cutting machine or 3D printer into the needed Cartesian-based "X", "Y", and "Z" directions. Mold or mold patterns can then be output through *CNC* (Computer Numerical Control) machining or routing of stock material, 3D printing equipment, and even plasma or laser cutters. The physical limitations of the CNC equipment's linear axes dictate the length, width, and height limits, or *build envelope*, that the machine is capable of working within—so a large mold or mold pattern may need to be divided into smaller pieces to fit on some machines.

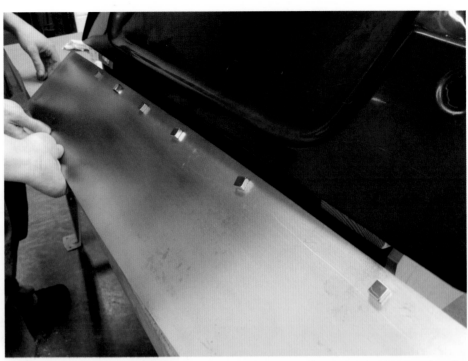

With steel parts, magnets can be used to hold a sheet metal flange form in place before laying up composite tooling.

With all of the high-powered tools currently available, try to avoid the pitfall of "technological overkill"—or designing molds with more complexity, expense, and cost than is truly necessary for the task at hand. *Even the best mold-makers use wisdom to pick a combination of low-tech and high-tech methods when devising their mold-making path!*

Section and Template Planning of Mold Patterns

One of the simplest mold pattern construction methods available is to sculpt a block of material using photographs or three-view drawings (top, front, and side) as references. This can require good drafting skills and planning for alignment of each drawing view to the block of material.

Another method for creating mold patterns and molds is to adopt the

Registration features on the flanges of this mold help align the mold sections to each other.

age-old boat building techniques called "lofting". With lofting, an object is drawn using traditional orthographic drafting methods (either manually or with a computer) and then sliced into enough parallel sections to adequately describe its overall shape. The object's contour at each of these sliced sections is then transferred to rigid construction materials, trimmed to size, and used to create corresponding sections for the actual pattern. These sections are set apart from each other at *station points*—or specific intervals marked on a rigid backbone, called a *strongback*. For composite mold-making, the space between these section templates is then filled with sculpting material (usually in the form of foam) or laid over with slatted material (such as thin wood strips), and then smoothed over to create the final shape for the pattern—producing a shape with relatively good accuracy.

The strongback can be as simple as 2x4 boards with sections secured in a "ladder" formation, but larger mold patterns may require a welded steel framework. Meticulously measure and fasten all section templates to the strongback to avoid *tolerance stacking*—which occurs when small variations in measurements made *between* templates compound over the length of the mold pattern, making the overall size either too big or too small.

To avoid this problem, measure section placement from a common point—typically from one reference end or side of the mold pattern.

Another variation on the section and template construction technique is to use thicker three-dimensionally CNC-cut sections derived from a computer model rather than spaced-apart, two-dimensional contour sections. These thicker sections can be cut up to the maximum "Z"-direction (or vertical) travel capabilities of the particular CNC machine, shaping the section and the space *between* each of them to save time over otherwise hand-shaping the transitions between sections.

Mold-making Materials and Selection Options

Of the several mold-making material options available, each has a molding use for which it is best suited, based on the material's shapeability, chemical compatibility, cost, and durability—though many mold-making quandaries can be solved using a creative mix of materials and methods. Only those materials most common to small shop fabricators are explained here, but additional options are available to those who seek higher part volume, accuracy, and quality from their molds.

Mold Chemical Compatibility

Beware of chemical incompatibilities between the mold and the materials going into it. For example, styrene vapor from polyester and vinyl ester resins and gel coats can cause paint on a mold pattern to crack or bubble, and may be incompatible with some plastics. An alternative to styrene-based resins is to use an epoxy surface coat and epoxy resin matrix.

Further, silicone used in contact with polyester resins will inhibit the polyester from curing—even when the resin is highly catalyzed. Likewise, sulfur-based clay can inhibit the chemical

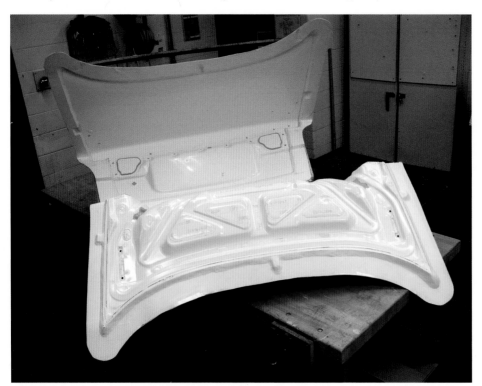

For parts composed of joined upper and lower skins (as with car hoods, trunks, and doors), matched molds can be fabricated to align the skins together.

Backup supports can be used on molds that require tight tolerances, and to keep composite tooling from warping over time. Steel tubing is used to reinforce this concept vehicle chassis mold (bottom right).

reactions within mixed liquid epoxies, so the two should not be used in contact with each other. However, such chemical interactions are rarely a problem with cured epoxy or metal molds.

Even when using a so-called "self-releasing" plastic (such as polyethylene, polypropylene, or Delrin) as a mold pattern or mold, it is still wise to use release agents. Three to five coats of buffed parting wax should be a sufficient release coating for most parts, but a backup application of PVA (polyvinyl alcohol) or other suitable liquid release works best in practice—especially with epoxy resins.

Mold Longevity and Material Selection

Aside from the shape, draft, and smoothness of a mold, the durability of the material it is made from will dictate a sizable portion of the mold's longevity. For this reason, consider the actual number of parts you intend to fabricate with a mold, any wear-inducing hardware insertion during layup, pressurization processes (such as vacuum-bagging, autoclave, or pressure vessel use), or level of heating it will endure, and then select a mold material to match those needs.

Wood

Wood is readily available, inexpensive, and easily shaped with common woodshop tools. It is most readily used with flat or shallowly-curved shapes that have dimensional depths less than an inch or so, although larger-sized shapes can be made by gluing-up or fastening multiple boards together. Wood is great for creating patterns, templates, sections in mold patterns, reinforcements, or supports and can be easily and accurately shaped with a CNC router—but laser cutting can also be used for thin plywood materials under ¼" thick.

As a natural product, wood is available in various densities and strengths, but it must be sealed with resin (using polyester, epoxy, or urethane), lacquer, plastic laminate (such as Melamine or

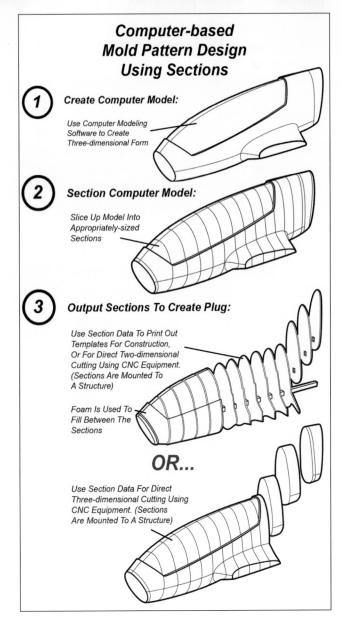

Computer-based Mold Pattern Design Using Sections

1 **Create Computer Model:**

Use Computer Modeling Software to Create Three-dimensional Form

2 **Section Computer Model:**

Slice Up Model Into Appropriately-sized Sections

3 **Output Sections To Create Plug:**

Use Section Data To Print Out Templates For Construction, Or For Direct Two-dimensional Cutting Using CNC Equipment. (Sections Are Mounted To A Structure)

Foam Is Used To Fill Between The Sections

OR...

Use Section Data For Direct Three-dimensional Cutting Using CNC Equipment. (Sections Are Mounted To A Structure)

Formica), or specialty sealers to block off its porous surfaces to prevent bonding with the composite when used as a mold surface.

Sheet Metal

Sheet metals can be formed to create widely ranging mold shapes, but producing complex contours with them requires some significant skill. Small, manageable sheets of mild steel and aluminum can be found at most hardware stores (usually supplied for use in home or commercial HVAC ductwork), but even larger sheets can be purchased through industrial suppliers. It can be readily bent, folded, cut, and joined into desired shapes with simple metalworking tools, and can be hammered and formed into large compound curved shapes with the right skills, tools, and time. They can also be polished to a mirror-like finish with cutting and rubbing compounds, but they should be reinforced and handled with care because they can be easily damaged, deformed, or dented.

Machined Metal

Machined steel or aluminum metal molds cut from billet tend to work best for high-volume and high-pressure moldings. For very simple shapes, traditional hand-controlled milling or turning equipment can produce usable molds, whereas more complex or compound curved shapes may require computer models and CNC-capable machinery for accurate production. Machined metal molds can be highly polished and are compatible with all common resin types, but they can be very heavy, and are expensive in material and forming costs. However, they are more recyclable than other mold material types.

Thermoplastic Sheet

Plastic sheet can be used to create small to medium-sized temporary molds with planar or compound curved surfaces. It can be formed with heat from an oven or heat gun, or by using vacuum-thermoforming processes. Sheet acrylic molds can also be reinforced with wood or metal backup supports, or by laminating fiberglass reinforcements to the back side of the mold with polyester, vinyl ester, or liquid acrylic resin matrices.

Machined Plastics (Thermoset and Amorphous Thermoplastic)

Machined plastic stock can be used for small to moderately sized molds or mold patterns where hard surfaces need to be constructed to high tolerances (often by means of CNC milling) and at high cutting speeds. Several types of plastic stock are available in solid sheets of varying thicknesses and can be cut, stacked, and bonded as needed. They can also be purchased with fillers (such as aluminum or other materials) for better machinability, thermally conductivity, and mechanically stability. They can also be highly polished to produce excellent mold surfaces. Please note that many commodity semi-crystalline thermoplastics will not produce a smooth surface when machined or sanded.

3D Printed Plastics (Thermoset and Thermoplastic)

A wide range of plastics are available for making 3D printed molds and mold patterns. FDM-based printing methods are currently the least

Wood vs. Foam Shaping Capabilities

Flat Wood Sheet(s):
Shallow Shapes Possible

Cut and Stacked Wood Sections:
Complex Shapes Possible
(Tends to Be Very Heavy)

Foam:
Complex Shapes Possible
(Tends to Be Lightweight)

expensive with the most thermoplastic material options, which includes the following recommended plastics (in ascending order of general temperature and strength characteristics for use as molds): PLA, ABS, ASA, PC, PC-ABS, Ultem 9085, and Ultem 1010. Soluble cores can also be 3D printed using PVA (dissolvable with warm water), HIPS (dissolvable with D-Limonene), and other professional, proprietary materials (such as Stratasys system's own ST-130). Consumer-grade SLA and DLP 3D printing processes can also be used to make molds with even better surface quality, but they tend to use expensive proprietary materials and have smaller build-size limits.

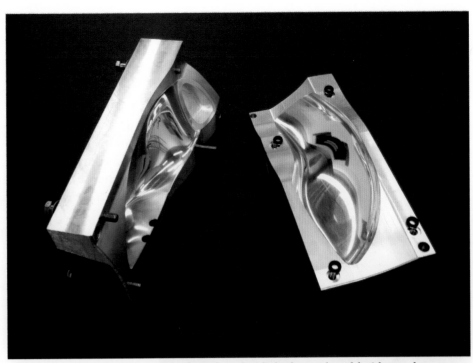

Machined and polished metal molds (shown here as cut from aluminum billet) are excellent for high-temperature and high-pressure composite moldings.

It should be noted that at the time of this book's publishing, 3D printed *metal* molds are also being experimented with for various composites applications—but speed, cost, and surface finish remain formidable barriers to using these on larger parts in the foreseeable future.

Mass-cast Thermoset Resins

Liquid casting resins can be used to create solid, complex molds relatively quickly when poured over a mold pattern that is positioned within removable forms. Mass-cast thermoset molds can be relatively heavy and expensive by volume, so they are best reserved for small to moderately-sized mold-making applications. They can also be made of high-temperature type resins, filled with metal powder for better thermal

Machined thermoplastic materials (as shown here using Delrin plastic) can be CNC cut very quickly. This 7" x 9" mold was created in less than an hour and only needs minor surface polishing before use.

Mass-cast thermoset resin can be formed over practically any mold pattern. Here an aluminum-filled epoxy is being used to mold a bladder-formed gear-shift knob.

High-density foam (as with this 40lb urethane foam material) is excellent for medium-sized parts, and it machines very quickly and cleanly.

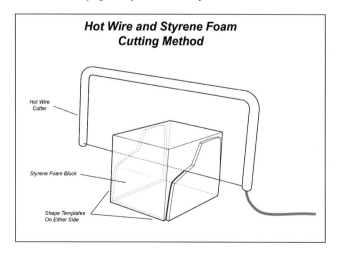

Hot Wire and Styrene Foam Cutting Method

Hot Wire Cutter

Styrene Foam Block

Shape Templates On Either Side

conductivity, or reinforced with fibers for high pressure applications.

Composite (F.R.P.)

Composite laminates make great molds because of their hard, high quality surfaces, their relative low weight, the ease of creating them with laminate materials (that may already be on-hand in a composites shop), and their relative low cost. Composite tooling is best created when formed over an existing part or pattern, and can be highly reinforced to increase its durability. Additionally, when used in conjunction with an elevated-temperature cure resin on parts that require very high tolerances, the mold can be constructed of the same composite materials that will be molded in it as a means to ensure exact thermal expansion matching between the parts and mold during processing.

Foam

Urethane, styrene, and other types of foams are widely used as composite mold-making materials because they can be easily carved, sculpted, or machined and have relatively low cost per volume. Foam comes in a wide range of densities (from less than one pound to over 40 pounds per cubic foot of volume) and corresponding durability. It is available in large blocks, sheets, or as two-part urethane liquids that expand and harden. Styrene foams can be quickly sliced with a hot wire (though polyurethane—or polyisocyanurate foams cannot), and all foams can be cut and shaped very easily with common woodworking tools or CNC routing equipment. PVC foam is typically available only in sheet form and is much more expensive than urethane or styrene-based foams—but it can be lightly thermoformed for certain shapes. Urethane foams have a higher chemical resistance than PVC or styrene-based foams, and are compatible with most resin types.

As foams are porous and susceptible to impact damage, they are best used when sealed with composite laminates or hard surface coats of resin—and even then only for a very limited number of molding cycles.

Plaster

Plaster is an age-old favorite for sculptors since it can be shaped very easily with hand tools, although it is generally too fragile to use as a long-

92

term mold—so it is best for one-off molds, mold patterns, or mold cores. Plaster comes in powder form, is mixed with water, and poured into a form, shaken to remove air bubbles, and fully sets once hard and dry. Plaster must be sealed with several coats of resin, lacquer, or specialty sealant before being used as a mold surface.

Modeling Clay

Oil-based, non-hardening modeling clay can be used to produce very complex, smooth, non-porous surfaces with excellent detail. It comes in very soft to very hard varieties, but is most workable when warmed in an oven between 120 and 150 degrees Fahrenheit—though any hotter and it can actually melt into a liquid! Modeling clay is expensive, so it is best used judiciously over a foam or wood armature or buck. Once shaped, it must be sealed with special coatings prior to one-time-use molding.

Silicone (and "Mother Molds")

Silicone is used for molding textures and undercut features that simply cannot be easily extracted from a rigid mold. In these cases, the silicone is typically used as part of a *mother mold,* where the silicone resin is set up over the surface of the part, allowed to solidify, and then rigidified by backing it up with fiberglass and epoxy resin (as explained in the next chapter).

Conclusion

In spite of the relatively complex nature of mold-making, several common guidelines are available to small shop fabricators to simplify their efforts as they endeavor to produce successful molds for composite projects. Having covered the previous points on mold design, the next chapter will explore the actual mold fabrication process using some easily accessible materials and methods.

References and Resources

Gougeon, Meade, *The Gougeon Brothers on Boat Construction: Wood and West System Materials.* (Michigan: Gougeon Brothers, Inc., 2005), 165-206.

John J. Morena, *Advanced Composite Mold Making.* (Malabar: Krieger Publishing, 2007).

Robert Quesada, *Computer Numerical Control: Machining and Turning Centers.* (Columbus: Pearson Prentice Hall, 2005), 2-71.

Smith, Z. *Advanced Composite Techniques.* Napa, CA: Aeronaut Press, 2005.

Stratasys, Ltd. *FDM for Composite Tooling 2.0: Design Guide.* Downloaded from Stratasys.com

Wanberg, John. *Composite Materials Handbook #1,* Stillwater, MN: Wolfgang Publications Inc., 2009.

Wanberg, John. *Composite Materials Handbook #2,* Stillwater, MN: Wolfgang Publications Inc., 2010.

Wanberg, John. *Composite Materials Handbook #3,* Stillwater, MN: Wolfgang Publications Inc., 2013.

Chapter Six

Fabricating and Using Molds

Having discussed the basics of moldability for composite parts, we will now cover the topic of actual mold fabrication. As previously explained, molds for composites can be made of several different materials in various forms depending on the chemicals, heat, and pressure used during processing of the parts made in them. This chapter will present several of the options available to small shop composites fabricators using many readily available materials and techniques.

Quick, Sheet-based Molds

Many types of sheet materials that are smooth and non-porous can be used as mold surfaces. This includes steel and aluminum sheet metals as well

Large, Class "A" surfaced parts can be fabricated even in small composite shops—as shown with this fiberglass concept car part made from composite tooling—using processes explained in this chapter.

as acrylic, ABS, polycarbonate, and polystyrene sheet plastics that can be formed, bent, and cut to shape. For flat molds, even tempered glass panels or Melamine/Formica-faced wood sheets can be very effective. Sheet metal molds have the benefit of being very resilient to the chemicals used in composite lamination processes. Plastic sheet molds can still be just as useful, albeit with a much shorter lifespan, and as long as there is good compatibility between the mold material and the chemicals used in it.

Prototype molds made from sheet materials are typically best formed as a single piece whenever possible—especially when an air-tight mold is needed for vacuum-bagged processes. For plastic molds made of multiple pieces, silicone sealant or modeling clay can work well for smoothing or sealing seams. However, clay seams can damage easily and may need to be repaired after each demolding process. For sheet metal molds, a bit of skilled welding, filing, sanding, and polishing can bring multiple metal pieces together into a smooth, unified mold.

Simple bends, curves and planar shapes are the easiest to create with sheet materials—though complex, compound curved surfaces are possible with advanced skills. Sheet metals can be bent, cut, rolled, or machined, and more elaborate shapes can be made through panel beating or use of an English wheel. After cutting and forming the sheet metal mold, use a file to round off corners and deburr any rough edges. Also, completely remove any rust, oil, or debris from the surface of the sheet metal, then polish and wax it before putting it into service.

Heating can be used to form simple molds using sheet thermoplastics. A strip heater can be used to create quick bends, a heat gun is effective for localized shaping and forming of the sheet, and an oven can warm an entire sheet of plastic at once to rapidly form the whole sheet (as with vacuum thermoforming described below). Remember to remove any protective film or paper backing from sheet plastics prior to heating! Avoid scratching or gouging the surface of the plastic while working with it—as scratch removal can be a very difficult and time consuming task, requiring extensive fine-grit sanding and polishing steps.

Heat forming used in conjunction with and vacuum processing (called *vacuum thermoforming*, or *vac-forming*) can produce inexpensive molds countless times using wood, plaster, or urethane

Sheet metal is an especially useful material for mold-making because it can be manipulated using common metal shop tools—such as the roller shown here.

Flanges can be easily formed in sheet metal with a bending brake (shown here).

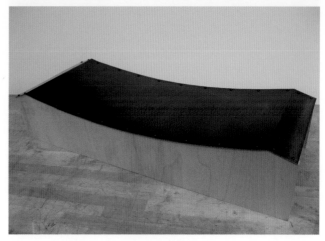

Once complete, sheet metal tooling can be supported using simple wood structures (shown here).

Sheet plastics (as with this opaque acrylic) can be easily heat-formed on a strip heater (shown here), heat gun, or oven.

Once sufficiently warmed, the sheet plastic can be bent to the desired angle and allowed to cool.

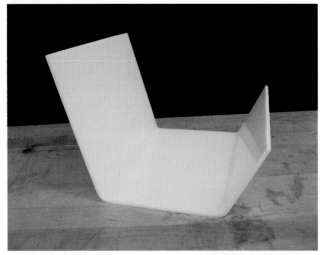

A quick mold like this can be fabricated using plastic sheet in under 10 minutes.

To heat form an acrylic plastic sheet in an oven, pre-drill through-holes in the plastic and then mount it to a wooden frame with screws (1/8" acrylic is shown here).

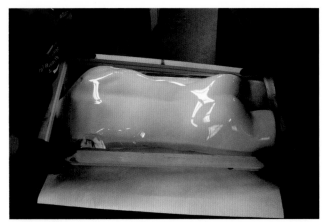

Once sufficiently warmed in an oven at 350-375° F, pull the plastic over a form (as shown draped over this mannequin torso for creating a composite backpack frame) and allow it to cool.

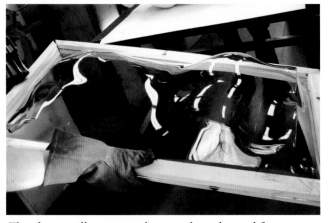

The plastic will retain its shape and can be used for a limited number of part molding cycles.

Once waxed, the mold is ready for use.

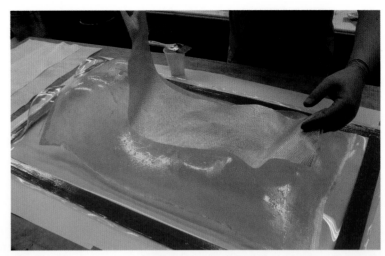

foam (but not styrene-based foam) mold patterns. Vac-formed molds are suitable for wet layup, vacuum-bagged, infused, and even pressure vessel processes—but they do come with a few limitations. Polystyrene (.040" to .100" thick), ABS (less than 1/8" thick), and acrylic (less than 1/8" thick) plastic vac-formed sheets are best used with epoxy or urethane resin matrix composite parts due to chemical compatibility issues with styrene-based resins. However, clear PETG (.040" to .100" thick) sheet plastic can be used with polyester resins, but it is a bit more finicky to thermoform than some other plastics.

Vac-forming methods have a slight learning curve, and usually entail a bit of trial and error with a vacuum-thermoforming machine until some good skills are built up—but this process can dramatically expedite small mold fabrication. Several designs for vac-formers exist online these days, with many of them deriving their magic suction powers from an off-the-shelf wet/dry shop-vacuum or vacuum pump, a reservoir tank, some valves and tubing, and some construction wood.

To perform the vac-forming process, the sheet plastic is clamped into a frame and then warmed with a heat gun or surplus shop oven until it is as flexible as a piece of thin, wet leather. This warmed plastic is placed over the mold pattern located on a vacuum platen, and the vacuum is quickly applied, allowing atmospheric pressure to push the draped plastic over the mold pattern. The plastic is allowed to cool and then it is removed from the mold pattern. The formed plastic piece is then trimmed and waxed as normal prior to use as a mold.

Another type of quick, simple mold-making process entails adhering drafted mold features directly to a flat sheet of material using fastening hardware, double-sided tape, adhesive, or RTV sealants to keep them in place during molding and demolding processes. Sharp inner corners on these molds can be rounded using small clay fillets that have been smoothed with a gloved finger or curved-ended stick. Mold release can then be

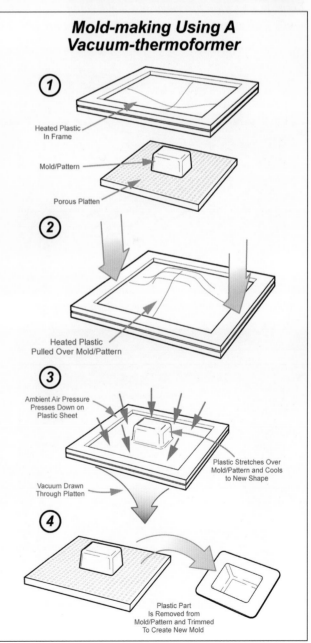

Mold-making Using A Vacuum-thermoformer

① Heated Plastic In Frame

Mold/Pattern

Porous Platten

② Heated Plastic Pulled Over Mold/Pattern

③ Ambient Air Pressure Presses Down on Plastic Sheet

Plastic Stretches Over Mold/Pattern and Cools to New Shape

Vacuum Drawn Through Platten

④ Plastic Part Is Removed from Mold/Pattern and Trimmed To Create New Mold

To create a vacuum thermoformed mold, clamp thin sheet plastic (polystyrene is being used here) into a frame...

...place the mold pattern over the vacuum platen...

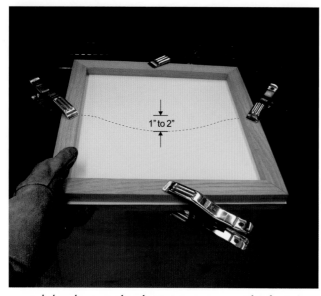

1" to 2"

...and then heat up the plastic in an oven until it begins to droop with the consistency of thin, wet leather.

added to the mold and composite parts formed directly over it.

"Bagged" Molds

One of the most time-consuming steps in creating molds involves creating air-tight, non-pourous, smooth surfaces for a mold or mold pattern (as described below with wood and foam mold surfaces). To shorten the time necessary to perform this task, thin plastic film (typically used for vacuum-bagging processes) can be applied over an unfinished mold form and pulled down using a vacuum source to create a moldable, pseudo-sealed surface—or a "bagged" mold—with the caveat that it will likely not produce a "Class A" surface. This process is useful for one-off or short production run parts, but can also be helpful for creating composite tooling and specialty "transfer" molds.

To perform this process, create a mold pattern from inexpensive materials (such as foam, wood, plaster, or clay) and then apply vacuum bagging film over the pattern. If the mold pattern has a flat bottom to it, it is easiest to first mount it to sealed flat stock, such as sheet metal, sheet plastic, or sealed wood. Sealant tape can then be used to seal the edges of the bagging film directly to this flat stock at the bottom of the pattern. More complex mold patterns can be sealed by wrapping a bag completely around the part itself.

Composite laminates produced over such bagged molds can also be vacuum-bagged—creating a "double-bagged" part with enhanced properties (somewhat similar to the "double-bagged" resin infusion process described in the following chapter).

A variation of this process uses styrene beads—like those used for bean-bag chairs, therapeutic pillows, and certain packaging applications—to create temporary molds. When contained in a sealed plastic bag under vacuum, the styrene beads are pressed tightly together by external atmospheric pressure and are immobilized in relation to each other by the friction between them. This property of the small beads makes it possible to use them as a type of transfer mold, where they can be placed in a bag over a form, evacuated, and then retain their low-fidelity shape until additional molding processes are performed over them. This can be especially helpful when creating generally shaped molds from human forms, but can be useful for other creative purposes, as well. Bagged styrene beads can even be somewhat sculpted with one's fingers when under low vacuum for free-form shaping, followed by applying a high vacuum to lock them in place before forming a permanent mold over them.

Foam/Wood-based Mold Finishing and Surface Prep

Wood, polyurethane foam, and styrene-based foams are all ideal for mold and mold pattern construction because they can be shaped quickly and have enough compressive strength to handle composite layup and vacuum processing. However, they all require special sealing prior to use as a mold surface.

One common method of sealing a foam or wood surface is to first apply a skin of fiberglass or carbon composite over the surface, closing any voids with filler, and then applying a resin sealer coating over the composite to fill any remaining pores in the surface. Satin and twill weave fabrics are the best choice for creating a protective composite skin because they lay very smoothly over porous, compound curved surfaces (including those with small pits or voids), and can help minimize finishing work. However, these still require additional smoothing steps after layup due to the space found between the woven threads in the fabric. Use sanding and sparing amounts of body filler to smooth these surface defects, and pay special attention to avoid sanding through the composite skin throughout this process. Anything larger than a pinhole will need to be filled, but simply pressing filler into the small holes with a gloved finger may be sufficient to seal many small defects. For very large mold patterns, inexpensive gypsum-based drywall compound works well to quickly cover broad areas. Once dry, this surface can then be shaped using common drywall tools, such as sanding screens and hand shapers, until major scratches are completely smoothed over.

Next, smooth the surface of the mold pattern with a sealer prior to polishing, prep, and composite tooling layup. Surface sealers, such as sprayable, polyester-based materials (like Duratec or Featherfill primer) are excellent at filling in small pinholes and leveling lightly scratched, textured, or porous surfaces. When properly thinned, these sealers can be applied using common HVLP spray equipment and will require only minimal spraying skills to produce good results. After curing, the sealer will yield a hard coating over the laminate skin that can

Place the hot plastic over the mold form…

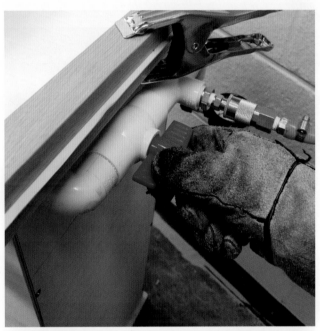

…and hold the frame firmly over the platen while turning on the vacuum.

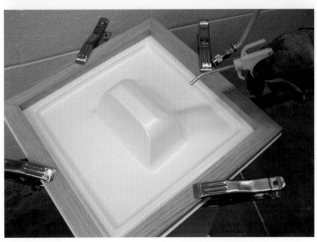

Use an air nozzle to quickly cool the hot plastic…

...and then remove the plastic from the frame and mold pattern. Use a utility knife to cut the formed plastic to size...

...and then wax it for use as a temporary mold for composites.

Sheet material can also be used to make quick molds by adhering additional features on top of it—as shown here with acrylic plastic features adhered to Melamine board to mold a carbon fiber bulkhead (see inset).

To avoid the hassle of surface finishing a foam or wood mold pattern, the pattern (shown here in styrene foam with clay repairs to it) can be placed over breather cloth on top of a non-porous sheet material...

...and then sealed around its edges with sealant tape and vacuum-bagging film.

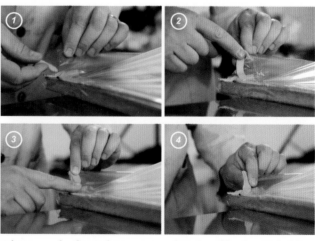

Pleats can be formed in vacuum-bagging film by: 1) holding up the excess film, 2) pressing sealant tape inside one face of the pleat, 3) pressing the other face of the pleat against the sealant tape, and then 4) pinching out any wrinkles or air bubbles in the sealant tape.

be wet sanded and beautifully polished for the easy release of composite tooling that will be fabricated over it. Take note that applying a composite skin, fillers, and surface sealer over a pattern will inevitably add thickness to it, which may cause problems if tolerances in the pattern's geometry are critical for the final part size or fit—so double-check surface and geometry accuracy frequently.

To save time, high-density foams (higher than 15 lbs per cubic foot), closed-grain woods (such as hard maple), and engineered fiber or particle boards may be sealed as simply as applying a resin sealer directly over their surface—eliminating the composite skin lamination process and finishing steps altogether. This simple sealing is not as robust as composite laminate sealing, though, so it is useful for only a couple molding cycles. This is especially true of sealed wood materials, as they are more susceptible to temperature and humidity changes that can cause cracks and separation in the sealed surfaces.

After successfully forming a smoothly shaped and properly sealed mold pattern, it is then possible to build the composite tooling over the waxed pattern.

Guidelines for Fabricating Composite Tooling

Fabricators who are familiar with typical wet layup methods generally find that building composite tooling is relatively straightforward and, apart from a few extra steps (such as flange form fabrication and prep), is exactly the same as an average wet layup procedure. Composite tooling is extremely cost effective for molding high-quality parts in low to moderate quantities—especially for medium to large-sized parts—and can even be used in forming and processing pre-preg materials if high-temp resin is used as the tooling matrix. Composite tooling is always formed over a waxed mold pattern, so the fabricator has the added ability of assessing the part design before wholly committing to making the tooling.

Flange Form Fabrication for Composite Tooling

As mentioned in the previous chapter, flanges are common features on molds for composites. When fabricating composite tooling, the flange supports and forms are best created before

Once the vacuum port has been inserted through the bag's edge and the whole bag has been fully sealed…

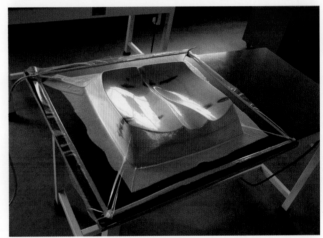

Turn on the vacuum pump and evacuate the bag. The resulting smooth surface can be used to mold a prototype composite part without needing any additional surface treatments.

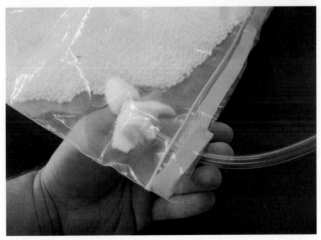

To create a styrene bead transfer mold, place styrene beads in a bag with a bleeder-cloth-covered vacuum line inserted into it, and then seal the bag with sealant tape.

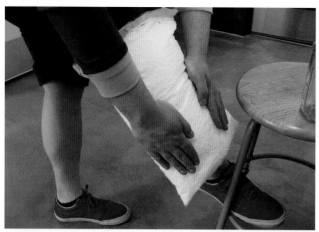

Place the bag over a form (in this case, the leg of a soccer-player in need of custom shin guards) and turn on the vacuum pump. The styrene beads will solidify in place as long as the vacuum is on.

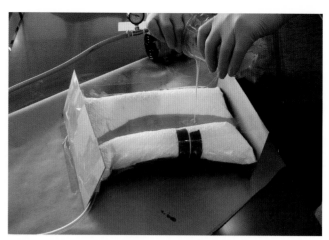

Next, pour two-part foam into the cavity of the form and allow it to cure.

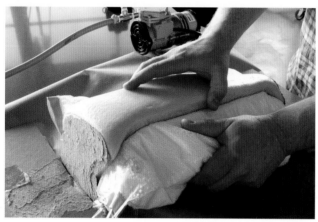

Turn off the vacuum and remove the cured foam from the beads (which may adhere to the plastic bag if the foam has reacted with too much heat)…

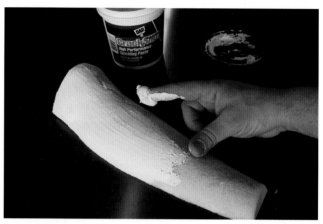

…and then trim the foam and smooth it with sandpaper. Use drywall compound to fill any open surface pores on the foam, as this will provide a smoother surface for molding in the next steps.

The new mold pattern can be used to create multiple vacuum-formed molds.

The resulting composite laminate is shown here after wet layup and vacuum bagging procedures. Once trimmed and upholstered, it's ready to hit the soccer field.

beginning the mold layup since composite mold flanges are most durable when they are laid up at the same time as the rest of the tooling.

Most molded composites require trimming after they have cured in order to create clean edges—so the mold must allow for extra edge material (or flash) to be laid up during lamination to account for this. If the mold pattern does not have enough height to accommodate this extra trimmed material, it can be built onto the mold pattern before creating the flange forms for the composite tooling using clay, or thick sections of sealed foam or wood. Maintain a good fit between these materials and the mold pattern to minimize any gaps.

Pre-wax the mold pattern, and then designate the location of the parting line long before you begin creating the flange forms. If the parting line is on the mold pattern itself, mark it on the mold pattern and then make cardboard templates to match the contours of this parting line. These contour templates can be transferred to other smooth, non-porous sheet materials (such as sheet metal or plastic) that can be used as the actual flange form molding surfaces. Flat, planar flange form surfaces are preferred, as they are the easiest to fabricate—especially when created by simply using a flat surface attached directly to the bottom of a mold pattern. However, flange supports for odd-shaped parting lines can still be made using formed sheet or other formable materials. Keep in mind

Mold Pattern Finishing Steps

1 Rough Sand Plug Surface...

2 Layup Composite Shell Over Plug...

3 Apply Polyester Primer As Sealer...

4 Wet Sand And Polish Final Surfaces...

A shaped mold pattern can be sealed with composite and resin materials, and then followed by polishing prior to fabricating composite tooling over the pattern.

Porous foam surfaces will require sealing before being used as a pattern for composite tooling. First, sand the foam smooth, then apply a skin of fiberglass and resin over the surface and allow it to cure.

103

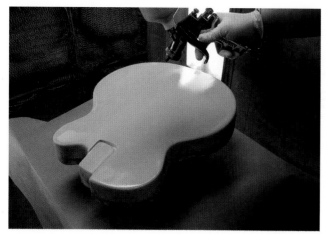

Carefully sand out any wrinkles of rough areas in the fiberglass skin, and then seal the laminate surface with a resin primer (as shown here spraying a polyester primer).

Once the sealer has cured, wet sand it smooth to at least 600-grit and then apply rubbing compound and wax to polish the surface. Composite tooling can then be successfully formed over the mold pattern.

When creating composite tooling, thoroughly wax the mold pattern first (as shown with this carbon fiber fender that needs to be replicated)…

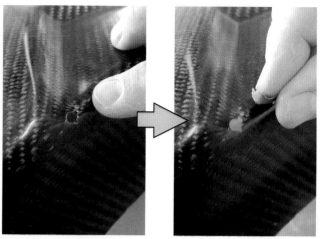

…and then use wax or clay to fill any surface imperfections on the pattern.

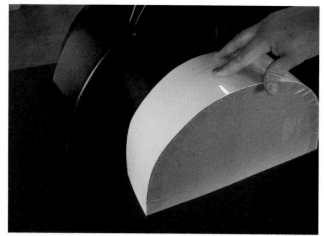

Add flange forms to the mold pattern, as shown here with a cardboard and sheet plastic construction covered in packing tape for easier release.

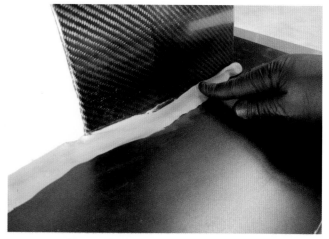

Use non-sulfur modeling clay to create fillets and seals at edges of the mold pattern.

that it is usually best to avoid sharp angles and tight corners with composites, but right angled flanges are common with composite tooling; they are just laid up in a way that minimizes voids while still sufficiently reinforcing them.

Start by fabricating a support structure for the flange forms using egg-crated cardboard, wood paneling, or foam core constructions. Secure the flange form supports so they will stay in place without sagging, sliding, or falling off the pattern throughout the duration of the layup. Flange form supports can be attached to the mold pattern with fasteners (such as screws, bolts, or nails), double-sided or sealant tape, or even modeling clay. With steel mold patterns, sheet metal flange forms can even be effectively attached to the mold pattern using strong magnets.

Some materials that make good flange form surfaces include plastic sheet (such as acrylic, styrene, polypropylene, or high-density polyethylene), sheet metal (steel or aluminum sheet stock), or wood sheet (Melamine/Formica faced particle board, MDF sheets, or Masonite). For a very quick, inexpensive means of sealing porous flange form surface materials (like wood or foam), simply adhering packing tape to the surfaces can be very quick and effective.

After attaching the flange form to the mold pattern, carefully wax all its surfaces, and then close any gaps between the pattern and

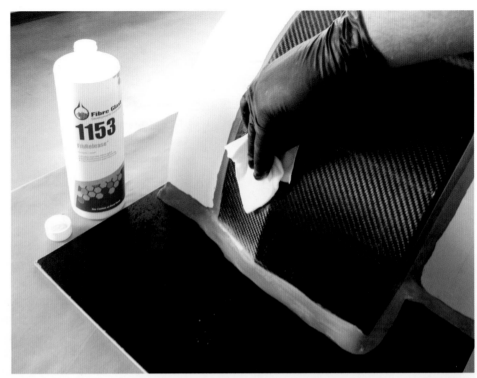

Apply additional mold release (such as PVA or other liquid-based release) over every surface of the mold pattern and flange forms before starting the composite tooling layup.

Next completely mix the gel/surface coat and apply it to the mold pattern and flanges forms.

105

Allow the gel/surface coat to cure to a tacky state before continuing with the tooling layup.

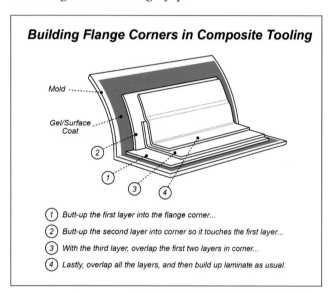

Building Flange Corners in Composite Tooling

Mold

Gel/Surface Coat

① ② ③ ④

① Butt-up the first layer into the flange corner...

② Butt-up the second layer into corner so it touches the first layer...

③ With the third layer, overlap the first two layers in corner...

④ Lastly, overlap all the layers, and then build up laminate as usual.

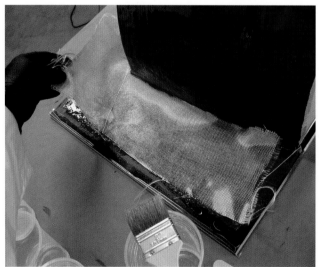

When the gel/surface coat is ready, brush laminating resin over the entire form, and then begin applying laminate plies one-by-one to build up the tooling.

flange form with modeling clay. Smooth this clay into all the corners with a gloved finger or curved-ended stick to seal them off and prevent resin from flowing between any gaps during the mold layup process.

Finally, apply mold release to all mold pattern and flange surfaces that will be in contact with resin—but do not disturb any of the modeling clay fillets through this process. Four to six applications of paste wax followed by a liquid release is usually sufficient prior to laying up composite tooling.

Laying Up Composite Tooling

Even if you intend to form expensive room-temperature epoxies and carbon fiber laminates with your composite tooling, inexpensive polyester resins and fiberglass reinforcements will often work just fine as the mold-making material. However, to avoid thermal expansion issues for high temperature moldings, high-temp resins may be needed along with using the same reinforcement fabric for the mold as will be used for the final production parts. For complex mold shapes, twill or satin weave reinforcement fabrics work best.

Apply tooling gel/surface coats to provide a tough, void-free coating for the composite tooling. Once the gel/surface coat has cured to a tacky state, apply a wet coat of laminating resin over the gel/surface coat, and then begin to add reinforcement layers and resin to build up the tooling.

In areas where there are tight corners (such as where the mold pattern meets a flange), create a transitional fillet of resin paste (made from resin and an appropriate thickening agent, such as colloidal silica) and apply it with a gloved finger. Make sure to avoid bubbles and uneven application of resin paste. Next, butt-up strips of reinforcement on either side of the corner, then bridge it with additional layers of fiberglass fabric to further reinforce it. Continue with this build-up of the mold and flanges until they are sufficiently thick and reinforced.

When creating composite tooling, be careful not to build up the thickness of the mold so quickly that it gets warm enough to affect the mold pattern or overheat the resin. For example, 1.5 oz fiberglass mat laid up at room temperature with polyester resin that has been catalyzed to 1% MEKP (or about 5 cc of MEKP catalyst per 16 oz of resin) will produce noticeable heat when it is laid up at a rate of only one layer every ten minutes. A layup performed any faster than this will very likely cause

Completely wet-out the reinforcement materials with resin while working out any bubbles from the laminate. Be sure to apply equal numbers of plies in all areas of the tooling during lamination.

runaway exotherm and overheat the resin. For situations requiring fast laminate buildup, less catalyst may be helpful, as long as it is catalyzed enough for sufficient curing. Slow-cure epoxies can be useful for small to medium sized molds, as they are less prone to exotherm problems.

Beware that unevenly building up composite tooling over a mold pattern while using high shrink rate resins (such as polyester or vinyl ester) can create waves or faint lumpiness in the mold surfaces. Additionally, reinforcement ribs added prior to full cure of the mold laminate plies can also create very distinct, tell-tale dips in the surface of the mold due to matrix shrinkage. To minimize these surface blemishes, the FRP mold layup can be performed in a "staged" approach. For the first stage, apply a uniform gel/surface coat over the part, allow it to tack up, and then layup one or two layers of lightweight reinforcement fabric (such as veil material) and resin over the coating to act as a protective shell. Allow this composite skin to also reach a tacky state of cure—a state at which most shrinkage has already occurred. Next, apply the remaining reinforcement plies necessary to rigidify and thicken the mold—as this will help isolate the areas of material shrinkage and leave the mold surface as smooth and flawless as possible. Lastly, add any needed reinforcement ribs and backup supports after the rest of the resin in the tooling has tacked up or cured, fastening them to the tooling or laminating them in place (as described below)

Multi-section Mold Layup with Composite Tooling

Multi-section molds are created in multiple steps, starting by building an initial flange at the

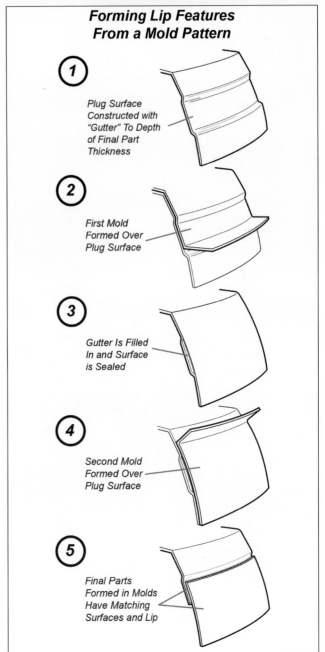

Forming Lip Features From a Mold Pattern

1. Plug Surface Constructed with "Gutter" To Depth of Final Part Thickness

2. First Mold Formed Over Plug Surface

3. Gutter Is Filled In and Surface is Sealed

4. Second Mold Formed Over Plug Surface

5. Final Parts Formed in Molds Have Matching Surfaces and Lip

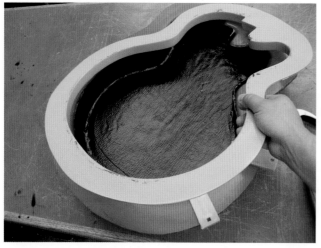

For parts that will require later seam bonding, a removable lip-former can be produced—as with this piece used to form a lip in a guitar body.

If additional strength is needed in composite tooling, wood or foam can be added to the back of the tooling and then laminated over with more composite material, as shown here.

Some composite tooling may require post curing in an oven—as shown with these pieces that will be used for high-temperature moldings.

Clay forms should be sealed before being molded over with composite tooling. PVA can be sprayed on as an effective sealer…

…and then followed by an application of a more rigid sealer, as shown with this HVLP sprayable polyester primer.

Carefully wet sand and polish the sealed surface of the clay form…

parting plane using the same methods for flange formation explained above—but they should include registry forms on them that have been constructed out of clay or wax. Next, layup the first composite tooling section and flanges as normal. After these first flange forms are removed, the newly formed flange registration marks will be visible—and the next set of mold flanges can be laid up and keyed into them.

To layup subsequent mold sections, make sure to apply sufficient mold release to the existing flanges. Seal any stray fibers or frayed edges on the existing flanges with packing tape or polyethylene flash tape to keep resin in the next mold section from fusing to them. Next, layup the matching flange and mold section over the previous flange to ensure perfect alignment between mold sections.

After this new mold section has cured, drill mold alignment holes straight through the mating flanges to accommodate securement bolts and washers before demolding the tooling from the mold pattern.

Composite Mother Molds

Complex details on the surface of a mold pattern are especially difficult to mold in composites, but can be formed using a hybrid mold composed of fiberglass and epoxy over silicone. This type of mold

…and then wax the surface before applying a gel/surface coat.

Composite tooling can then be laminated over the gel/surface coat once it has tacked up…

109

...and the tooling can be built up to the required thickness. Allow the composite tooling to fully cure before attempting demolding, trimming, and finishing steps.

When creating a mass-cast thermoset mold, fully enclose the mold pattern with release-coated forms. This particular mold required two mating mold sections, so registration marks have also been added in the corners of the forms.

Thoroughly mix the liquid casting resin and pour it into the form over the mold pattern.

Allow the casting resin to fully cure before demolding.

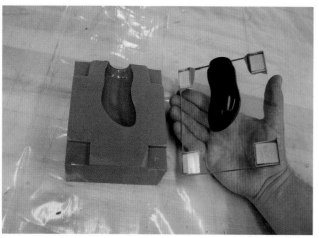

For this mold, the forms were removed...

...and then repositioned to cast the second half of the mold. (Note that the corners of these forms also need to be sealed with RTV or clay to prevent leakage of the casting material.)

110

uses the flexible qualities of silicone to capture important details from the mold pattern, but it is then backed up by the rigid structure created by a fiberglass laminate (called a "mother mold"). To create a fiberglass mother mold, apply release over the mold pattern (mostly out of good practice—as silicone is generally self-releasing), then brush on silicone rubber material made specifically for use with a brush. Fill in all details as completely as possible while leaving a relatively smooth outer surface on the silicone. Allow the silicone to fully cure, and then apply a mixture of epoxy and chopped fiberglass over the silicone. After the fiberglass composite has cured, carefully remove it from the silicone, and then peel back the silicone from the mold pattern. The silicone can then be nestled back into the fiberglass shell for molding of a new part. Please note that parts made in this silicone form will likely need to be created using thickened epoxy putty or slurry in order to fill in the shape details—but once these details have been formed and smoothed over, additional reinforcements and epoxy resin can be laminated over them to complete the part.

Backup Supports for Composite Tooling

Most resins will exhibit some amount of creep (or permanent deformation of the material when placed under prolonged load), so composite tooling should be reinforced to reduce this. Backup supports added to the mold will help in this regard, and can be made by laminating on ribs of wood, crating supports, polyurethane foam and composite, or even angle iron or steel tubing. Carbon fiber reinforcements added to the tooling can also slow the effects of creep in a mold because of their inherent stiffness.

Mold-making Over Clay Forms

The versatile nature of clay allows it to be rough-sculpted very quickly, or to take on significant detail when sculpted with the proper tools and skill. With a bit of surface prep work, composite tooling (or even one-off composite parts) can also be created over a clay form. Sulfur-free modeling clays work best when used in conjunction with polyester and vinylester resins—unless the clay surface has been completely sealed (as explained below).

Additional casting material was mixed and poured over this waxed mold and pattern...

...and the mold halves were demolded after cure.

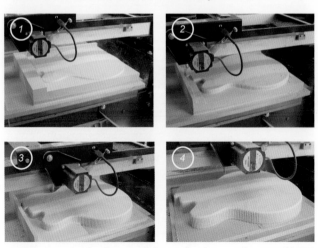

CNC routing of soft materials can be done rather quickly in multiple passes, as shown here.

CNC milling of harder materials (as shown here with aluminum) requires considerably more machining time…

…followed by laborious hand smoothing…

…and then additional polishing.

Soft clay has better workability than hard clay—but hard clays can better withstand the poking and prodding of a layup brush during composite lamination. Consequently, warming up (and thus temporarily softening) hard clays tends to work better for many clay forming and composite tooling tasks. Modeling clay can also be expensive and heavy, so it is best used as a skin (around ½" to 1" thick) over an armature—which can be built up by using firm finger pressure to apply small bits of warmed clay at a time to the armature. (Please note that a comprehensive demonstration of clay sculpting techniques is out of the scope of this book, but can be studied more thoroughly through a quick reading of fine art sculpting and transportation design books.)

Clay mold patterns can take considerable time to fully shape and smooth, but mold flange forms for the clay pattern can be built using additional clay—simplifying this task significantly.

Prepare the clay's surface for composite tooling layup by first sealing it, then creating a hard resin shell over it, and finally applying mold release agents. This will help keep the composite laminate from sticking to or chemically interacting with the clay. To seal the surface, apply multiple coatings of liquid PVA (polyvinyl alcohol) using an airbrush or refillable paint application system, allowing each coat to dry before re-application. Follow the PVA coating with an additional layer of catalyzed, sprayable polyester resin-based primer (such as Duratec or Featherfill) to produce a hard protective shell over the PVA. Follow this with careful wet sanding (to *at least* 600-grit, though up to 1000-grit will work even better) and polishing—but avoid sanding or polishing through the hard resin shell! Apply release agents to the surface and then perform all composite tooling lamination steps, as described above.

After lamination and curing of the composite, demold it as usual. Demolding will likely destroy the clay mold pattern and require extensive cleanup of any remaining clay bits from the sides of the tooling with naphtha or mineral spirits. After cleanup steps, Inspect the final surfaces of the composite tooling and use polish and wax to prepare it for service.

Mass-cast Thermoset Plastic Molds

Many types of small molds (including open, closed, or matched molds) can be created relatively quickly by casting liquid resins over a mold pattern. These molds can be used for a wide range of processes, including wet layup, vacuum-bagging processes (including resin infusion and pre-preg layup and processing), and expandable cores.

Casting resins are available in a range of viscosities, with lower viscosity resins being most useful for molding over patterns that have fine details—as the thin resin will flow more easily around these details and leave less voids. Prior to casting a mold, ensure that all mold forms are secure and free from gaps that could allow the liquid resin to escape. Casting resins tend to be rather expensive, so it is best to devise ways of filling up unused mold volumes with foam, wood, wax, or clay blocks that can withstand the exotherm and post-cure temperatures of the casting process before pouring resin into the mold cavity. If a space-filling block is lighter than the actual resin casting material (which is a common problem with metal-filled resins), securely fasten the block to the mold form so it will not float or shift during casting. *Completely mix the casting resin and hardener before pouring to avoid soft spots in the final cast mold!*

For clamshell molds, pour the first half of the mold over a well-waxed mold pattern that has registry marks fastened to the mold forms around it. This will help ensure proper fitment with the second half of the mold that will be poured over it. After allowing the first half to cure, remove the mold forms and reposition them as needed to pour the second mold section. Before pouring the second half of the clamshell mold, remember to apply mold release to all surfaces of the first mold section and mold pattern. Once the second half of the clamshell mold has cured, remove the mold forms and carefully demold the mold sections and mold pattern. Mass-cast molds can be somewhat brittle in thin sections and sharp corners, so it is wise to round off corners with a file or sanding block where necessary. In some cases, corners can be strengthened with resin-soaked fiberglass roving that has been placed in the mold corners and allowed to cure to a tacky state prior to casting the rest of the mold.

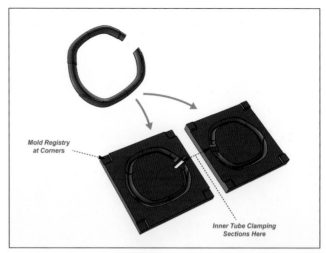

Molds can be made directly from a computer model, as shown here with some prototype composite steering wheel molds that used inflatable-bladder processes.

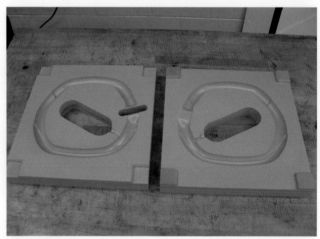

The molds for this steering wheel were CNC routed directly into MDF boards, sealed with a polyester primer, and then polished and waxed prior to use.

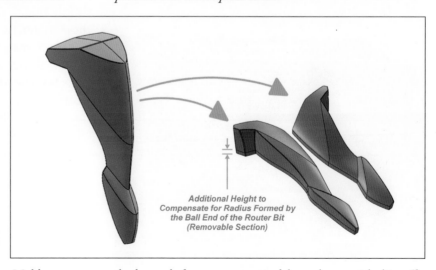

Mold patterns can also be made from computer models, as shown with this coffee table leg that was to be CNC routed from wood.

113

The final pieces where then cut, assembled to each other, smoothed, sealed, and then used as a mold pattern for some high-temperature composite tooling.

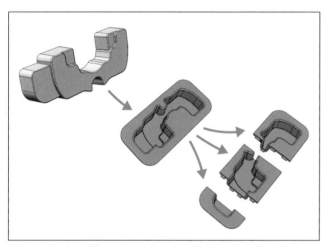

3D printed molds may need to be split into smaller pieces—as illustrated here. The desired part is shown at the top left, the resulting mold shape is shown at center, and the 3D printable mold pieces are shown at the bottom right.

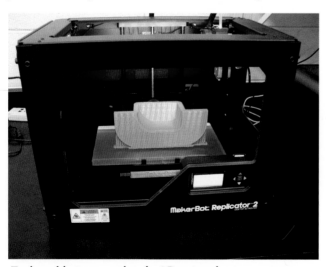

Each mold piece can then be 3D printed...

Direct Digitally Output Molds (CNC Cut, 3D Printed, or Laser-cut)

3D models can be output to directly fabricate molds, but this avenue of mold making comes with its own set of processing requirements. For example, CNC cutting requires material preparation and fixturing, surface smoothing, and even polishing (for metal) or sealing and polishing (for wood, foam, and clay) of mold surfaces before putting it into service. 3D printed molds will also require surface finishing and sealing (depending on the required surface quality), and laser-cut molds may require some assembly, smoothing, or sealing themselves.

CNC Cut (Machined or Routed) Molds

When using CNC cutting methods to directly make a mold from a 3D computer file, consider ways in which to efficiently use the mold-making materials before actually cutting. Many materials can be cut and joined together to avoid wastefully discarding large volumes of material in the form of chips or dust—not to mention the actual machine cutting time or tool wear saved by not cutting unneeded material. CNC cutting machines are also limited in their ability to perform deep cuts into dense or hard materials—so be aware of the depth-of-cut limitations for the particular machine you intend to use.

For small metal molds, CNC cutting, wet sanding, and polishing can often be done in the same time required to make composite tooling over foam, wood, clay, or plaster mold patterns—simply due to the laborious sealing and finishing these materials require. However, as the mold size increases, material costs and CNC machine time for metals begin to outweigh the material and labor costs associated with other less-costly materials. Keep in mind that the actual CNC machine cutting time depends heavily upon the material used: steel cuts slowly, aluminum cuts at medium speeds, wood and thermoplastic materials can be cut quickly, and foam or clay can be cut fastest of all.

3D Printed Molds

Current 3D printing capabilities make it possible to "grow" molds for composites using a 3D computer model of your part—which can save a great deal of mold-making effort. Well-planned, 3D printable molds can be designed to incorporate edge flanges, edge channels for the securement of bagging materials, and even to include integral supply lines for resin infusion.

The layering steps inherent in the building process of 3D prints produces visible topographical imperfections and surface porosity that typically needs to be smoothed out and sealed with sanding and filling prior to use as a composite mold. Sprayable surface sealer (such as an automotive polyester primer) works very well for this task, but other brush-on resin sealers are also available.

…the mold pieces can be joined with adhesive…

Since most 3D printers have small build volumes, large molds may need to be divided into sections that can be joined together with an appropriate adhesive after printing. Mold sections are most accurately joined together through the use of alignment features (such as tabs and slots, or holes for pegs or fasteners). Once joined, fill and smooth out any seams prior to surface sealing steps. The final sealed, wet sanded, and polished surfaces of the 3D printed mold can be waxed and laid up over with composite laminates just the same as other mold types— while taking into account the thermal limitations of the 3D printed plastic. Additionally, if all sides of the mold have been sealed, it can also be used with vacuum-bagging processes for even better laminate consolidation and surface quality.

Laser Cut Molds

CNC laser-cutting equipment can be used with an appropriately sectioned computer model to create

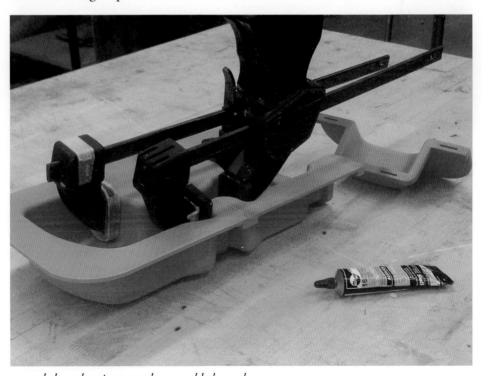

…and then the pieces can be assembled together.

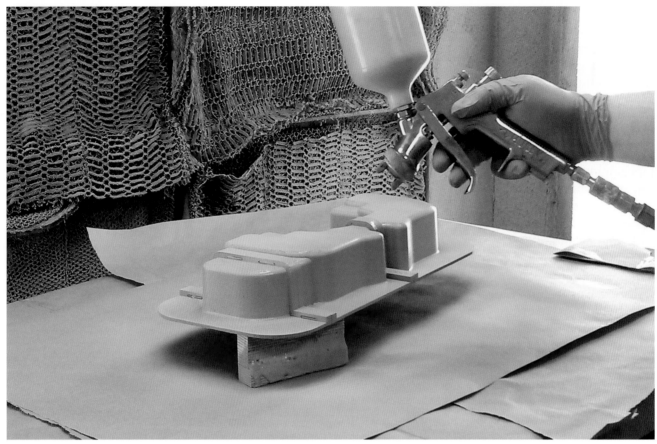

Additional surface sealing, wet-sanding, and polishing will likely be required before using the mold.

Some molds can also be laser cut—as shown here making parts for a filament winding mold—using 2D vector data created from a computer model or drawing software.

mold templates, mold sections (spaced at station points on a strongback), or even thin sections stacked back-to-back (with alignment accommodations built in) to create a solid, final mold piece. Thin plywood or amorphous plastic sheet materials tend to work best with this mold fabrication method, and may require additional steps of surface sealing and finishing prior to use as an actual mold pattern or mold surface. This method of mold-making is generally limited to small molds, given the restricted cutting area found on most commercially-available laser cutters or laser-cutting services.

Remove all protective paper from laser cut plastics before molding.

Conclusion

Depending on a laminate part's geometry and processing requirements, several mold-making options are available to small shop composite fabricators. These mold-making processes range from low-tech, low cost methods, all the way to more costly, computer-controlled, high-precision methods. But with a completed, high-quality mold in hand, composite layup can begin—which can be further enhanced by the advanced techniques demonstrated in the next chapter.

References and Resources

Wanberg, John. *Composite Materials Handbook #1*, Stillwater, MN: Wolfgang Publications Inc., 2009.

Wanberg, John. *Composite Materials Handbook #2*, Stillwater, MN: Wolfgang Publications Inc., 2010.

Wanberg, John. *Composite Materials Handbook #3*, Stillwater, MN: Wolfgang Publications Inc., 2013.

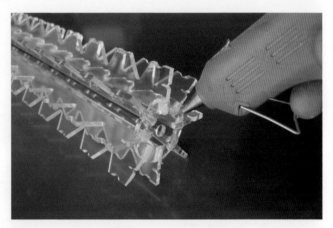

This particular mold was assembled with removable hot glue joints between the pieces...

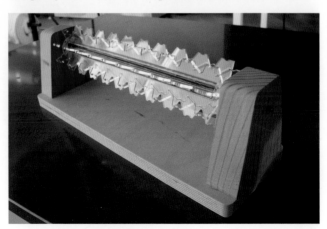

...and then mounted to an ad-hoc wood support using a ¼" steel rod as an axle so it could be rotated during winding of the reinforcement filaments.

Chapter Seven

Improved Composite Techniques

The strongest, lightest, and highest quality composites are those that have tighter laminate consolidation, lower void content, and better control of fiber-to-resin ratios. This chapter will discuss and demonstrate several of the methods available to small-shop fabricators to create these types of superior composites.

Tube Forming Processes

Roll-wrapping and *mandrel lamination* are relatively simple composites molding methods that can produce long, straight or tapered tubes with minimal mold complexity. Roll-wrapping is a method of simply wrapping common, broad good

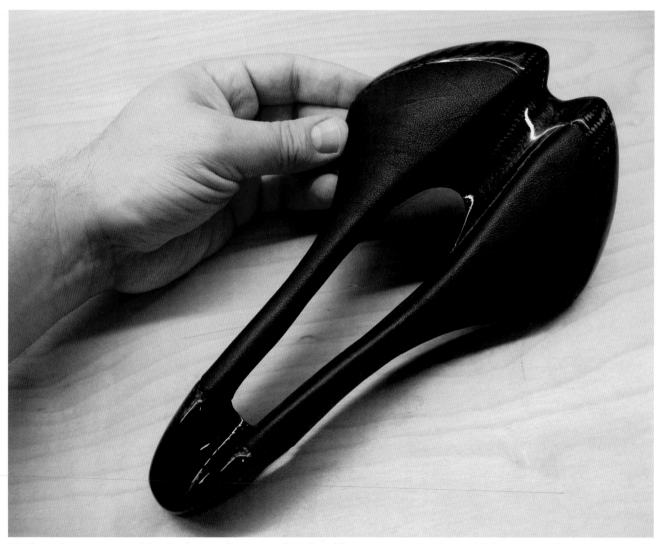

High-quality composites (like this low-void prototype bicycle saddle) require some advanced fabrication techniques—several of which are described in this chapter.

reinforcements around a mandrel, while mandrel lamination is commonly used with filament wound, woven, or sleeve fabric reinforcements.

Heat-shrink tape or tubing is usually applied over the composite on a mandrel to pressurize the laminate and help squeeze out excess resin and voids. It is also possible to wrap electrical tape adhesive-side out around the composite on the mandrel to provide this consolidation pressure, or to use advanced vacuum-bagging techniques.

The mandrel's surface should be very smooth and uniform in diameter to ensure good release of the composite. A machined and polished metal tube or rod can work well for this, but a PVC pipe or a wooden dowel covered in layers of craft/butcher paper (to act as a removal sleeve) and then wax paper can also be effective. Apply sufficient mold release (if using a metal mandrel) and then apply masking tape around the ends of the mandrel to keep them clean for later sealant tape adhesion.

Pre-cut any reinforcement materials prior to lamination on the mandrel. Resin can be added to the reinforcement before or after placing it on the mandrel, but make sure the material is fully impregnated. Apply as many plies as required for the lamination.

After layup, consolidate the laminate with the heat shrink tape or heat shrink tubing. To do this, first adhere silicone or mastic tape around each end of the mandrel, and attach the shrink tape (*with the release-side against the laminate*) to the silicone tape, wrapping it in a spiral up the length of the mandrel, overlapping it least ½ to ¾ the tape's width. Use a heat gun to slowly heat the shrink tape, starting from the middle of the mandrel, rotating it for even heating. The heat shrink tape will begin to contract, squeezing out any excess resin—but beware of any spurts of pressurized resin that may shoot out. Heat shrink tubing can be used in a similar manner— but it is slid over the outside of the laminate rather than wrapped around it. Heat shrink tubing also produce a slightly more uniform laminate surface, but with less consolidating pressure.

Roll-wrapping can be performed with wet laid-up or pre-preg material (though pre-preg tends to work a bit better), but it is best performed over a metal mandrel. Lay out the impregnated reinforcement flat on a table surface, firmly placing the lengthwise face of the release-coated mandrel over the edge of the reinforcement. Next, press down on the mandrel while rolling it across the pre-

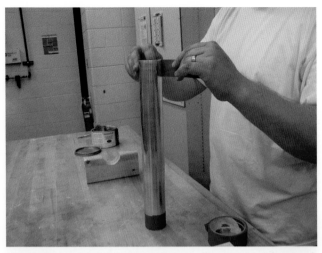

To perform mandrel lamination or roll-wrapping, first apply mold release to the mandrel and then tape the ends of the mandrel to keep them clean during the lamination process.

Slide resin-impregnated reinforcements over the mandrel and smooth them against the face of the mandrel.

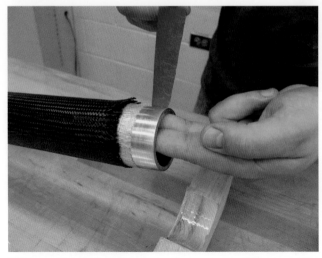

When all laminate plies are in place, remove the tape from the ends of the mandrel...

119

…and then apply sealant tape to the clean mandrel ends.

Adhere heat shrink tape (release side down) to the sealant tape, and wind it down the length of the mandrel over the laminate.

Attach the heat shrink tape to sealant at the other end of the mandrel. Use a heat gun to warm the tape uniformly down the length of the mandrel.

preg laminate, picking up and rolling the laminate over the mandrel's surface. Use high downward pressure during wrapping to minimize voids, rolling the laminate over the mandrel until the required number of plies have been built up over it. Finally, apply heat shrink tape (as described above), and then heat cure the pre-preg in an oven (as directed by the pre-preg manufacturer). These laminates can all be demolded as explained in the next chapter.

Manual Filament Winding

Filament winding generally requires elaborate equipment to wind reinforcement filaments onto a mandrel—but this process can be greatly simplified to still create effective structures. To perform filament winding, the filament must be held taut during winding, it must wetted with resin, and also laid down in a controlled manner. However, off-the-shelf equipment can be modified to perform these sequential tasks in a coordinated way—and still produce excellent results.

Manual filament winding equipment is almost unheard of these days, so a handheld, 3D printable "manual filament dispenser" has been developed by the author to fill this niche application. (Files for this device are available for free download at www.grabcad.com under the author's name.) A small post is located at the back of this apparatus onto which an adjustable-tension fly fishing reel can be mounted with hose clamps for holding reinforcement filament. A holster is located at the front of the device for a modified 12oz. "FIFO" (First-In-First-Out) bottle—which is a condiment dispenser available through several online distributors of restaurant wares. The FIFO bottle has a small, flexible membrane in its lid that works very effectively at keeping too much liquid resin material from running out—but it is also effective for squeezing off excess resin from a continuous filament that has been passed through it. To decrease the possibility of resin spills out the opposite end of the bottle, two dispenser lids (from two separate bottles) can be used to cap both bottle ends. Filament can be wound onto the fishing reel, and then one strand of filament can be passed through the top and bottom caps of the bottle. Mixed, slow-cure resin can be poured into the top of the bottle, then the bottle can be capped and set into the snap-fit holster at the top of the device. Once the filament tension has been set on the reel, the manual filament winding process can be performed over a form or mold, as demonstrated.

After sufficiently winding the filament around a form, cut the filament from the reel, pour out any remaining resin, and then clean out the FIFO bottle with acetone or lacquer thinner. Allow the resin to fully cure, and then demold the finished filament wound fabrication, as needed.

Compression Molding

Compression molding creates high quality, low void laminates by compacting them from either side. For small shop fabrications, however, compression molding is generally produced using common clamping tools to create shapes with shallow depth, minimal surface curvature, no undercuts, and no vertical features (such as ribs or fins).

To create compression molded flat panels, thick wood boards that have been surface-sealed (such as with Melamine or Formica) or plastic coated (as with packing tape, polyethylene film, or acrylic sheet) can work very well as rigid mold surfaces. Seal off porous mold edges with packing tape, and then apply release coatings.

The laminate can be laid up as usual, and a core layer can be added between plies prior to adding a top mold over the laminate. Place the mold set between polyethylene film or into a plastic bag to minimize resin spills. The mold boards can then be compressed using evenly spaced wood clamps.

When the resin begins to gel as it cures, tighten the clamps to close any spaces left by partially squeezed-out resin. Allow the laminate to cure and then demold and trim it (as instructed in the next chapter).

When compression molding shallow and well-drafted shapes, a flexible insert (such as mass-cast silicone) can be used as a pressure "distributor", along with clamps attached to the molds. Create one rigid mold side with a flat bottom by machining plastic or wood, or mass-casting it over a form. Next, produce an offset to the mold (to compensate for the thickness of the laminate) using tape, sheet wax, or clay. The remaining mold cavity can be used for casting tin or platinum cure silicone resin that has a final Shore A hardness of 30 to 40. Once the silicone has fully cured, remove it from the mold, trim it, and then remove the offset material from the mold.

Heat shrink tubing can be used in place of heat shrink tape by simply sliding it over the laminate...

...and then using a heat gun to warm the tubing from one end of the mandrel to the other. The final cured laminate can be removed as shown in the chapter on Demolding, Trimming, and Finishing.

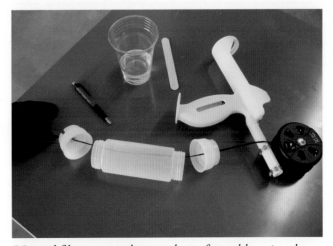

Manual filament winding can be performed by using the author's 3D printable filament dispenser (available at www.grabcad.com). Wind filament onto the attached reel, and then thread it through the ends of the dispenser bottle.

Pour some mixed, slow-cure resin into the dispenser, attach the top cap…

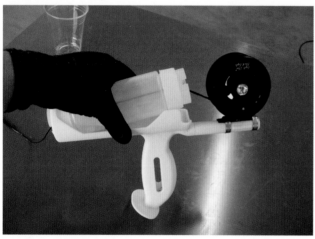

…and then holster the dispenser bottle into the device. Adjust the tension on the reel as needed for best dispensing of the filament.

Apply mold release to the mold form…

Apply release agents to the mold, perform the composite layup, and then place the silicone insert over the laminate in the mold. Backup the silicone insert with a release-coated board and attach clamps to pressurize the mold set. Once the insert is properly compressed, allow the laminate to cure completely.

After the laminate has cured, remove the mold clamps, carefully extract the self-releasing silicone insert, and demold the finished part.

Vacuum Bagging

Vacuum-bagging is a technique that uses atmospheric pressure to compact a sealed and vacuum-evacuated composite laminate. The higher the atmospheric pressure around the evacuated laminate, the better consolidation of the composite (and less voids)—so autoclave or pressure-vessel processing are often used to enhance this process. Vacuum-bagging is effective on nearly all open shapes, and can even be adapted to some enclosed or hollow shapes with a bit of creative planning. These techniques can be used on wet, dry, or pre-preg layups, and with or without sandwich cores—but keep in mind that it requires air-tight molds with flanges, or molds that can otherwise be completely sealed within a bagging envelope (described below). Mold seams and holes can also be closed off with sealant tape to avoid air leakage during vacuum bagging procedures.

To perform vacuum-bagging, prepare the mold with release agents, and then lay up the laminate, as usual, including any cores that may be required in the laminate. Next, apply the appropriate vacuum-bagging materials (as described below).

Peel/release ply is a release-coated cloth that is applied directly over a composite laminate when secondarily bondable surfaces are needed. This ply has pores that allow excess resin to flow through it while creating a rough surface on the final, cured laminate.

Release film (also called "perforated film") is a thin polyethylene, nylon, or Teflon film perforated with small holes to limit the amount of resin flowing through it, and also acts as a release layer over the peel/release ply.

Bleeder/breather cloth is a non-woven material used to wick up excess resin (the "bleeder" function) and transport air out of the laminate to the vacuum pump (the "breather" function). Typical four or five ounce bleeder/breather cloth will work well for most applications where an autoclave or pressure vessel is not being used. After applying all the required vacuum-bagging plies, add an extra strip of breather/bleeder cloth where the vacuum connector will be positioned through the vacuum bag. This extra cloth will serve as an air evacuation pathway to the vacuum line while providing extra padding to keep the vacuum connector from leaving an imprint on the part during cure.

Bagging film is made from flexible plastic films and is placed over the mold to completely seal off air from the open face of the laminate. When fully evacuated, bagging film helps compress the bagging materials against the composite. Bagging film comes on rolls, but can also be purchased in "envelope" form (as a flattened tube of plastic film) that only needs to be sealed at its ends.

Sealant tape is a high tack silicone material used to close off the edges of the vacuum bag. Avoid getting dirt, debris, or resin on it to help it maintain a good vacuum seal. Create "pleats" and "tucks" as needed with the bagging film and sealant tape to avoid tight spots in the bagging film. Mold corners, deep features, and jogged flanges often require large pleats to allow the bagging film to conform into them.

A **vacuum pump** is attached to the sealed vacuum bag to evacuate the molded laminate. Vacuum

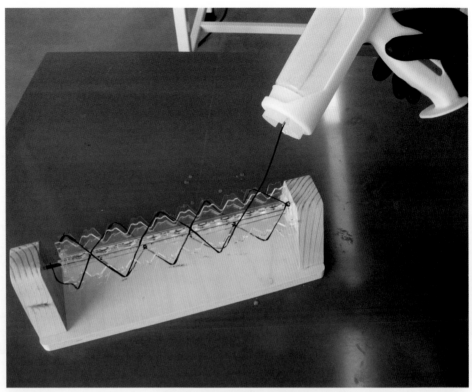

..attach the end of the filament to the mold form, and then begin the filament winding process, rotating the mold as needed to control the placement of the filament.

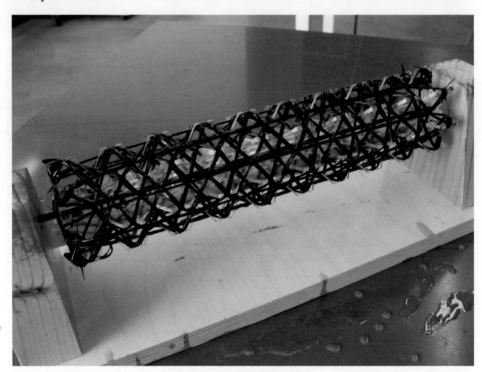

Once the filament has been fully wound (as shown with this completed isotruss), clean and dispose of any remaining resin from the dispenser bottle, and allow the part to completely cure before removing the mold form.

To perform compression molding on a panel, wet out a sheet of reinforcement onto a flat mold face, and then wet out the corresponding foam or wood core material.

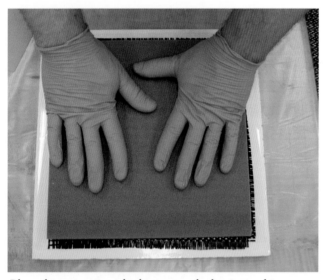

Place the core resin-side-down over the laminate skin…

…and then wet out the top face of the core with resin.

pumps create a vacuum that is significantly higher than a typical shop vacuum, and can be left on for prolonged periods of time without problem. Take special care to maintain a vacuum-pump as the manufacturer recommends for longest pump life. A less expensive alternative to a vacuum pump may be a ***vacuum generator***—which is a device with no moving parts that attaches to a compressed air line (capable of 3.5 CFM or more), yet produces a high vacuum. Connect a ***vacuum gauge*** to the pump and at other locations over a bagged part to measure the level of vacuum within the system.

Vacuum connectors and ***vacuum lines*** join the vacuum bag to the vacuum pump system, and are commonly available in various sizes at many hardware stores. Multiple connectors and vacuum lines can be connected into a manifold system for multi-bag setups. Also, a ***bleed-off*** valve is typically placed in line with the vacuum bag to control how much (and how quickly) vacuum is applied to the bagging system.

The vacuum line inlet can go either through the bag, or at the bag's edge seal. To apply a through-bag connector, place the lower half of the vacuum connector inside the bag and seal the bag's edge. Make a small cut in the bagging film with a utility knife, and then fasten the top half of the connector through the bag to the bottom half of the connector, as recommended by the manufacturer. When inserting the vacuum line through the sealed bag edge, wrap a ring of sealant tape around the vacuum line a couple inches from the line's end and then insert it into the vacuum bag. The sealant-taped vacuum line can then be tacked to the bag's seal and closed off with additional bits of sealant tape until completely closed. Be sure to enclose the bag-covered end of the vacuum line with bleeder/breather cloth to keep the bagging film from closing off the end of the vacuum line when evacuated.

Always place a ***resin trap*** between the vacuum line and the vacuum pump to keep resin from flowing into the pump. Resin traps should be able to accept vacuum line fittings, but can be constructed of practically any container that is air-tight, such as a Mason jar with sealed fittings in the lid, sealed PVC pipe sections configured in a "T", or large, purpose-built units available from composites suppliers.

When applying the vacuum, check for even pressurization on the laminate and avoid "bridging" of the bagging materials—a problem that can be corrected by throttling open the bleed-off valve on the vacuum and adjusting the bagging materials, as needed. It is typically a good practice to leave the vacuum pump on long enough to provide assistive pressure to the part until it has cured to a hardened green state, even if your vacuum connector is equipped with a built-in shut-off valve. Remember that the part should not be removed from the mold until it has fully cured. Once cured, peel away the bagging materials from the part, and then demold, trim and finish it (as explained in the next chapter).

Please note that proper vacuum-bag processing with pre-pregs may require compaction, debulking, or consolidation steps! These additional processes entail vacuum bagging the laminate after laying up every few plies, and may further include slightly warming the pre-preg and compressing the plies tightly against the mold face using assistance from an autoclave or hydraulic press—depending on the shape of the mold and the laminate thickness.

Pressure Chamber Processing of Vacuum-bagged Parts

As previously mentioned, an autoclave or pressure vessel can be used to improve the quality of a vacuum-bagged part. Unfortunately, autoclave processing may be out of the reach of many small shop fabricators—so unheated pressure chamber processing of a vacuum-bagged or double-bagged resin infused part (described below) can be a great alternative. The results of this kind of processing are excellent surface quality, minimized voids, increased laminate strength, lower part weight—and as close to a perfect composite part as is possible using wet layup or resin infusion processes. With a quick modification of some common paint pressure tank equipment, it's possible to create a small, unheated autoclave-like pressure vessel to closely replicate the processing quality of an autoclave at a fraction of the cost.

Paint pressurization tanks are commonly available to hold either 1 or 5 gallon buckets of paint (with prices between $100 and $350), and can be pressurized from 50 or 90 PSI, depending on the strength of the tank. These pressure levels are enough to produce a noticeable improvement over un-pressurized laminates—but the size constraints of the tanks limit them to processing only smaller parts. These tanks are easily modified for use as a pressure vessel by changing just a few fittings on

Apply the remaining laminate layer(s) over the core...

...and wet them with resin, as needed.

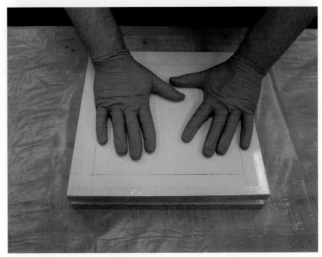

Place the other waxed mold face over the sandwich laminate...

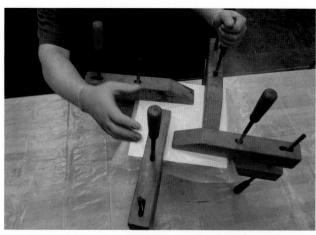

...and then place the whole mold system into a bag (to catch resin spills) before attaching clamps uniformly over the mold set. As the resin begins to gel, tighten the clamps a bit more to ensure better consolidation.

Curved compression molded shapes can be made by: 1) laying up wetted laminate onto a rigid form (as shown here with plastic-lined wood), 2) adding shaped foam over the laminate with release-coated plastic liners on other side, 3) applying clamps around the form, and then 4) demolding the part once fully cured.

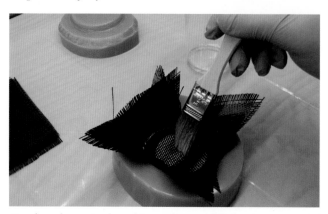

For deep shapes (such as this earphone mold), laminate material can be placed in the mold (as with this mass-cast mold)...

them, but before using the pressure vessel, make sure to adhere to the following precautions:

1) All of the safety features of the original pressure vessel should remain intact.
2) Never pressurize the tank until all safety locks on the lid are in place and fully secure.
3) Never exceed the pressure limits or ratings of the pressure vessel. Don't assume that the safety pressure release valves on the pressure vessel are infallible!
4) Do not include a heat source inside the pressure vessel—this will increase the pressure within the vessel, possibly exceeding its safe operating pressures.
5) Fully equalize pressure between the interior and exterior of the pressure device before removing the safety locks on the lid or attempting to open the pressure vessel.

In general, remember that a vacuum can make things *implode*, while pressure can make things **explode**! Both of these results a can be equally exciting, but an explosion can be significantly more dangerous. *A pressure vessel is a potentially lethal device if used incorrectly—so be sure to follow all safety guidelines for the tank and be sure to use good common sense during every step of the pressurization and depressurization process!*

A paint pressurization tank comes with at least two ports in its lid: one for adding air pressure, and one for extracting paint. For processing composites, the paint outlet tube can be refitted to accept a vacuum line for attachment to vacuum-bagged molds through the lid. Common plumbing and air fittings from the local hardware store can be used for this purpose, but make sure all threaded connections are tight and sealed with Teflon tape or pipe thread sealant. Attach a vacuum-gauge to the vacuum line on the outside of the lid to monitor the vacuum levels of the part during tank pressurization.

Process a vacuum-bagged or resin infused part as usual, connecting it through the vacuum line in the lid of the pressure vessel during evacuation. Completely remove all air leaks in the sealant tape on the bagged part, and then place it in the tank. Seal and lock the tank, and then slowly pressurize the tank, monitoring the vacuum gauge to ensure that it is maintaining adequate vacuum—though a small drop in vacuum levels is common. Allow the laminate to fully cure, then slowly depressurize the tank with the pressure release valve. Once the internal pressure has dropped completely, open the tank and remove the mold from the vacuum line. Demold, trim, and finish the part, as usual.

Resin Infusion (V.A.R.T.M.)

Resin infusion (also referred to as Vacuum-assisted Resin Transfer Molding—or V.A.R.T.M.) is an out-of-autoclave process that can produce very repeatable, cost-effective parts with excellent fiber-to-resin content. It does this by moving liquid resin from a supply source (such as a resin-filled bucket or cup) into an evacuated *preform* (composed of dry fabric layers placed in a mold) by the application of pressure (such as atmospheric pressure or a piston system). The speed of laminate impregnation through infusion is dependent on several factors, including the placement of the resin supply lines and vacuum lines, the permeability of the reinforcement fiber, the resin viscosity, the use of flow media, and the ambient air pressure. Remember that resin flow will always follow the path of least resistance and will fill any evacuated spaces in the mold—whether they contain reinforcement or not.

Some benefits of resin infusion is that it does not require brushes or rollers, protective clothing or respirators, and has a practically an unlimited dry layup time. It can be used on parts of any size, but is most effective on shapes that are easily accessible from at least one side. Hollow forms can also be infused, but can be much more difficult to process.

Molds used with resin infusion should be as robust and air-tight as any mold used with other vacuum bagging processes. Prepare the mold as usual using appropriate release agents. Gel coats and surface coats can still be used with infusion—although they will shorten the dry layup window for the part based on the cure time for the coating.

Reinforcements can be laid directly into the mold or adhered to the mold walls using moderate amounts of spray adhesive. Beware that loose-weave reinforcement (such as twill, satin, leno, basket, and knit) will infuse more readily than tight weaves (such as plain weave or unidirectional fabrics). Also, core selection for infused sandwich structures is limited to closed-cell foams, wood, or specific structural flow media. Some foam cores (like Divinymat) are scored or scrim-backed to facilitate resin flow on both sides of them during

…and a formed silicone piece can be placed over the laminate, and the excess reinforcement edges can be trimmed off.

A second mold half can be placed over the silicone…

…and then compressed with clamps.

Once fully cured, the clamps and silicone can be removed…

…and the part can be demolded.

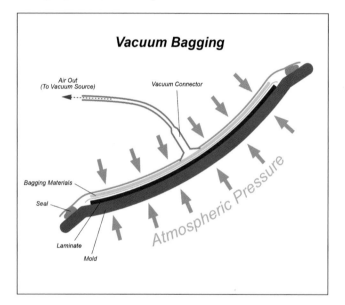

Vacuum Bagging

Air Out
(To Vacuum Source)

Vacuum Connector

Bagging Materials

Seal

Laminate

Mold

Atmospheric Pressure

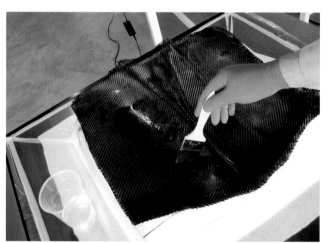

To perform vacuum-bagging processes, layup the laminate as usual (in this case, a prototype seat bottom is being formed over a bagged mold)…

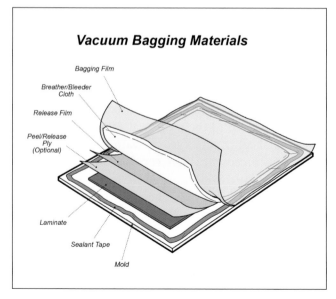

Vacuum Bagging Materials

Bagging Film

Breather/Bleeder
Cloth

Release Film

Peel/Release
Ply
(Optional)

Laminate

Sealant Tape

Mold

…and then apply sealant tape to the edge of the mold.

infusion processes. Many of these cores facilitate resin flow between the laminate and core interface through small channels that have been scored into them, or by means of scrim cloth or other flow media that has been bonded to them. *Actual honeycomb cores should not be used with resin infusion as their cells will simply fill with excess resin.* Some honeycomb-like cores (such as Lantor Soric) are also available, but they can be relatively heavy once infused. Additionally, keep in mind that cores, inserts, and molded-in fasteners will require special attention for proper processing.

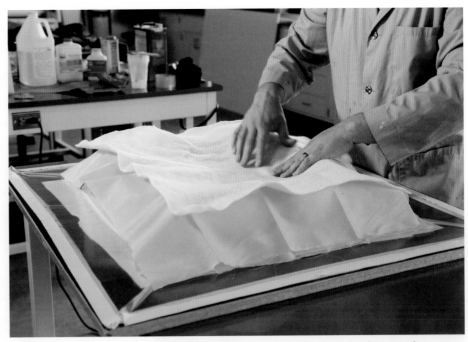

Apply bagging materials in the proper order over the laminate, ensuring that the laminate is completely covered and not contacting the breather/bleeder cloth.

Successive reinforcement plies should be adhered to the laminate stack using only sparing amounts of spray adhesive between them—as too much adhesive can slow resin flow during infusion. Be sure to press each new ply of reinforcement tightly against the mold's walls, tight features, and corners to minimize material bridging and voids.

Always place peel/release ply on top of the laminate stack prior to adding vacuum and resin lines, or flow media. Small bits of sealant tape or flash tape can be used to help immobilize these items, if necessary. It is common to use highly-porous flow media to help enhance resin flow over the laminate during infusion—with some flow media types being more flexible or porous than others. *Structural flow media* that becomes part of the laminate is also available (such as SAERflow made by SAERTEX) for helping infuse very thick laminates.

Vacuum lines are typically placed on the perimeter of the

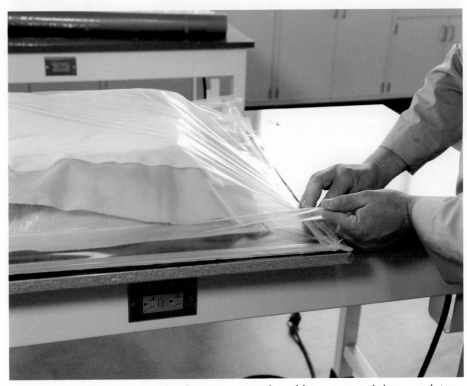

Place bagging film over the other bagging materials and laminate, and then attach it to the sealant tape, removing all gaps and wrinkles in the seal.

129

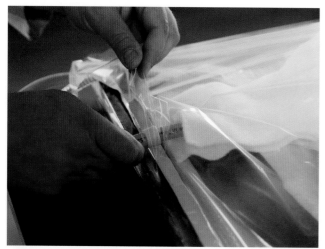

Insert the vacuum line, covering the end with breather cloth to keep the vacuum bag from closing it off.

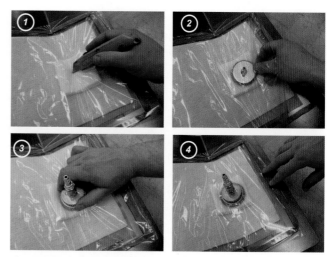

A vacuum connector can be used by: 1) cutting a slit in the bagging film, 2) placing the bottom part of the connector inside the bag, 3) connecting the top of the connector through the slit in the bag to the other half, and 4) sealing the bag.

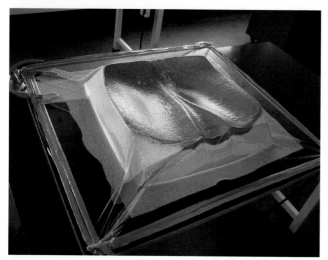

Once the vacuum is applied, double-check for and correct any vacuum leaks to get the best results. Excess resin will wick into the breather/bleeder cloth as the laminate consolidates and cures under vacuum.

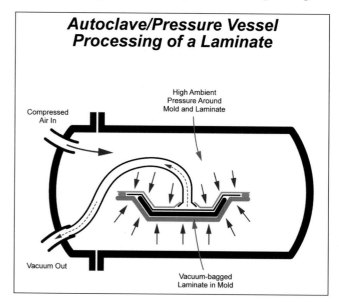

Autoclave/Pressure Vessel Processing of a Laminate

High Ambient Pressure Around Mold and Laminate

Compressed Air In

Vacuum Out

Vacuum-bagged Laminate in Mold

High-pressure laminates can be created by modifying a paint pressure tank for use as a pressure vessel.

First, remove the fittings from the lid that normally act as the paint outlet for the pressure tank.

part, but this is dependent on the geometry of the mold or part. Small or narrow parts (less than a couple feet in width) may even be set up with the resin line on one edge of the reinforcement stack, and a vacuum line on the other. Also remember that a resin trap is needed with resin infusion because resin will often overflow out through the vacuum lines once the laminate has been thoroughly infiltrated. Gas-permeable and fluid-resistant tubing (called *Membrane Tube Infusion*—or MTI hose) specifically made for resin infusion is available to keep resin from flowing out of the mold, but a resin trap

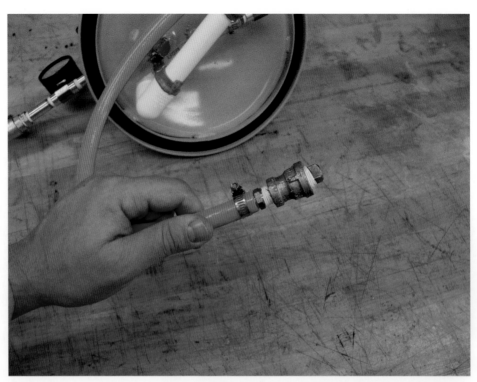

Next, add fittings that can be connected to the mold of a vacuum-bagged or infused laminate. (The fitting shown here has been capped for pressure leak testing, but can be removed for actual processing of a part.)

is still recommended when using this type of tubing in the event of membrane failure. Another option to keep resin from flowing into the vacuum line is to provide two to four inches of additional peel ply (without flow media over it) between the edge of the laminate and the vacuum outlet (if enough space is available in the mold)—which will create a section through which air can flow out, but resin will flow only very slowly toward the vacuum line.

After placing the resin and vacuum lines in the mold, use sealant tape and bagging film to encapsulate the whole system, similar to vacuum bagging processes, adding tucks and pleats where needed. A complete seal is *crucial*, so firmly apply the sealant tape, apply the vacuum, and track down any leaks at the edge of the bag.

Keep a vacuum over the preform for several minutes (or up to an hour in humid climates) prior to infusion to help evaporate

Attach a vacuum-bagged laminate to the vacuum line in the lid of the pressure vessel...

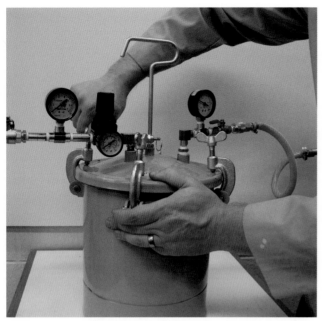

...and then completely seal the lid. Next, slowly pressurize the tank and check for leaks. Once the part has cured, release the pressure and remove the part.

The final part should have excellent surface quality, low voids, and tight laminate consolidation.

Vacuum Only   *Vacuum with 40 psi Pressure*   *Vacuum with 60 psi Pressure*

out any residual moisture that may be present in the laminate stack. Mix up an appropriately low-viscosity resin in a cup or bucket, and place the open end of the clamped resin line into it. As a rule of thumb, resins below 200 cps tend to give the best infusion results, though thicker resins (up to roughly 1000cps) may still work if they are slower-cure types and are given enough time to infuse.

Resin can flow very quickly through the laminate if done correctly, so be prepared to crimp off the resin line with a small clamp as soon as necessary. If you notice small trails of bubbles forming during infusion, these may be a sign that there is a small leak in the bagging film or sealant tape—so use additional sealant tape to close these off. Once infusion is complete, stop the resin flow and discard any remaining resin in the resin supply container.

Remember that successful infusion is not guaranteed on the first try, and may entail running through several test parts until arriving upon the proper placement of vacuum and resin lines—especially for large or complex parts. Adjust the placement of vacuum lines, resin lines, and location and amount of flow media until the best parts are produced.

Occasionally, an otherwise well-infused part will have a dry spot or small un-infused area. This can often be remedied by using a resin-filled syringe to inject a small bit of resin through a slit in the vacuum bag over the dry spot, and then immediately sealing up the slit with some sealant tape.

For better consolidation pressure on an infused laminate a "double-bagging" procedure can be performed over the infused laminate. To do this, place some bleeder/breather cloth (to ensure even pressurization over the laminate) and a second sealed bag over the infusion bag. This second bag must completely enclose the first bag, while still allowing the original vacuum line(s) to exit. For some small molds, it may be easier to simply enclose the whole mold in a sealed envelope bag. Keep in mind that the double-bagging process will require very wide mold flanges—so plan mold making efforts accordingly. Upon evacuation of the outer bag, the vacuum level on the inner bag may be dropped slightly (usually with a bleed-off valve) to avoid squeezing out too much resin from the infused laminate.

Allow the laminate to cure under vacuum to maintain consolidation pressure on the laminate during cure. After the laminate has cured, the bagging and infusion materials can be removed in the same manner as with a vacuum-bagged part. Demold, trim, and finish the part as usual.

Infusing With Liquid Acrylic Resin

Resin infusion takes practice and conscientious attention to detail. When infusing liquid acrylic resin, these skills are needed to their maximum levels—simply because acrylic resin requires very tight processing controls for best results. For example, there should be absolutely no leaks anywhere in the bag or vacuum system, since oxygen keeps the acrylic from polymerizing and fully curing. Even degassing the mixed resin in a vacuum chamber can be very helpful in removing bubbles that can compromise the quality of the composite. Take additional precautions to avoid igniting the flammable acrylic vapors, including not running the vacuum pump within three feet (1m) of the infused part or open containers of the resin. It is also recommended to include a vapor chiller between the resin trap and the vacuum pump to keep acrylic vapors from contaminating the pump's oil. Also, acrylic resin can have a softening effect on sealant tape, so flash tape should be used to immobilize in-bag materials in lieu of sealant tape. In spite of these particular quirks associated with acrylic resin, it can provide some welcomed processing

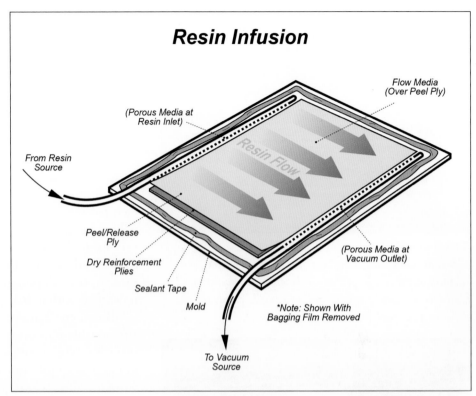

Resin infusion processes are performed by enclosing a reinforcement preform in a vacuum bag with the appropriate infusion materials (as shown above), evacuating the preform, and then allowing resin to flow into the preform from a resin supply source.

To infuse a laminate, stack the dry laminate plies onto the mold surface, and then add peel ply, flow media, and bagging film on top.

133

A clamped resin inlet can be placed through the sealed bag edge into spiral-cut tubing laid over the flow media. A vacuum outlet can be placed on the opposite edge of the laminate through spiral-cut tubing as well. Apply the vacuum and check for leaks.

Place the open end of the resin inlet into a container of mixed resin, then remove the clamp on the resin line to start the resin flow.

Resin should flow through the laminate stack toward the vacuum line. Once the resin has fully infused the laminate, clamp the resin line to stop the resin flow.

freedoms not found in traditional thermosets—namely, the ability to be thermoformed (as previously demonstrated), and a higher degree of recyclability.

Pre-preg Layup

Pre-preg lamination is significantly less messy and easier to perform than wet layups. However, pre-preg can also cost nearly three times as much as traditional materials (even with the cost of resin factored in), has a limited shelf life (after which it will eventually cure on its own), is available from very limited sources, and requires special processing to work effectively. In spite of these hurdles, though, the full potential of pre-pregs can still be unleashed with a little preparation and practice.

Broad good pre-pregs are supplied in rolls with a removable film on at least one side because of their surface tackiness, so they must be firmly pressed in place in a mold to work out large voids and wrinkles. Pre-preg requires warming with a heat gun and finessing with a rubber squeegee or gloved hand to successfully form it onto complex mold faces. It cuts very easily and precisely with a utility knife or scissors and doesn't produce frayed edges—making it possible to speed up a layup by pre-cutting (or *kitting*) patterns and plies beforehand. Pre-preg plies also do not easily slide into position over each other, and can take a bit of work to separate if firmly pressed together. Gloves *must* be worn during pre-preg layups to keep skin oils from affecting the bond between pre-preg plies.

Once all plies have been properly positioned in a mold, the pre-preg laminate will need to be pressurized and heated. Pressure is commonly created by vacuum-bagging the laminate, followed by atmospheric pressurization (with an autoclave) to between 50 and 150PSI—but other pressurization means are possible, as well. Heating the resin matrix slightly liquefies it, allowing it to flow between the laminate plies and bond them together—while at the same time filling voids as it cures. Because of pre-preg's heat processing requirements, it must be laid up in molds that will maintain their shape, strength, and rigidity at elevated temperatures and pressures—and high-temp mold release is always required. Metal or composite tooling made with high-temp resin work very well for processing pre-preg layups—but take into account the thermal expansion of your particular mold material when creating dimensionally critical parts. Also, keep in mind that thick, insulative molds will take significantly more time to warm and cool than thinner ones.

Pre-preg must be processed with the proper rate of temperature ramp up, holding at the required temperature(s), and then controlled rate of cooling for best material properties. To facilitate this, thermocouples can be placed in several locations over the laminate or built into the mold to accurately monitor the temperature of the mold/laminate system.

Once fully cured and cooled, the part can be quickly demolded, trimmed, and finished.

Internal Pressurization Methods

Special molding methods are required to create hollow, high-pressure laminates. Such hollow parts also require the use of a clamshell mold systems that are strong enough to withstand the pressures (and even temperatures) of the molding process. Two common molding methods capable of creating hollow parts involve *trapped rubber molding*, and *inflatable bladders*.

Trapped Rubber and Pre-preg Laminate Fabrication Techniques

With trapped rubber molding, a pre-preg composite laminate is enclosed in a mold in contact with a high thermal expansion rubber insert. When heated, this rubber insert expands faster than the mold itself, forcing the laminate against the mold walls under high pressure to produce tightly consolidated, high quality composite components. Significant pressure (up to hundreds of pounds per square inch) can be produced by a trapped rubber expandable insert, so a robust clamshell type mold is required. This mold must be able to be completely sealed to keep the insert from expanding into cracks or seams, and it must be able to withstand the curing temperatures of the pre-preg materials. Metal molds or high-temp mass-cast resin molds work well for such applications.

To form the silicone rubber insert, first create a dummy part in the mold (using clay, wax, tape, or composite laminate) to help create a gap for the laminate between the mold and the rubber insert. Next, cast a 30 to 40 Shore-A platinum-cure silicone rubber into the mold over the dummy part. Once cured, remove the insert, trim off any flash

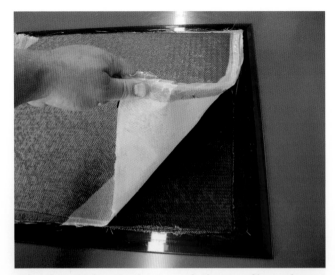

After the resin has cured, remove the bagging film and infusion materials...

...and then demold the part.

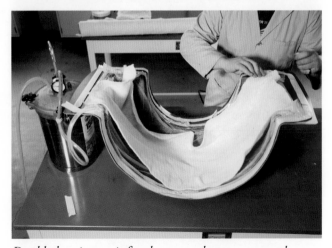

Double-bagging an infused part can better compact the laminate. To do this, place breather/bleeder cloth over the bagging film of the uncured, infused laminate.

135

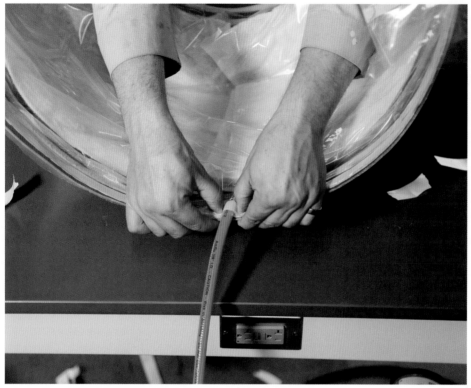

Apply bagging film over the part and use sealant tape to seal the bag's outer edge and around all other existing vacuum and infusion lines on the part. Insert the vacuum line and apply vacuum to outer bag.

at the seams, apply mold release to the mold walls, and then proceed with pre-preg layup in the mold.

After laying up the pre-preg part, apply a high-temp nylon film over it, followed by adding the rubber insert. Securely close the mold and heat process the molded pre-preg, as required by the pre-preg manufacturer. After cure, allow the mold to fully cool, open the mold, remove the rubber insert, and then demold, trim, and finish the part as usual.

Inflatable Bladder and Laminate Fabrication Techniques

Inflatable bladders are also used to compress a composite laminate against the mold faces of an enclosed mold, but they can be used on complex shapes that are difficult of impossible for trapped rubber molding. Bladders have one or more air inlets on them, and are composed of flexible, air tight materials. These bladders are best used with pre-preg materials, or with thick resin matrix wet laid-up composites. Unlike trapped rubber molding, they can develop very uniform pressures on a laminate—but they often require special sealing hardware and connectors for pressurized air delivery into the bladder.

Inflatable bladders must be correctly designed (being flexible, tough, and airtight) so they can be inserted and expanded correctly in the mold. The primary purpose of the bladder is to create a barrier that seals off the pressurized air from the laminate as it compresses

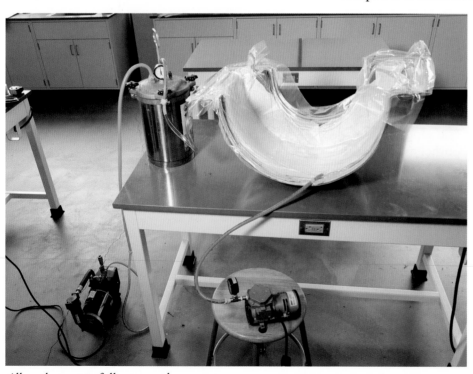

Allow the part to fully cure under vacuum.

136

the composite against the mold—so it should not be allowed to overstretch and burst within the molded part. Some materials that fit the requirements for a bladder include edge-sealed nylon and polyethylene films, latex rubber, silicone (which can also be fiber-reinforced for better longevity), and even properly sealed bicycle inner tubes (which come with the benefit of having their own built-in valves). When using thin films to make bladders, it is best to slightly oversize them to avoid too much stretching. Latex bladders can be custom made, but stock shapes are also readily available, along with thin-walled tubing, party balloons, or even run-o'-the-mill latex condoms. If the bladder material will likely bond with resin in the composite, it can be sheathed in release film.

Molds for bladder-formed parts only need to be heat resistant when used with pre-preg materials, but they should be strong enough to withstand bladder pressures that range from 20 PSI to over 150 PSI, depending on the desired consolidation and acceptable void content. As a result, these molds should be securely fastened together with hardware or clamps. For some inflation systems, good ways to seal the bladder include using a sealing flange (either flat or tapered) to hold the end of the bladder securely at the mold opening, or to use o-rings and a sealing plug to capture the bladder opening and seal it off at an inlet port. Always test a new mold to ensure it can handle the intended pressure exerted by the bladder prior to actual molding.

Pre-preg composites tend to work best with bladders, but thick liquid resins will work as well if their viscosity is between 5,000 to 15,000 CPS. Pre-preg is especially helpful in making truly seamless parts with a bladder as its stiffness can help bridge the joint between mold halves when bringing clamshell mold sections together. The natural closed structure of woven sleeve reinforcements makes them useful in fabricating wet laid-up tubular parts, although it can be helpful to partially inflate the bladder prior to putting the impregnated laminate into the mold. After layup, securely close the mold and inflate the bladder as slowly as possible to allow the bladder to gradually push out any air bubbles rather than trapping them in place.

Cured parts can be demolded by completely releasing pressure from the bladder, unclamping the mold halves, removing the bladder, and extracting the part.

To perform pre-preg layup, first treat the mold surfaces with a high-temperature mold release instead of paste wax.

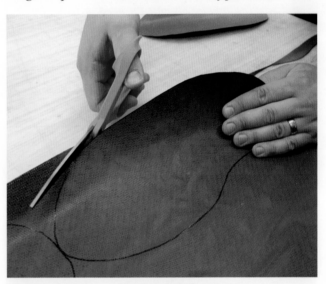

Cut out the pre-preg plies, as needed.

Peel back the protective film from the pre-preg...

...and press the pre-preg ply onto the mold surface.

Use a heat gun on its low setting to soften the resin and loosen the fibers to help the laminate plies conform to complex mold surfaces.

Use a rubber squeegee to press the pre-preg into tight corners and to remove voids in the laminate.

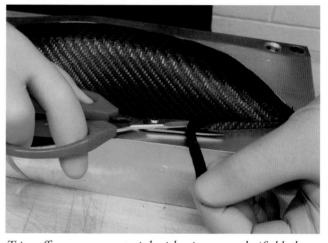

Trim off any excess material with scissors or a knife blade.

Trapped Rubber Pressurization

Rubber Insert

Laminate

Release Film

(Optional Lip/Overlap)

Thermal Expansion Pressure

Two-part Mold (Heated)

Conclusion

To form the highest quality composites requires processes that can adequately pressurize a laminate with the proper fiber-to-resin content—all to produce a low-void, optimized composite laminate. These quality requirements can be fulfilled in several different ways, though each one involves a good degree of skill and practice. Once these parts have been optimized and cured, the final processing steps of demolding, trimming, and finishing can be performed—as described in the next chapter.

Pre-preg materials work well with trapped rubber moldings. Place all the needed plies into a heat and pressure-resistant mold...

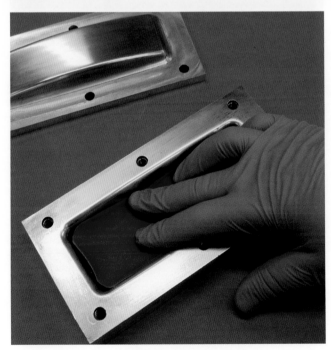

...and then insert the trapped rubber components to the mold system. Here, silicone rubber sheet material helps pressurize a prepreg laminate for a gas pedal.

Next, close the mold with appropriate hardware...

...and then place the part in an oven to cure it based on the pre-preg manufacturer's recommendations.

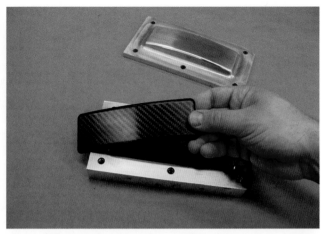

Once fully cured, allow the mold and part to cool, then demold the part.

One method of sealing an inflatable bladder includes using a tapered flange to clamp the end of a latex tube, and then fastening the flange to the mold.

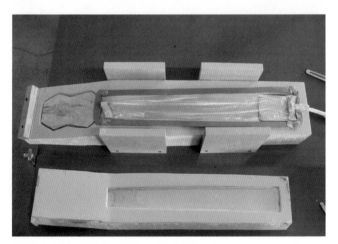

Inflatable bladders can also be made using bagging film, sealant tape, and air fittings, as shown in this mold for an 8-string guitar neck.

A bicycle inner tube can also be used as an inflatable bladder, as shown in this steering wheel mold. To form sleeve-woven reinforcement over an inner tube, the tube will need to be cut...

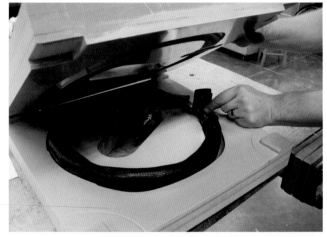

...and the reinforcement material can be slid over the inner tube and placed in the mold. The ends of the inner tube can then be folded over and clamped shut. The mold can then be closed and the inner tube inflated to pressurize the laminate.

Once fully cured, pressure can be released from the inner tube, the mold can be opened, and the part can be removed.

Lastly, the inner tube can be extracted from the center of the hollow laminate.

References and Resources

Arkema, Inc. *Vacuum Infusion of ELIUM Resin: Process Guide To Vacuum Infuse ELIUM Thermoplastic Composite Parts*, www.arkema.com, 2018.

www.fibreglast.com/product/vacuum-infusion-Guide

www.sollercomposites.com

https://www.webstaurantstore.com/tablecraft-12sv-12-oz-invertatop-dualway-first-in-first-out-fifo-squeeze-bottle/80812SV.html

Wanberg, John. *Composite Materials Handbook #1*, Stillwater, MN: Wolfgang Publications Inc., 2009.

Wanberg, John. *Composite Materials Handbook #2*, Stillwater, MN: Wolfgang Publications Inc., 2010.

Wanberg, John. *Composite Materials Handbook #3*, Stillwater, MN: Wolfgang Publications Inc., 2013.

Wanberg, John. *Composite Materials: Step-by-step Projects*, Stillwater, MN: Wolfgang Publications Inc., 2014.

Chapter Eight

Demolding, Trimming, and Finishing Processes

Molded and cured composite laminates generally require additional part cleanup and finishing before putting them into service. This often entails removing extraneous material, smoothing out edges, adding holes, adhering other components, or applying a surface finish to the final part—all of which are discussed in this chapter.

General Demolding Tips

Before demolding a composite part, make sure it is fully cured and is no longer tacky or rubbery when touched—this will keep it from sticking to the mold or deforming when demolded. Depending on the geometry and rigidity of the part, several tools and

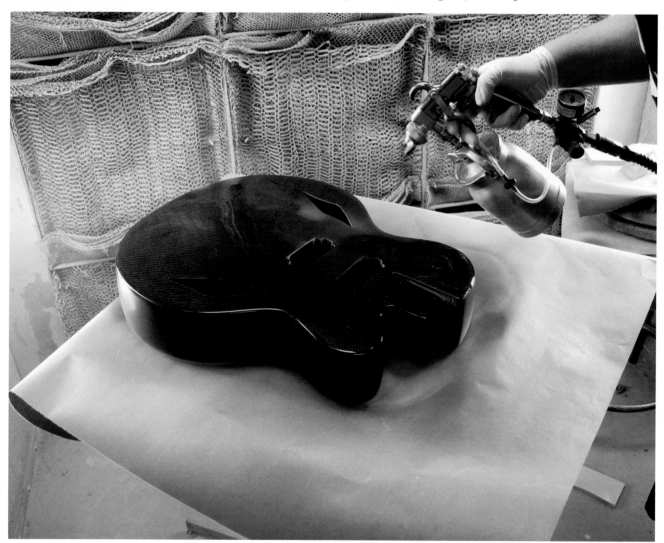

Clear coats are also available through several composites suppliers for application with a spray gun—and they can produce some very good results (as seen here).

methods may be required to remove the laminate. In general, the most effective tools for releasing a part include plastic wedges, an air nozzle and compressed air, rubber mallets, running water (for releasing PVA), and a jig or press (for mandrels or other difficult laminates). Never use screwdrivers, chisels, or other metal implements that may damage the mold. Additionally, before demolding a part, it is wise to clear the work space so there will be enough room to work around the mold and approach it from all sides. The following guidelines can help determine the best demolding methods to use.

Demolding Flat Panels

Flat, rigid, or slightly curved laminates are by far the easiest parts to demold. Small panels can be removed by carefully inserting and twisting a plastic putty knife or plastic wedge between the mold and the edge of the laminate. For larger panels, carefully slide a plastic putty knife between the mold and laminate and then run the putty knife around the perimeter of the laminate. Carefully insert several wedges into the resulting gap and slowly drive them in with a rubber mallet. Rigid panels will tend to separate from the mold all at once, while more flexible laminates may need to be released one area at a time until they can be pulled away from the mold surface.

Demolding Compound Curved Parts

For composites that have large sections of compound curvature or complex mold flanges and parting lines, several techniques (and a great deal of patience) may be required to remove the part, depending on how well the part has adhered to the mold. Always start with the least intrusive demolding methods before resorting to more extreme ones. Demolding large, deep, or complex components, often requires working from one edge to the other, little by little to remove the part from the mold.

When demolding a vacuum-bagged or resin infused laminate, peel off and discard all bagging materials prior to demolding the actual laminate. This can be a deceptively laborious step, especially for parts that are small, deep, have considerable shape changes within them, or where the breather/bleeder cloth has contacted and adhered to the laminate. In general, it is easier to completely remove one layer of the bagging material at a time, when possible.

Composite parts can be fabricated in practically any size, but the methods for demolding, trimming, and finishing them are all very similar—as discussed in this chapter.

To demold a flat panel, simply slide a plastic putty knife or wedge beneath the panel's edge, working it around the edge of the part until it begins to lift from the mold face.

For deeper or curved parts, press the laminate edge away from the mold face (when possible), and then drive wedges into the gaps.

143

Once the part is free, remove it from the mold.

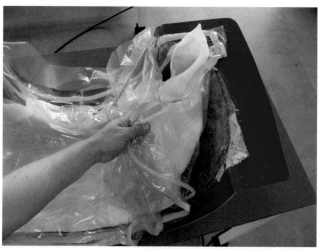

To demold a vacuum-bagged or infused part, remove the bagging and infusion materials before demolding the part itself. It can be helpful to only remove single layers of material at a time.

If infusion lines have become lodged onto the surface of the infusion materials, a short sideways tap with a chisel at the base of the infusion line can help loosen it—but avoid damaging the laminate!

Completely remove any peel ply, sealant tape, or flash tape from the surface of the laminate.

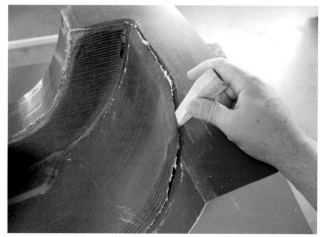

Use a wedge to lift the edges of the part from the mold face, and then remove the part from the mold.

To demold a mandrel-formed part, first remove any heat shrink tape…

To demold the laminate, start by inserting a plastic putty knife between the mold and the edge of the composite. If there is a flange and enough flash to grasp onto, try to pry the composite away from the mold using a gloved hand. Carefully drive small wedges into the gaps created by prying the composite away from the mold surfaces, avoiding any extreme flexure of the mold or composite part. In areas where the demolding seems to be working most effectively, replace the small wedges with larger ones, carefully tapping them in with a rubber mallet until the part comes free. *Do not tap wedges in so far that they begin to break the laminate—which will be evident by a heart-wrenching, crunching or crackling sound!*

If a large part will not release with the wedges, try blowing air into gaps between the mold and the part with an air nozzle or air nozzle-equipped wedge. Lightly feather the air trigger to puff air into the void between the part and the mold. The part should eventually float free from the surface of the mold as air pressure pushes it up from below.

Demolding a Mandrel Laminate

To remove the laminate formed over a mandrel, first remove the heat shrink material over the laminate. If heat shrink tape was used, carefully cut the heat shrink tape at one end and unwrap it. Small pieces of residual heat shrink tape can be removed with a utility knife blade, but avoid nicking any of the mandrel's surfaces.

To remove heat shrink tubing from a laminate, use a seam ripper tool (available at fabric stores) to cut through the tubing. Cutting the tubing in a slightly diagonal direction with the seam ripper can help it cut through the tubing more smoothly.

To remove the laminate from the mandrel, the mandrel will need to be pressed from out of the center of the laminate. A simple press system can be constructed by drilling a hole in a hardwood board (such as oak or hard maple) that matches the diameter of the mandrel, and then using bar or pipe clamps to apply even pressure on the mandrel. When pressing out the laminate tube, it may make a slight "pop" or crackling sound as it releases and slides down the face of the mandrel. If the laminate does not quickly release from the mandrel, it may be helpful to firmly tap the laminate in several spots with a rubber mallet to loosen it. Once loose, the laminate should slide relatively easily off the end of the mandrel.

…or remove heat shrink tubing with a sewing seam ripper.

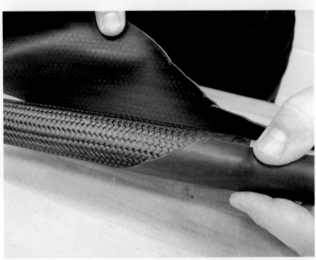

Heat shrink tubing can be easily peeled away from the laminate once cut up its length.

To demold the laminate from the face of a straight mandrel, cut a hole (slightly larger than the diameter of the mandrel) in a block of dense wood, dense plastic, or aluminum.

145

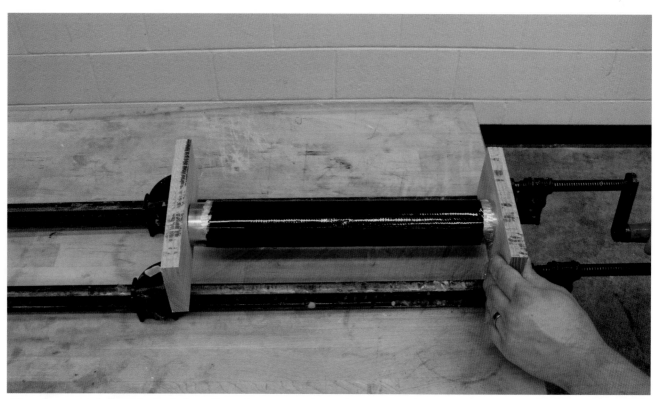

Place the mandrel through this hole, and use clamps to apply axial pressure to the laminate to drive it down the length of the mandrel, as shown here.

The laminate can then be removed completely from the mandrel.

146

To dissolve styrene foam in a moldless laminate, pour a solvent (such as acetone) onto the foam. It will begin to immediately breakdown.

When possible, clear away melted plastic and pieces of foam to expedite the removal process.

Laminate surfaces can be cleaned up with acetone and a scrubbing pad, followed by additional sanding.

Use fasteners inserted through drilled holes in the matched flanges of multi-section molds to secure the mold sections in place.

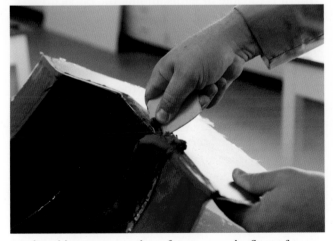

To demold composite tooling, first remove the flange forms, and then scrape off any leftover clay material from fillets or seals.

Clay can be cleaned from the tooling using a rag soaked in mineral spirits.

Use a rotary tool to trim back any rough edges on the tooling (note the use of a shop vacuum here to remove trimming dust)…

…and then sand the trimmed edges smooth with a sanding block.

To demold composite tooling formed over a clay mold pattern, remove the mold pattern, then carefully scrape away the remaining clay from the surfaces of the tooling.

Dissolving "Moldless" Part Forms

Styrene foam in moldless composites can be dissolved away using acetone, lacquer thinner, kerosene, or styrene monomer liquid—since styrene foam is very susceptible to solvent attack. Keep in mind that it is not possible to dissolve urethane, vinyl, or epoxy foams in this way. Take care to use adequate ventilation and avoid skin contact with any solvent used to dissolve the styrene foam. Allow the solvent to evaporate from any dissolved foam prior to disposal. Cleanup of dissolved styrene foam residue from a composite laminate can be sped up by using a putty knife to scrape away any gummy, melted material. Further cleanup can be done with an acetone-soaked scrubbing pad, followed by rough sandpaper.

If urethane or vinyl foams need to be removed from a laminate, they can be broken, chiseled, chipped, scraped, or sanded out of the composite—a task which can be particularly time intensive, but that can be made easier by using low-density foams instead. Any remaining rough, aesthetic surfaces can be filled with body filler, smoothed with sandpaper and high-build primer, and then painted (as discussed below).

Demolding and Finishing Composite Tooling

Allow composite tooling to fully cure before demolding it to avoid permanent deformation of any uncured material. For added tooling strength, post-curing is recommended, but this is best performed while still on the mold pattern—if the pattern is capable of withstanding the post-cure heating temperatures.

Demolding and finishing procedures for composite tooling are the same as for other molded composites—taking special care to minimize damage to the mold pattern in the event that it will be needed for future mold repairs. Mold flanges should be trimmed to produce smooth edges, which can be done most easily using a cutoff wheel attached to either an electric or air-powered rotary tool. Trimmed edges should be leveled with a file and then wet-sanded using a block to smooth the final edges. Rough, stray fibers can be removed from the back of a mold using a file, sandpaper, die grinder, or disc sander.

Use fine-grit wet sandpaper to remove any blemishes in the mold, such as scratches or material left by the mold pattern. Larger protruding blemishes can be smoothed with a fine-tooth file. If you find any large pores or bubbles (larger than ¼" in diameter) in the mold surface, grind them out with a rotary tool, clean them with acetone, and then fill them with tooling gel coat or epoxy surface coat. Allow these spots to cure, then smooth with wet-sandpaper, starting with 220 grit and then working progressively up to at least 600 grit. Follow wet sanding with progressively finer polishes to thoroughly smooth the tooling surface prior to molding any parts.

Demolding Stubborn Parts

Occasionally, a part will not release from a mold as planned. This can often be frustrating, especially when expensive composite materials were used in the part's layup and there may be the chance that extreme removal steps will damage either the laminate or the mold. In the process of removing a stubborn part, however, always start with the least invasive removal methods first.

Mold patterns or composite parts that have considerable thickness to them can sometimes be removed by fabricating a make-shift removal jig that employs large-threaded screws to extract the seized component from the mold. Sturdy wood or scrap metal tubing that is braced against the mold flanges work well for this purpose. Drill holes in the wood or metal that will allow screw threads to pass through them, and then tighten the screws into the stubborn material until they begin to pull it out.

When less extreme methods fail to remove a stuck part, more aggressive tactics may be needed. Try employing several moderate blows to the back of the mold with a rubber mallet—but avoid any severe, damaging force on either the part or the mold. These blows can often help loosen the part, making it easier for wedges or air nozzles to take effect.

In most cases, it is usually best to sacrifice the part rather than the mold, simply because molds generally take more time, effort, and expense to build than the laminates that go in them. To destructively remove a part, carefully chip away at it, little by little, with a flat blade screwdriver or chisel, paying very close attention that you do not drive the tool through the part and into mold surfaces. When applying prying forces to the part, use the edge of a plastic wedge to pry against rather than

If some of the sealer material is attached to tooling, carefully scrape it away, as well, or use an air nozzle to help force it off the mold surfaces.

A piece of hard plastic sheet can be used to scrape the mold faces without damaging them.

Trim and smooth the flange edges, then wet sand and polish any surface imperfections left on the mold before applying release agents and using the mold.

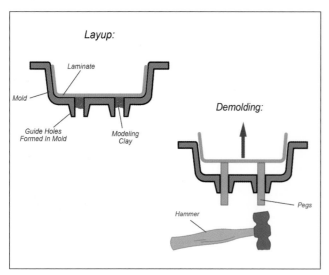

Part removal accommodations can be built into some molds prior to use (as shown above).

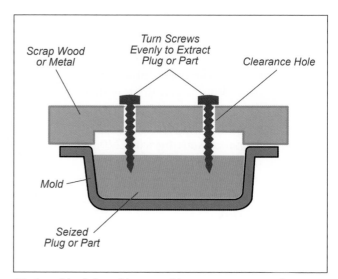

To demold solid, stubborn mold patterns, a removal jig (shown above) can be helpful.

Some stubborn parts can be loosened with a quick blow to the back of the mold with a rubber mallet.

If a mold pattern is stuck to the surface of composite tooling, it can be carefully chipped way…

…and then removed from the tooling. Be careful throughout this process to minimize mold damage and subsequent mold repair steps.

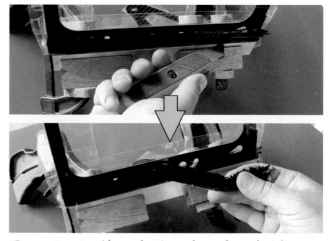

Green trimming (shown here) can be performed with a knife or scissors.

directly against the mold. After removing all the rogue laminate pieces, inspect the mold for damage and make repairs as needed.

"Green" Trimming Laminates

Extraneous, accessible wet laid-up laminate that extends beyond the edge of a mold (called flash) can be trimmed with scissors while still in the "green-cure" state. This can reduce the number off rough, sharp edges on the part and save some time and hassle when trimming the part after demolding. When resin in the composite is cured to a gel-like state (evident by its rubbery feel while still being only slightly tacky to the touch) the fibers are nearly completely immobilized, but can be easily trimmed with a utility knife or scissors. When green trimming, avoid cutting off all the flash on the part's edge—as some extra material can still be helpful to provide extra leverage for pushing against during demolding.

Handling and Cleaning Demolded Laminates

After demolding, a composite may have several hazardous edges or hardened threads that need immediate attention before the part can be handled safely—so wear leather or canvas gloves to protect your hands. Sheet metal snips or hand shears work well for pre-trimming a cured part to cut off any hazardous protruding stray fibers or jagged edge material.

Parts created in PVA coated molds tend to pick up at least a little of the PVA when demolded. This film is very easily removed by running it under warm water and rubbing it lightly with your hands or with a dishwashing scrubbing pad. Other release agents deposited on the laminate can be removed with acetone and a rag prior to applying any surface finishes.

Best Tools for Trimming Cured Laminates

Hacksaw cutting works well for straight or large diameter cuts on small or odd-shaped parts—but it can be laborious and time consuming. Gel/surface coatings may chip when the teeth of the blade push the gel coat *away* from the laminate, so make sure the blade is oriented with the teeth pushing

Before trimming a laminate, it is sometimes helpful to cut off excess flash with scissors or metal shears.

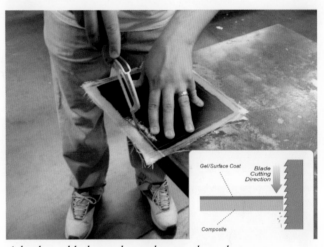
A hacksaw blade can be used to cut through most composites, but make sure the teeth are cutting downward into the gel/surface coat, as shown (see inset).

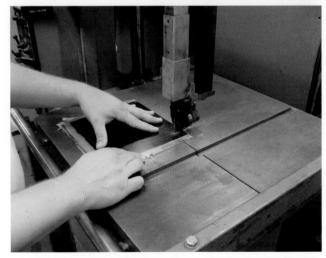
Bandsaw cutting can be very effective for flat laminates, but be sure to use a carbide blade.

151

A rotary cut-off wheel is the tool of choice for cutting most composites. These are available for small jobs, but also come in larger sizes for bigger or thicker laminates.

Curved cuts can be accomplished with a cut-off wheel by making successive straight cuts, as shown here.

A rotary file (see inset) can be used to make very curved cuts...

...as seen with the trimmed laminate here.

downward into the gel coat side of the composite during cutting.

A bandsaw (with fine-toothed carbide-blade) tends to work very well when quickly trimming flat panels or for straight or large diameter edge contours. With bandsaws (as with hacksaw cutting above) gel/surface coated surfaces should be facing upward during cutting. Carbide blades with fine teeth are recommended for maximum blade life.

A fine-toothed jigsaw can be used similarly to a bandsaw, especially for parts that require cuts in the middle of the part rather than just around its edges. Again, carbide blades work best with jigsaws. Also, bandsaw and jigsaw cutting of acrylic resin composites tends to work better than using a rotary tool, as these produce less heat during cutting operations and are less prone to melting the thermoplastic matrix.

A rotary tool and abrasive cut-off wheel are the best for most straight line and large diameter cuts—but is best used with a dust mask or respirator. Air-powered type rotary tools tend to blow away trimming dust as they cut, but electric types work best in lieu of a compressed air supply. Pairing a rotary tool with a shop vacuum to directly remove any cut site debris significantly minimizes hazardous airborne dust. *Avoid creating too much friction and heat with the*

When drilling composites, always use a sharp bit, slow spindle RPM, and high plunge rates to minimize overheating the matrix in the composite.

Cut edges can be cleaned up and smoothed by simply sanding them.

cutting wheel to minimize resin breakdown at the cut edges!

A rotary tool with a rotary file works well for creating tight radius or highly curved cut lines on parts of practically any size. Straight-line control is difficult with this tool, so cutting guides or CNC cutting equipment are recommended. This tool is not recommended for trimming aramid laminates because aramid fibers tend to fill the teeth of the rotary file during cutting, decreasing cut efficiency.

Abrasive water-jet equipment is best for cleanly cutting aramid fabrics, thick laminates, stacks of multiple laminate sheets at once, or when performing mass-production runs of a part. It can be extremely cost prohibitive for small-scale composite applications, and is limited to two-dimensional cutting.

A CNC router works best for trimming production parts where aramid fabrics are not used—though some specialized bits are available for this purpose. Laminates must be fixtured in place for accurate trimming, which may require custom jigs or fixturing hardware. Three-axis versions work well for most planar or slightly contoured parts, while five-axis versions are required for parts with complex trim lines and large or bulky contours in multiple axes. CNC trimming is most cost effective when used in situations where tool paths and program changes are

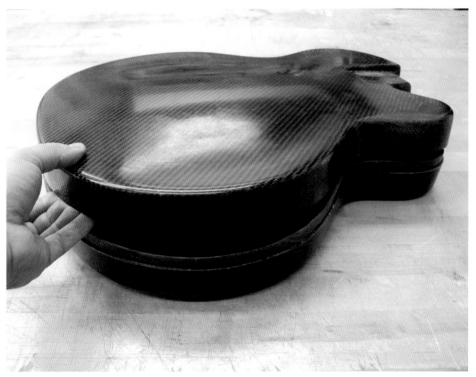

When secondarily bonding two parts together, check for good fit between the parts, thoroughly sand the bonding faces with 80-grit sandpaper, and then use acetone to completely clean the bond site.

Apply thickened resin or structural adhesive to bond components together, then use clamps to hold the components in place until the joint has fully cured.

154

infrequent (such as with large production runs). Diamond-patterned teeth, diamond coated, and cobalt-based metal bits tend to produce the longest cutting tool life.

Drilling Composites

As with cutting, drilling into composites requires special attention to avoid edge delamination or overheating of the matrix during processing. Holes should always be drilled using sharp bits to minimize heating during drilling operations. Cobalt drill bits and carbide drill bits work best for drilling—although they tend to be much more expensive than high-speed steel bits. Drill holes using "slow speeds and high feeds"—that is, with slow bit RPM while feeding the bit into the laminate with moderate to high pressure. When possible, water can be used as a coolant to help keep the drill site cool.

Finishing Trimmed Laminate Edges

Trimmed laminate edges often require filing and sanding to further smooth them prior to use. A metal file can help level unevenly trimmed edges very quickly, and wet-sanding can be used to further refine the edge without producing airborne dust. Using a block, a piece of high grit wet-sandpaper, a wet sponge, and a water-filled basin or running water, work over the trimmed edge until the final edge dimensions and shape are achieved. Apply water to the composite as needed to float away any sanded debris. Once it has been trimmed and the edges finished, the part is then ready for secondary bonding, surface treatments, or immediate use.

Secondary Bonding

Some part simply cannot be molded with all of their required features at one time. Such parts may require additional molded features (such as brackets, mounts, or even entire part sections) to be secondarily bonded onto them. Secondary bonding, while not the preferred method of joining composite components, can still be effective for rigidly mounting parts to one another.

Before attempting to bond composite components to each other, prepare their bonding surfaces by sanding them with a coarse grit sandpaper or a file to create sufficient "bite" for

Finishing mandrel-formed laminates can be aided by turning the part in a lathe and using emery cloth sandpaper to smooth the surface.

Other laminates can be sanded (as with this moldless part) using 120 to 200-grit sandpaper. If possible, sand composite parts over a downdraft table or use wet sandpaper to minimize dust.

Before applying fairing/surface fillers, completely clean the surface of the composite using an air hose or acetone.

155

The surface of most un-coated, sanded composites will likely have pores in it that need to be filled, as evident here.

the adhesive to key into. Smooth surfaces will bond poorly, and may just simply release from each other instead of bonding.

Clean the sanded bonding surfaces with high-pressure air, and then wash away any remaining dust residue with acetone. Mix resin with a thickener such as colloidal silica or high density filler to create a paste that has the consistency of peanut butter. Apply this adhesives mixture to the cleaned bonding surfaces. Join the parts together and clean up any excess resin paste that squeezes out the edges using a round-ended stick.

Clamp the parts in place until the resin has cured completely (as recommended by the resin manufacturer) before putting the bonded parts into service.

Sanding, and Applying Fillers/ Fairing Materials

Sanding can quickly remove material and smooth laminate surfaces to produce high-quality parts. Electric or air-powered sanders work very well for large jobs, but simple hand sanding with a block works well for small parts. Use coarse grits (80 and 120 grit) for very fast material removal, and then work up to finer grits (320 to 600 grit) for better surface quality. Wet-sanding is the preferred method of smoothing composite surfaces to minimize airborne dust. Wet-

Thoroughly mix all fillers before applying them to the surface of the part. Smooth the filler over the surface as much as possible with a spreader before it begins to cure.

156

sandpaper is commonly available in fine grits (from 220 to 1200 or higher), though more coarse grits are sometimes available from specialty paint suppliers.

Occasionally, pores or surface roughness will developed in uncoated laminates during molding. These surfaces can be smoothed by first rough sanding them (to 120-grit), and then applying fairing compound or body filler with a spreader—which typically involves considerable sanding and good craftsmanship to produce a high quality surface. If needed, custom fairing compound can be created using resin mixed with a low-density fillers (such as glass microspheres and colloidal silica) until it achieves an appropriate peanut butter-like consistency.

Filling surface blemishes can be problematic where a bare composite is intended to be visible. In some cases, fairing compound can be pigmented to match the color of the laminate, and then applied carefully and sparingly to the surface. Keep in mind that sanding into the reinforcement weave of a carbon fiber or aramid composite can produce some unsightly visual imperfections that may be very apparent once a clear coat is applied over the surface—so sanding should be minimized or avoided on these aesthetic surfaces whenever possible. If a clear coat will be applied over a laminate, beware that sanding above 400 grit can sometimes cause clear coats to bead up or create

Next, sand the filler smooth with 220-grit sandpaper, frequently checking the surface for shaping accuracy.

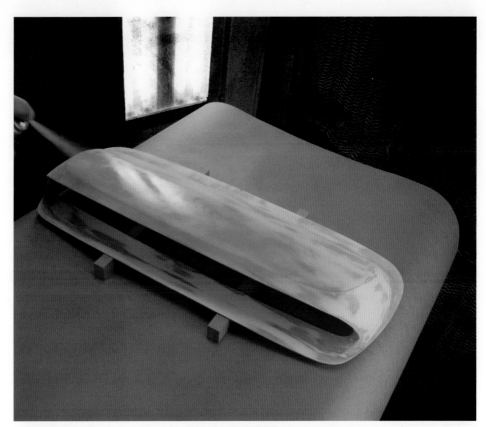

Repeat the previous two steps until the surface appears to be completely smoothed. To find any additional areas for smoothing, spray a sandable primer over the filled surfaces.

157

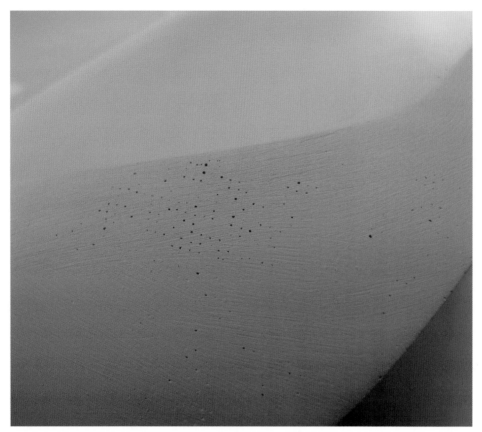

Once primed, any remaining surface imperfections will be much more noticeable. Use additional filler or glazing putty to correct these before adding final surface treatments.

The finished, primed piece can then be prepped for final paint.

unsightly "fish-eye" flaws in the coated surface.

Upholstery Over Composites

Upholstery materials generally adhere well to composite secondary structures—as with vehicle interior panels, motorcycle seating, and various furniture applications. Upholstery adhesives will generally bond well over most sanded laminate surfaces, but staples can also be used to adhere upholstery materials to fiberglass and aramid composites. For some situations, upholstery may be a good option to avoid labor-intensive laminate surface finishing steps as it is very effective in hiding various surface imperfections.

Coating and Finishing Composites

Paint/Lacquer

Apply primer to the composite that is compatible with the paint system to be used for the final coats. Fill any additional pores that may appear between these primer coats. When the primer has dried, apply paint either from a spray can or spray gun. Also, acrylic matrix composites tend to accept solvent-based paints very well, so lacquer-based paints produce good results on these composites.

Polyurethane Finishes

Many acrylic and urethane paints (including clear coats) provide the UV protection required to shield epoxy-based composites from damage. They are commonly available from automotive body and painting supply stores, many of which carry good information about the protection their paints can offer. These paints come in an endless variety of colors and are usually best applied with a spray gun, though for small jobs spray cans will often do an acceptable job.

Resin/floodcoating

To show off the weave of a composite (as is common with carbon and aramid-hybrid weaves), a "flood-coat" is usually in order. A flood-coat is a thick coating of resin that is either sprayed on (typically using a UV-stable polyester or vinyl ester-based coating) or brushed over the composite and then allowed to cure. Flood-coats can produce a highly polished or "wet" surface look as they easily fill in small voids and pores, leaving a clear, smooth, level shell over the composite. Flood coats can even be tinted with dyes to produce colored, translucent effects.

One drawback of using flood-coats, though, is that they can add unnecessary weight and their "pretty" coating can easily chip, fracture, or separate from the composite if it is significantly impacted or flexed. Such performance deficiencies are further compounded by the fact that damaged flood-coat surfaces are extremely difficult to repair, usually requiring complete sanding and removal of the affected area followed by a recoating of resin.

Care of Composite Tooling

Treat composite tooling with care to ensure long service life. Occasional cleaning with water and mild soap will help keep dust and other contaminants off the mold, but solvents work best when removing resin residues. D-Limonene works well for most basic cleaning tasks, but sparing amounts of acetone or lacquer thinner can also get the job done. *Never use paint stripper (with methylene chloride) on composite tooling—it is very efficient at breaking down resin matrices!*

When gel or surface coats are not used for molded composites, a thin film of cured resin may build up on the surface of a mold over time. This may be apparent by a faint, ghost-like fiber pattern

To adhere upholstery directly to a composite part, mask off any areas that need to be protected from adhesive, sand the bonding surfaces and clean them with acetone, and apply adhesive to the bonding surfaces.

Carefully apply the upholstery, making sure to press out any bubbles or wrinkles.

Remove the masking tape and inspect the part.

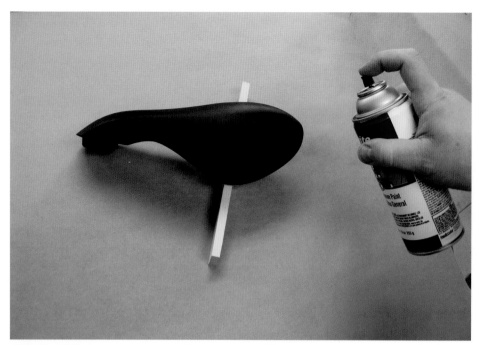

Seams on bonded parts can be hidden on carbon fiber parts by first smoothing them with filler, than spraying flat black primer over the seam, feathering out the paint on either side of the seam.

that is visible on the mold surface. To remove this film, scrape the tooling surface with a piece of hard plastic (such as acrylic) to remove most of the hardened resin film. Next, apply cutting/rubbing compound onto the mold's surfaces, and then buff and polish it until it has regained its original gloss. Reapply release agents to the mold, as usual, before reuse.

Never store heavy objects or shop materials on or in composite tooling, and always support it by its flanges. If composite tooling needs to be stored for long periods of time, backup supports can be used to maintain its proper shape, it can be stored over the original mold pattern, or polyurethane foam (as two-part mixed urethane foam poured into the waxed mold) can provide support to the mold during storage. Also, it is wise to apply a good coat of mold release on a mold before storing it for any long period of time to simplify future cleanup efforts.

Conclusion

A composite part is not truly complete until it has been demolded, trimmed, and cleanly finished. A good level of craftsmanship is needed throughout these final treatment processes, but will inevitably result in a well-executed composite part. However, even the best finished parts are still subject to wear and tear over time, so the next chapter will cover repair methods for composite laminates.

When clear coat is painted over the part, the primed seam will become virtually invisible.

160

Flood coats can be added over a well-sanded and acetone-cleaned surface. Try to minimize the amount of bubbles in the clear coat during application with a brush.

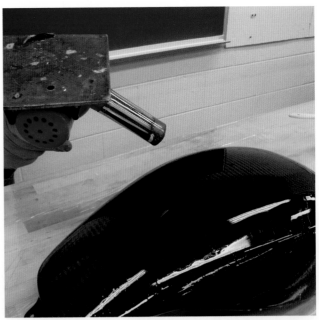

With some flood coats, bubbles can be removed by warming the resin with your breath or a heat gun—though in some cases, a carefully applied MAP gas torch may be needed.

Once cured, the flood coat can be further smoothed with fine-grit wet sanding and polishing to produce a high quality finish.

Clear coats are also available through several composites suppliers for application with a spray gun—and they can produce some very good results (as seen here).

References and Resources

Wanberg, John. *Composite Materials Handbook #1*, Stillwater, MN: Wolfgang Publications Inc., 2009.

Wanberg, John. *Composite Materials Handbook #2*, Stillwater, MN: Wolfgang Publications Inc., 2010.

Wanberg, John. *Composite Materials Handbook #3*, Stillwater, MN: Wolfgang Publications Inc., 2013.

Chapter Nine

Repairing Composites

Composites can be damaged in a variety of ways including impact, stress fracture, heat, wear and abrasion, or environmental or chemical exposure. The type of repair needed will depend on the specific type of damage found in the composite. This chapter will describe some simple repair methods for correcting damaged composite laminates.

General Repair Guidelines

Regardless of the different types of damage possible in a composite, there are four general steps that must be performed, as discussed below:

Some repairs are difficult to do while some may be nearly impossible, as shown with these damaged carbon fiber bike frames: 1) Faint surface damage is indicative of deeper delamination, 2) A severe fracture like this can be difficult (though not impossible) to rebuilt and realign, 3) This disbonded section will only require surface prep and more adhesive, 4) A missing head tube and deep delamination damage like this can virtually scrap the part.

- Assessing damage
- Preparing the composite for repair
- Adding material to the damaged area
- Surface finishing

Assessing Damage

Damage in uncoated fiberglass composites is evident by discoloration in the laminate—but coated, painted or opaque composites (like carbon or aramid) are much more difficult to assess. Even mere surface scratches may be indicative of even more damage beneath.

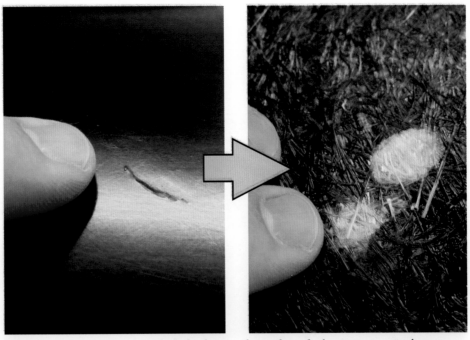

A slight dent in the surface of a laminate may indicate further damage, as evident on the back of the laminate.

Several industrial methods of detecting damage with a composite include utilizing ultrasonic, x-ray, or thermal methods, but the average fabricator rarely has access to such equipment. However, simply tapping lightly on an undamaged composite will produce a certain audible tone, while the tone from a damaged area in a laminate will produce a comparatively duller tone. Using this tapping technique, the breadth of damage in the laminate can be determined and then marked (often with a permanent marker) and used to help guide the next steps of the repair.

Depending on the extent of the damage in a composite part, the fabricator may need to make a judgment call about whether to repair the part or to replace it. This judgment may not only be determined by the amount of damage but also by the skill level of the fabricator, the available tools, the suitability of the repair materials available, the

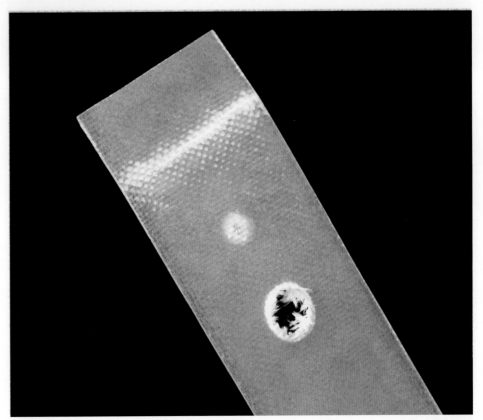

Fiberglass can be damaged in several ways, as shown here: delamination from bending (top), impact delamination (middle), and edge delamination caused by a dull drill bit (bottom)

163

A rotary tool can be used to increase the bondable area to repair a gouge (as shown here), though the laminate should not be ground down too deeply.

After using acetone to clean the damaged section of the laminate, apply catalyzed gel coat to the damaged area.

cost of the labor involved in the repair, the critical structural and engineered requirements of the part, and even the availability of a replacement part. If the scope of the repair is outside the fabricator's capabilities or resources, it may be more advantageous to replace the part or seek additional professional repair assistance.

Preparing the Composite for Repair

Practically any sizable damage found in a composite will have at least compromised the resin matrix in the laminate. Fiber fracture is also common in parts damaged through excessive stress or impact, but both matrix and reinforcement deficiencies must be addressed to correct the damage. Adequately repairing the composite will require some form of an adhesive bond of new material to the original material in the part. Adhesives do not generally bond well to dirty, wet or smooth surfaces, so the damaged area must be properly prepared prior to any subsequent repair steps. Completely sand the damaged area with 80-grit sand paper. Depending on the type of damage found in the composite, this sanding procedure may be done either by hand or with the use of power tools. Hand sanding is the preferred method of surface prep, but skilled use of a power sander can significantly speed up the process as

Once the gel coat has tacked up, seal off the surface of gel coat from the air with a sprayed coating of PVA.

Once the gel coat has cured, wash off the PVA…

…and use progressive grits of wet sandpaper (from 220 to 1000) to smooth the repaired area. Be careful not to sand through the original gel coat!

Sanding can be followed by progressive grits of polish.

If done correctly, it will be difficult to identify where the original damage was located.

long as care is used to avoid over-zealously sanding the laminate to the point that it is incurs further damage. Sufficiently clear all sanded surfaces with shop air or a vacuum, followed by a generous wipe-down with acetone. This will help provide a clean surface for enhanced secondary bonding to the original material by the adhesives used in the repair.

Adding Material to the Damaged Area

After properly preparing the damaged area, add composite material to be to reinforce the sanded area. If the damage is merely cosmetic, only body filler or surface coatings may need to be added over the carefully sanded surfaces to complete the repair. Where structural damage has been sustained, the actual ply orientation of the laminate in the affected area will need to be determined and new material added to correspond with those ply orientations. Care should be taken to ensure that the resin and reinforcements used in the repair will match the original material as closely as possible to retain the original strength of the composite. Mat fiber laminates require much less attention to fiber orientation as the fibers in them are very randomly arranged.

This particular step of repair should be performed under "clean" conditions to keep dust or humidity from affecting the quality of the repair. Avoid contamination of the

A small grinder can quickly taper the surrounding damaged area of holes in a laminate. For smaller areas of damage, an electric rotary tool can also work well. Clean all sanded areas with acetone.

repair site by keeping it away from any dust, grease, oil (including those from one's own ungloved fingers), or chemicals that may compromise the bond.

Surface Finishing

Repairs will often add bulk or additional surface "imperfection" to the repaired area on the component unless they are smoothed over and cleaned up. For structural applications, the surface quality of the part may not necessarily be a high priority, but wherever the aesthetic quality of the surface is important, additional finishing steps will be needed. This will include sanding, polishing, and in some cases, complete recoating of the surface with gel coat or paint, as described below.

Tape is then placed on the opposite side to prevent seepage from the liquid resin that will be used in the subsequent repair steps.

Cosmetic/Surface Repairs

Some of the simplest, least invasive composite repairs are those that are performed on scratches, nicks and cracks in a surface coat, gel coat, or paint. These types of repairs are all considered to be "cosmetic" in nature in that the structural integrity of the part is not affected by the damage. Even small holes drilled in a composite may be considered cosmetic damage if they do not significantly weaken the surrounding laminate, but nonetheless need to be removed from the composite for the sake of aesthetics.

Light scratches in a gel or surface coat that do not

Thick, high strength epoxy tends to work best for a variety of repairs. West Systems' G/flex epoxy is used for the repair here, though thickened epoxy also works well.

Several layers of resin-wetted material should be added over the damaged sections to match the thickness of the laminate.

After the epoxy has cured, remove the tape and roughen up the surface of the repair to promote bonding with the gel coat that will be added next.

Catalyzed gel coat is added over these roughened sections of the holes. This is allowed to tack up, and followed with a sealer coat of PVA.

go through the coating may be quickly fixed with only minimal wet sanding using fine grit sandpaper followed by progressive grits of polish and final buffing.

Paint coatings are generally much thinner than gel or surface coats so scratches in them may require more aggressive sanding to smooth out the scratch, followed by glaze-putty filling and repainting of the surface—in the same way that painted metal surfaces are repaired.

If a scratch extends *through* the gel or surface coat, but not into the composite below, first use sandpaper to grind out the surrounding area slightly to give the filling and coating materials more bondable surface area. Small scratches or cracks in a gel coat may need to be widened. Any blisters in a gel coat will need to be removed, roughened up and thoroughly cleaned. The next step in repairs like these is to smooth over the sanded area with an appropriate filler. Common polyester-based automotive body filler is an effective, inexpensive material that can be quickly smoothed and then coated over by a gel coat, surface coat or paint. For more demanding cosmetic repairs that need to resist cracking, micro-balloon filled epoxy works very well. Epoxy-based fillers tend to form a more tenacious bond with the surrounding composite materials than their polyester-based counterparts do, so they will give increased performance at the repair site. Epoxy also exhibits less shrinkage during cure than polyester, so it will pull away from the edges of the damaged area less than polyester will.

Small holes may be filled using body filler in a similar manner. If the hole is not too big, the filler will be able to bridge the gap created by the hole and effectively close off the defect. Enough filler should be used in such situations to fully adhere to a large surface area behind the hole to keep the filler from simply pushing out of the hole after cure. After the hole is filled and smoothed, it can then be recoated with gel or surface coat or paint.

Large holes on a non-structural part will require a bit more work to repair than small ones. The surface area around the hole should be sanded down, covered on the opposite side, and reinforced with new material and resin. Once cured, the surface area around the hole can be filled with body filler (if needed), coated with gel coat or paint, smoothed and then returned to service.

Refinishing a composite with a new layer of gel coat can require a good amount of skill and

After the gel coat has cured, these sections are then progressively wet sanded to be flush with the surrounding, original gel coat…

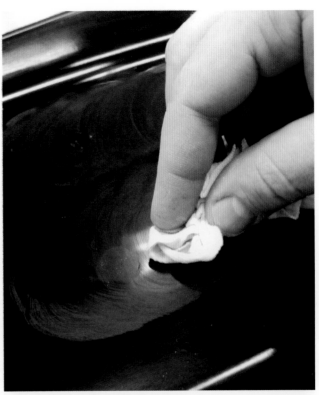

…and polished to a high luster.

The final results of the repair will be difficult to detect.

More extensively damaged laminates may require considerable work to repair. Luckily, the broken piece of this laminate was still available and would not have to be completely rebuilt.

The scope of damage in this laminate is evident in the delamination visible on the back of the part.

considerable effort. Small touch-up jobs are not as laborious, but they will still take a bit of effort to match the color of the original coating. Color matching can be performed manually by using a neutral color gel coat and then adding pigment to it until it reaches the desired color. Some composite material suppliers also offer a wide range of gel coat colors and corresponding color sample books to accurately determine the right color needed to produce a "seamlessly" repaired surface.

Before refinishing a laminate with gel or surface coat, sand the surface with 80 grit sandpaper and then thoroughly clean the surface with acetone. The gel or surface coat can then be applied over this roughed surface. After a polyester gel coat has begun to tack up, it should be covered by two to three sprayed coats of polyvinyl alcohol (PVA) to seal it off from the ambient air and promote full curing of the gel coat's outer surface. Polyurethane-based paints are also very effective in refinishing a surface and will give good wear resistance without some of the hassles of gel coat application. Gel coat, surface coat and polyurethane paints will all require some fine-grit wet sanding and polishing to produce a high-quality finished surface.

Composite Skin Repairs

When damage extends beyond the coating on the composite, additional repair measures will be required. Depending on the amount of damage in

The damaged area should be ground down to a gradual taper...

170

the laminate, this may require extensive sanding and grinding of the composite to remove all of the damaged fibers and matrix materials. Sanding of the damaged area should be done in a way that will create a taper from the surface of the composite down through the damaged area, as shown. As a general rule of thumb, each ply in the laminate should be sanded to a taper at the rate of about .5" per ply. Completely remove the damaged area of the composite so that the resulting edges are smoothed or circular in shape rather than abrupt or angular. Take note of the fiber orientation of each ply within the laminate during the sanding step; the orientation of the reinforcements within the repair layers will need to match those of the corresponding plies in the original composite. In cases where the composite skin has been damaged all the way through the laminate, the entire damaged area may need to be removed. Repair plies will then need to be temporarily supported with some kind of form or mold until the new materials have fully cured.

Sandwich Composites and Core Repairs

A damaged sandwich composite will require additional repair steps (as well as possible engineering support) if the core has been compromised. In such cases, it will be necessary to sand the outer skin of the laminate with the proper taper and then to remove any damaged sections of the core. Replacement core material will need to be bonded in place and then laminated over by new composite materials.

The easiest sandwich composite repairs are those in which only one skin of the sandwich has been damaged. In these situations, the remaining skin of the composite helps to support the repair materials that are added to the laminate. When both skins of the sandwich composite are damaged, a temporary mold or caul plate is required to support the repair materials until they have cured.

Conclusion

Many types of damaged composites can be repaired using a few common, simple steps. With a bit of damage analysis, surface prep, material replacement and final finishing, a composite can be returned to service—with nearly the same degree of quality it had when it was first manufactured.

…until all the delaminated areas are removed.

Sheet metal can be used to create temporary molds, as shown here with a couple ad-hoc, waxed forms that will help align the surfaces of the repair area.

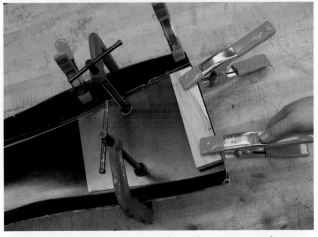

These forms are then clamped in place. Notice the piece of wood used to increase the clamping pressure of the spring clamps employed here.

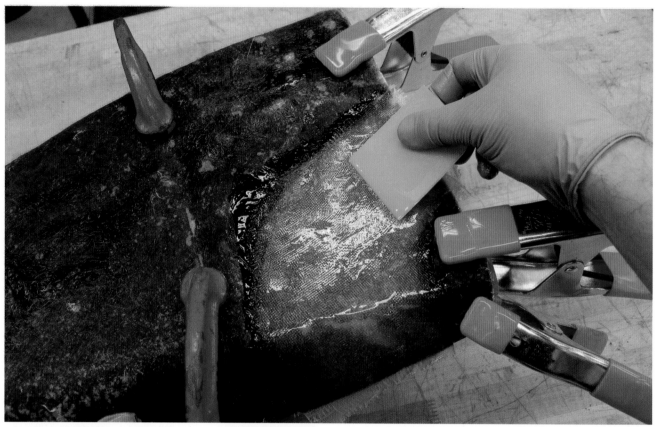

The repair can then proceed (as described above) over the damaged area on the back of the laminate.

After the repair has cured, remove the forms…

...slightly taper the gel coated area with a grinder...

...and apply body filler to smooth the surface.

Body filler can be smoothed with sandpaper and a sanding block...

...and then sealed with paint or gel coat—though finishing a gel coated surface can require considerable wet sanding and polishing.

References and Resources

Wanberg, John. *Composite Materials Handbook #3*, Stillwater, MN: Wolfgang Publications Inc., 2013.

Conclusion

This book contains quite a few tips and tricks for working with composite materials—but the techniques here are really just the tip of the iceberg in terms of what can be done with composites. If you've never fabricated composites before, but have read through this entire book (or have even thought about using some of the methods used here), you may have realized that there is a lot to learn when using these materials. They're not exactly like any other readily-available materials, and they take some serious honing of one's skills—and a LOT of patience—to really master. But that does *not* mean they aren't worth the effort to learn to use. Having passed through the refiner's fire (many times) in learning composite fabrication techniques myself, I sympathize what all those who have struggled and persevered in their attempts to create a solid, high-quality project using composites—especially on a tight budget without access to big-industry tools. As a result, I have tried to distill down as much useful information as possible for this book to at least get people started on the right foot with these materials. But be aware that this book really should only be the *start* on your journey to proficiency when using composites. Seek out other sources (both in print and online), ask questions of other seasoned professionals and practitioners (rather than just theorists), but above all else, *practice, **practice**, **PRACTICE!**...*as that is really all that can truly build your fabrication skills. And once you've completed a respectable composites project, give thanks for what you've been able to accomplish—it will do your heart good!

Nearly all titles published by Wolfgang Publications over the last 25 years can be purchased NOW.

Just punch the ISBN (International Standard Book Number) and/or the title, into your browser. Bingo - a sheet metal book from 1995 or a biography published in 2018 are in print and available from bookstores and on-line vendors.

ISBN Number	Title
9781929133208	Advanced Airbrush Art
9781929133239	Advanced Custom Motorcycle Assembly & Fabrication
9781929133536	Advanced Custom Motorcycle Painting
9781935828761	Advanced Custom Motorcycle Wiring- Revised Edition
9781929133147	Advanced Custom Painting Techniques
9781929133321	Advanced Pinstripe Art

9781929133123

Advanced Sheet Metal Fabrication

9781935828822	Advanced Tattoo Art: How-To Secrets from the Masters
9781929133864	Airbrush Bible
9781941064368	Airbrushing with Vince Goodeve: How to Airbrush 2 and 4 wheel Hot Rods

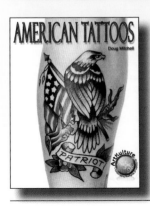

9781929133970

American Tattoos

9781929133666	Body Painting
9781929133437	Building Hot Rods

9781935828716

Colorful World of Tattoo Models

9781941064504	Composite Materials Bible
9781929133932	Composite Materials Fabrication Handbook #2
9781929133765	Composite Materials: Fabrication Handbook #1
9781935828662	Composite Materials: Fabrication Handbook #3
9781929133369	Composite Materials: Step-By-Step Projects
9781935828792	Custom MC Fab
9781935828853	Enthusiasts Guide: Honda Motorcycles 1959-1985
9781941064023	Gloria A Lifetime Motorcyclist
9781929133826	Guitar Building Basics: Acoustic Assembly at Home

9781941064337

Harley-Davidson Evo, Hop-Up & Rebuild Manual

175

Nearly all titles published by Wolfgang Publications over the last 25 years can be purchased NOW.

Just punch the ISBN (International Standard Book Number) and/or the title, into your browser. Bingo - a sheet metal book from 1995 or a biography published in 2018 are in print and available from bookstores and on-line vendors.

ISBN	Title
9781935828952	Harley-Davidson Sportster Hop-Up & Customizing Guide

9781929133697

Harley-Davidson Twin Cam, Hop-Up & Rebuild Manual

ISBN	Title
9781941064320	Honda Mini Trail - Enthusiast's Guide: All Z50, 1968 - 1999, 49cc
9781935828853	Honda Motorcycles Enthusiasts Guide - 1959 to 1985
9781929133017	Hot Rod Hardware
9781929133703	Hot Rod Chassis How To

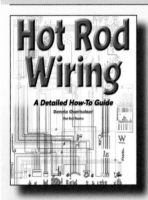

9781929133987

Hot Rod Wiring: A Detailed How-To Guide

ISBN	Title
9781929133710	How Airbrushes Work
9781929133802	How to Airbrush Pin-Ups
9781935828730	How to Build a Cafe Racer
9781929133178	How to Build a Cheap Chopper
9781929133062	How to Build a Chopper

ISBN	Title
9781935828006	How to Build an Old Skool Bobber
9781929133727	How to Fix American V-Twin Motorcycles
9781929133475	How to Paint Tractors & Trucks
9781935828693	How-To Airbrush, Pinstripe & Goldleaf
9781929133499	How-To Chop Tops
9781929133833	Kosmoski's New Kustom Painting Secrets
9781935828891	Learning the English Wheel
9781941064535	Pete Hill - A Motorcycle Legend
9781929133604	Power Hammers
9781929133901	Sheet Metal Bible
9781929133468	Sheet Metal Fab Basics
9781935828860	So Cal Speed Shop's How to Build Hot Rod Chassis
9781929133093	Sportster/Buell Engine Hop-Up Guide: Harley-Davidson
9781935828754	Tattoo Bible Three
9781929133840	Tattoo Bible One
9781935828051	Tattoo Bible Two
9781929133789	Tattoo: Behind the Needle
9781929133277	Técnicas Avanzadas de Pintura a Medida
9781929133635	Triumph Motorcycle Restoration: Pre-Unit
9781929133420	Triumph Motorcycle Restoration: Unit 650cc
9780964135895	Ultimate Sheet Metal Fabrication
9781929133314	Vintage Dirt Bikes